RANDOM REMINISCENCES OF A POLICE OFFICER UNDER TWO FLAGS

RANDOM REMINISCENCES OF A POLICE OFFICER UNDER TWO FLAGS

D.G. Bhattacharyya

GYAN PUBLISHING HOUSE
New Delhi–110 002

RANDOM REMINISCENCES OF A POLICE OFFICER UNDER TWO FLAGS

(Police)

Rs. 890

ISBN: 81-212-0781-9

Published in 2003 in India by
Gyan Publishing House
5, Ansari Road, Daryaganj
New Delhi–110 002

Phones: 3282060, 3261060, Fax: 3285914

E-mail: gyanbook@vsnl.com

visit our web site At http:\\www.gyanbooks.com

Lasertypesetting by: Varsha Graphics, Delhi
Printed at: Mehra Offset Press, Delhi

Respectfully Dedicated

To

Shri Atal Bihari Vajpayee

Prime Minister of India

Contents

Preface

I am writing these reminiscences 30 years after my retirement from service in 1971 and mostly relate to events which occurred between the years 1927 and 1971. I did not keep a diary or notes nor was I in the habit of keeping a diary at any time in my life.

As I had to depend on what I still remembered small mistakes in facts, figures and details of some events are most likely to occur. After completing my writing I have remembered several important events during my service life which should have been incorporated in these reminiscences. I have not tried to add them because it will be a time and labour consuming task to locate the pages where these additions should find entry in order to keep sequence or relevance.

Those readers who know most of the events, occurrences and circumstances are requested not to find fault for any errors, omissions or lack of sequence in these reminiscences now put on paper.

Besides actual occurrences I have incorporated my views, impressions and appreciation of events, policies, practices and problems in India omission of which would have made this book of reminiscences incomplete.

Writing of this book could not be completed without very willing co-operation and indefatigable efforts on the part of my steno-typist Miss Mala Sarkar who undertook typing of the manuscript several times with a smiling face. Besides I am thankful to D.C. Nath of New Delhi, a former service colleague, Partho Dutta, a friend, Mrinal Sarkar, a colleague, for helping me in my work.

My appreciation goes to Mr. Amit Garg, Chief of Publication Department, Gyan Publishing House without whose patience and willing co-operation this book could not be printed and published.

Lastly, I am thankful to Inder Malhotra, a veteran journalist and a senior political analyst well-known to all statesmen, journalists and intelligentsia in India, for writing an introduction to this book.

February 28, 2002   D.G. BHATTACHARYYA
Calcutta

Foreword

Well before I went to Calcutta (as Kolkata was then called) to live and work for *The Statesman* in the late Sixties I had known D.G. Bhattacharyya ("Durga", to friends) and was impressed by the high respect he enjoyed for his personal and professional qualities. I was to see more of these as years went by. He was born in 1913 in a family of Zamindars that later switched to business. But, while negotiating unfamiliar waters, it suffered serious losses and had to shut down shop. The young scion, having graduated in science from the Calcutta University in the early Thirties, had no option but to seek employment. It was the era when the sun was supposed never to set on the British Empire of which India was the brightest Jewel in Crown. So young Bhattacharyya competed successfully for the Imperial service simply called the Indian Police (IP) that was to the legendary ICS what IPS has been to the IAS since Independence.

Both before and after 1947 his was a distinguished career. He was awarded the Police Medal as early as in 1952. During the brief but brutal war with China in high Himalayas in 1962 he was posted to the border areas. In fact, since before the World War II until his retirement in the rank of Inspector General of police at the time of the war for the liberation of Bangladesh, he was witness, from a ringside seat, to a succession of historic events. These included the glorious march towards freedom, the searing tragedy of the Bengal Famine in 1943, the horrendous Calcutta riots three years later that presaged India's partion and so on. He also had the good fortune to come into close contact with three of India's Most Towering Sons—Tagore, Gandhi and Nehru.

Retirement did not persuade Bhattacharyya to hang up his boots. On the contrary, it opened up new vistas of brisk activity for him. He founded and ran one of the exceptionally successful security agencies and indulged in his several passions such as tireless travelling across the world. A keen sportsman in his younger years, he gave up hunting, shooting and fishing to concentrate on still and cine photography. In 1979, the sudden death of his wife was a shattering blow to him. His response to this terrible tragedy was to set up a charitable trust in her memory. It remains engaged in numerous welfare projects in the city he loves. Indeed, for a police officer he is a man of many parts.

This should explain why his numerous friends and admirers have been urging him to write his memoirs so that the younger generations—especially those engaged in the increasingly difficult task of policing the country—can benefit from his recollections and reflections on India during most of the twentieth century. This he has done with remarkable candour and without any pretensions. His Random Reminiscences would reward any reader who chooses to savour them.

In order to give his readers a glimpse of one of his many facets let me recount an anecdote that Bhattacharyya has not mentioned in his book for whatever reason.

Shortly after I had shifted from Delhi to Calcutta, Prem Bhatia, my professional guru and personal mentor as also a contemporary and close friend of Bhattacharyya, was staying with me. He was on his way to Singapore to take over as High Commissioner, having done a stint earlier in Kenya. Soon enough, however, he returned to his real love-journalism.

Understandably, Durga, who was then DIG (CID), rang me up to say that he must meet Prem. I immediately asked to him to join us for a drink. I was then living in one of the lovely bungalows in Tivoli Park (now, alas, demolished and replaced by multi-storied monstrosities) and one had to take a few twists and turns to reach it. I thought I should save him some bother and therefore requested him to jot down the directions to reach my house.

Durga's reply was characteristic: "Inder, please remember what my job is. I know exactly where you live."

Inder Malhotra

New Delhi **Inder Malhotra**

1

A New Life and Making of a *Sahib* out of a Native Rebel

On a cold and misty morning in February 1936, a young Bengalee in a suit and a *topee* on his head peeped out of his second class compartment trying to see the name of the railway station with low platform when the train guard came and told him that it was the destination of the young man who should get down with his luggage, take a *tonga* (a horse drawn two-wheel cart) and proceed to the Police Training College (in short PTC) Sardah in the district of Rajshahi, now in Bangladesh. The young man got down and unloaded his baggage which consisted of a suitcase, a hat box and a long steel trunk commonly known as an officer's kit box which could also accommodate a long ceremonial sword in its scabbard. After the train whistled off and left, a huge bulky young European appeared out of the mist and approached him enquiring if the young man was Bhattacharyya, actually D.G. Bhattacharyya, a newly appointed Asstt. Superintendent of Police and posted to PTC Sardah for training. The young man realised that someone had come to receive him at the railway station and his unspoken apprehension to find the right way out to the Training College disappeared. He quickly confirmed that indeed he was D.G. Bhattacharyya, a newly appointed ASP and was bound for the PTC. The tall gentleman was found to be smoking a pipe even at that early hour and extended his hand saying he was Chitham and mumbled some other words the Bengalee young man could hardly understand. Chitham was wearing a coat and sleeping suit, i.e. coat and *pyjama* and had a dressing gown on top. He took charge of the young man and his luggage, hired two *tongas* on one of which Chitham and the Bengalee young man sat together and the other *tonga* escorted by his bearer or another low grade employee of the college carried the luggage.

The young Indian mentioned above was none other than myself, D.G. Bhattacharyya, a Bengalee and the writer of these memoirs.

After covering a distance of three or four miles we reached a very large campus of the College. We drove on past several buildings to reach a small red building where we got down and I was ushered into a room which was to be my own for the next one year and three months. Chitham said many things with the pipe in his mouth and I failed again to understand all his mumblings. However, I came to know that one Muslim young man Jabbar who *salaamed* me on entering my room, was to be my personal bearer. Chitham further told me not to bother about parade that morning and advised me to have a shave and a bath and go to the main mess-building which had bed rooms, a living room, a billiard room and the dining room. I was told that Chitham who was staying in another room in the same red building would call me out to accompany him to the main mess for breakfast.

At 8-30 a.m., I got a call and accompanied Chitham to the mess building at a short walking distance and met a group of other ASP trainees numbering six British and Irish officers and four Indian officers three of whom were Bengalees and a Punjabi domiciled in Bengal who could speak Bengali fluently. His name was Harbanslal Bery and he belonged to my batch of trainees. He had arrived two days earlier and was found to be already friendly with both European and Indian officers and had free and relaxed manners. I had met him also as a recruit of the same year in the Calcutta office of the Inspector General of Police, Bengal, on the 2nd floor of the Writers' Buildings in Dalhousie Square, now known as Benoy, Badal and Dinesh Bag.

All the officers warmly shook hands and some spoke a few words of advice also. These officers were (1) Adam, (2) G. Walker, (3) W.Walker, (4) S.M. Ghosh, (5) A.M.A. Kabir, (6) M.A.H. Maswood recruits of the previous year, i.e. 1935 and William, J.R. Chitham, W.W. Jameson, H.L. Bery and myself of the current year, i.e. 1936. I later found out this overlapping of training of fifteen months' had an important purpose namely, not only to give enough time to complete training in the long and varied theoretical and practical courses to the officer cadets under training but also to bring the new generation of recruits in close contact with the somewhat older recruits, who had already absorbed a year's training and were half way to complete their full training in different districts to become eventually superior police officers of the lowest rank, i.e. assistant superintendents. This contact gave an opportunity to the senior members to give good advice to their juniors, give them a rough idea of the whole administration and what the new juniors were supposed to do. The advantage of the juniors was that they could ask questions, even foolish or awkward and get a correct answer or be warned not to be too inquisitive in the beginning. The juniors had also the advantage of watching their seniors in a formal function or social situation and learning how to behave or learn what respect openly or discreetly to give to outside dignitaries and visitors and to wait to watch them to act in a certain way in a novel situation. Thus, they might learn to do the same thing in the same or improved way according to their abilities.

On the morning of my arrival my three senior Bengalee officers decided to solve the problem of my learning correct table manners at the breakfast table and they told me the usual order in which cutlery is placed on the table and what food would be served in what form and how to take such food with the spoons, forks and knives and in what order. Although I had eaten food in hotels and restaurants in Calcutta but so much cutlery and crockery with napkins in silvered rings were not provided in those establishments. The usual practice was to put a new recruit in between two older recruits, preferably of the same nationality. I sat between Ghosh and Kabir and Bery was placed between Kabir and Maswood. We were also asked to observe the fellow seniors to learn what to do in eating a meal in the European style warning that we should not take the cue from the one sitting across the table on the opposite side who will act in the opposite way being in a mirror image position to us. I remember I smoothly finished the breakfast meal which I found tasty and wholesome.

After breakfast I went to the office of the Principal of the college who was one W.G. Thrupp. He asked a few general questions and volunteered the information that he was going away from the post of the Principal and one S.G. Taylor would be his successor. His successor would help me in buying a horse because it was customary for a trainee to buy and own a horse to ride, to play polo and to take part in other sports like hunting with hounds and to take part in point-to-point races.

I returned to my room, lay down and fell asleep as I had not been able to sleep well in the train for fear of missing the station of destination. My bearer Jabbar woke me up saying I should go to the main mess to have my lunch. On arrival in the building I was introduced to all other trainees to whom I was not introduced during breakfast hours. Of the two Indian trainees of my year, Bery was more free and chummy with all others even if they had been total strangers a day or two before. I behaved as per my own nature and habit and was somewhat reserved in conversation or in establishing camaraderie with others. As a matter of fact, I did not believe in going out of my way or going forward to establish friendly relationship with my colleagues or for that matter with any one whatever be his position in service or society.

There was a formal ceremony of initiation of a novice trainee namely 'SCONCING' which involved filling up a large silver bowl with beer or any non-alcoholic drink and making the trainee drink up the whole bowlful of liquid without stopping for breath. If one failed, one had to stand a round of drinks to others and try another day. Both Bery and myself succeeded in drinking a bowlful of orange squash and water at the first attempt.

During breakfast, luncheon and dinner, each trainee was served by his personal bearer who wore liveried dress and stood behind his employer. All the personal bearers were fully trained and conducted themselves in a faultless manner. I went to the dining hall of the main mess building and was seated in between Ghosh and Kabir as before who were supposed to help and guide me in observing proper table and eating manners. Three or four course luncheon was usually served and I was taught that soup should be taken by using the roundish soup spoon from near to far side so as not to spill any soup on one self. About use of the rest of the cutlery I was half accustomed and did not find any difficulty in following the correct procedure. Food served in the mess was mostly English or Anglicised version of Indian dishes like chicken or mutton curry and rice, chutney etc. The mess had an excellent cook who could cook different kinds of food at lunch and dinner and lunch and dinner were mostly four course meals, namely soup, fish, meat or chicken and dessert. The kitchen served varieties of well known soups, fish and meat and chicken dishes and a large number of good desserts in the form of pudding. Breakfast was more or less stereotyped namely, Kellog's cornflakes or rice flakes, Quaker oats porridge, eggs, bacon, toast, jam or marmalade some local fruits like bananas, apples, mangoes, lichis etc. We had been buying and consuming many packaged and tinned food imported from abroad, namely Kellog's cornflakes, Quaker oats, marmalades, jams of such brand names as Chivers or Cross and Blackwell, IXL, tinned sardines, tinned pineapples, Heinz mayonnaise, baked beans, English bacon, Californian asparagus, different imported sauces, namely, H.P. sauce, Worcester sauce, Anchovy sauce, tomato ketchup and many such items. Each officer took up the duty of acting as the mess secretary by turn for a month. If an Indian trainee wanted to live a European or rather English style of living in post training service life and had a good cook and a trained house bearer, he did have adequate training and first hand experience to run a suitable household.

I went round the common rooms like dining room, living room, billiards room in the main mess house and went and saw some private rooms. There were about half a dozen residential rooms, four single and two double bedded rooms to accommodate eight officer cadets (trainees) in all.

In the forenoon Jabbar, my personal bearer, had emptied the contents of the kit box and the suitcase and kept them in two wooden almirahs except boots and shoes which were kept outside.

At 4-30 pm I was served tea in my room and thereafter took a stroll to see the grounds of the college namely, parade ground, soccer-cum-cricket field, polo ground which served as parade ground also, tennis court, physical training and the horse riding training centres.

It was customary to have bath twice a day, i.e. morning and evening. There was no electricity or telephone in Sardah which was a village and we had pressurised incandescent lamps both in the bedroom and throughout the building and we used battery powered torch lights during our outdoor movements. There were pull *punkhas* as substitutes for electric fans and there were *punkha* pullers to work during the summer months.

The college in Sardah was a joint training centre of officer cadets of the Indian (Imperial) Police Service, Dy. Superintendents of the Provincial service and sub-inspectors of Bengal and Assam as well as constable recruits of Bengal only.

The precincts and the grounds of the Training College were situated in excellent open area with good surroundings. The big river the Ganges or the Padma flowed past the grounds and there were no large or crowded villages surrounding the site of the college. There were no places of amusement like a cinema or theatre, gambling dens, liquor shops or any red light area in the vicinity nor any place of sporting activities or clubs except what the college campus contained and provided; even the railway or bus station was at a distance. There were no telephones, no electricity and the trainees were segregated from urban luxuries and contamination from urban vices. The river Ganges was a source of pleasure to watch its flow and floods during the monsoon. The river provided some scope of waterfowl shooting in winter months. It was a great pleasure to walk along bank of the river or to ride on a horse. On the other side, i.e. the right or south bank was the district of Murshidabad with its headquarters at Berhampur.

The college grounds contained such buildings as the offices, class rooms, messes which housed the officer trainees, sub-inspector cadets and barracks for trainee constables, stables for horses, residence of teachers and trainees as well as the Principal's bungalow. Besides there were parade ground, polo ground and cricket ground which were inside the polo grounds, physical training centre, training centre to teach riding, rifle shooting range and other facilities.

Most important building was the IP trainee officers' mess building which had four single and two double bed rooms, a living room, a billiards room, a dining hall. Detached but adjacent were the kitchen and pantry. The IP officers' mess had a smaller building nearby having three more single rooms to accommodate three officers but two could if necessary be accommodated in one room. There was another officers' mess which accommodated provincial gazetted officers namely Deputy Superintendents of Police of both Bengal and Assam. During my time there was only one Dy. Supdt. cadet, named Bhabani Kanta Barua, who later became the Inspector General of Assam and we became fast friends after our retirement. Besides there was the Principal's office, class rooms both for the gazetted officers, sub-inspector cadets and constables.

Training was of two types namely theoretical teaching given in classes held indoors. Theoretical training was given in law, accounts and two languages namely Hindi and Bengali. All officers except those with Bengali as mother tongue had to learn all the subjects and pass departmental examination held by the government in Calcutta. The Bengalee officers had to learn all the subjects except Bengali like the rest.

Practical training was mostly done outdoors and consisted of learning drill and to act as a commander or in-charge, physical training like jumping over low barriers, scaling a high wall top of which one must grasp with one's hand by jumping, climbing up by grasping a long hanging rope by hand, etc. Riding, i.e. to learn riding a horse, in all its four gaits, namely, walk, trot, canter and gallop, to fix a saddle with stirrup on the back to put a bridle with reins in the mouth of a horse. Further he had to learn to have a proper seat and grip and also not to fall off if a horse reared or bucked. Then there was training in shooting with a musket, rifle and revolver and to learn proper grip of the butt, correct aiming etc. During our training year, we got hold of a Hotchkiss machine gun and we took turns for handling and firing with it.

Besides some items of outdoor sporting activities like playing hockey with the officers and jawans, cricket, tennis and playing polo were compulsory, especially hockey and polo. One had to learn the basic rules of the games and develop skill in actual play. The only indoor game provided for was billiards, carolina, slosh for which a good billiards table and cues were provided in the billiards room. There was also a box of ivory mah-jong set, which is an old Chinese table game of four people played with painted tiles. The tiles were kept in a nice brass bound wooden box which some British boys jokingly gave the vulgar name of 'Brass Bound Buggery Box'. As the game appeared to have complicated rules I never tried my hands at it.

During my training period of 15 months or more I studied in the indoor classes and took part in all the outdoor games and indoor game of billiards only. I had the knack of learning any game in a short space of time and quickly reaching a stage of low proficiency but could hardly attain excellence. As it happened sometimes we used to play by wagering small sums of money and this I did mostly with my colleague James Jameson who almost always lost to me and shelled out small sums of money and cursed himself profusely because he was generally a better player and won most of the games when no bets were on.

S.G. Taylor joined to be the Principal and Head of the Institution. He asked Bery and me to buy our horses; a sum of Rs 600 was sanctioned by the government to buy a horse. I tried to buy a horse during one of my visits to Calcutta and tried out 3 horses in the maidan in that part which is now known as the Brigade Parade Ground, none of which suited me as they were not comfortable rides. I was, however, thoroughly shaken when I tried out a smallish black mare which bolted with me across the maidan then on to Khidderpore road and across the tramway lines past running buses, motor cars and street cars. I could not control her and fortunately she stopped on her own to my great relief. After that incident I had no desire to try out horses on my own and both Bery and myself asked the Principal to find suitable horses and buy them for us. Sometime later the Principal got two horses—a horse for me and a mare for Bery. Both had some defects and we later learnt that he bought them from one Mcpherson, a friend of his who was the Principal of the Veterinary College and Hospital in Calcutta. Both of us were dissatisfied with our mounts and thought that the Principal had bought the two horses to oblige his friend. My horse had an uncomfortable ride and was hardly suitable to play polo which game requires a horse able to take quick turns to chase the ball. It was soon found out that Bery's mare had *Kumree*, i.e., weakness in the rear of its back due to an illness she suffered in the past but which was temporarily cured by Mcpherson, the veterinary doctor, but the disease left its marks on the body of the mare and she became unfit to play polo and was later destroyed. Bery had to be lent a PTC horse to ride and play polo.

After I gained confidence in horse riding I used to go out alone on horseback along the river bank and sometimes into the villages nearby. Some of us used to ride a horse on bare back, i.e. without the saddle and stirrup but with the reins in the mouth but this required skill and confidence. One day when riding bare back and returning to the mess, the horse bolted and all efforts on my part by hard pulling of the reins could not stop the horse. It ran between two barracks and tried to go through a low door beyond which there was a tank. As I did not dare to throw myself out from the back of the running horse I was sure to hit my head hard against the lintel and die on the spot if the horse had not suddenly stopped before going through the door and I had a providential escape. There was another occasion when I had a fall from the horse and one hind leg lightly hit me on the head. I was taken to the college hospital and the Surgeon stitched the wound which was a superficial wound on the scalp and I was administered on antitetanus injection.

There was an old passenger bus which had wooden seats and an engine, steering wheel and a clutch but had no brakes. One could therefore start the bus and travel but could not stop the car by applying brakes: Having no other vehicles available I continued to practise driving which I learnt in a rudimentary way in Calcutta and used to move about on the maidan and sometimes along the wide bund on the river bank. One day, however, I could not control the bus and it rolled down the embankment on the dry land side. I hurried back to the mess and told my colleagues about my predicament. Some of us including *jawans*, i.e. recruit constable, went to the spot with ropes and we tried to pull the bus back to the top of the *bund*, i.e. embankment but failed to do so because of the steepness. Ultimately we had to dig a trench to make the slope somewhat gradual and managed to pull out the bus.

I do not remember the exact details but there was another occasion when my horse which was tethered to a river bank tree, freed itself and strayed on to the soft muddy river bank of the Ganges or the Padma and got its four legs sunk into the treacherous sandy mud. It started braying in panic and I tried to extricate it out by pulling on the reins but did not succeed. Again I ran to the mess and told my colleagues and the riding master about the predicament. A number of us along with jawans and the riding master went to the spot and tried to put bamboos under the belly and help the horse to get itself free. Our efforts failed for a long time and I ran the danger of losing my horse which would have had to be shot and killed. However, the riding master had past experience of such a situation and he made the men manouvre in such a way as to put the bamboo poles thrust under its belly to raise the whole torso of the horse and free the legs from the mud and succeeded in getting the horse out of the soft mud and take it walking back to its stable.

We trainees not only organised and took part in the cruel sport of hunting poor village jackals, foxes, civet cats with hounds but we had to take part in a "point to point race" over a course which had low hurdles and narrow stretches of water to jump over and whoever could complete the course first got a small trophy. In the race William who was the best rider amongst us and had a good horse won the race and the prize. Actually winning the race or playing good polo of a low standard prevailing in the campus depended more on the horse than on its rider or player.

The mess had a 12 bore shotgun and an .8 bore duck gun. A local *shikari* named Abbas used to tell us tall stories of his exploits and success in shooting leopards in the bushes of the nearby village and sugarcane fields. There were leopards in adjoining village jungles and they used to maraud on goats and duck and chicken in the villages. One day he came with the news of a leopard being seen in a nearby village and wanted to take us to hunt the leopard. Bery and I accompanied him to the village and learnt that the leopard had taken shelter in a sugarcane field. Abbas promised to guide and assist us. He took me and Bery each with a gun and Abbas had his own gun. We walked a mile or two and reached a vast stretch of sugarcane fields with the sugarcanes still standing and making visibility limited to a few feet. Abbas got some villagers together who would conduct a beat to drive out the leopard towards the guns. We found that there were no trees except Babul trees with big thorns on their branches and it was nearly impossible to climb a tree where from to shoot the animal if it was flushed out. There were two feet wide aisles, i.e. uncultivated strips of clear land to demarcate each owner's cultivated plot and we could stand there. Doing so was very dangerous because a leopard coming out would be visible only at a distance of 3/4 feet. We told the *shikari* about the danger of being mauled severely even if we managed to shoot at the leopard and wound or kill it but he assured us that there was no real danger and I and Bery ought to be near each other and he would take his position alone at a small distance. We were foolhardy to agree and took our positions. The beat started and ended but fortunately the leopard did not come out. We tried another patch of sugarcane field and drew blank. Then we decided to leave after the villagers told us that the leopard must have heard sounds of our conversation and walking and must have slunk away from the area. We searched for *shikari* Abbas and after quite some time we saw Abbas coming towards us with blood streaking from some small wounds on his body. We ran to him enquiring why he did not fire his gun (we heard no gun shot) and allowed himself to be mauled by the leopard. He would not give a reply but a village boy told us that Abbas had not been mauled by any leopard but had injured himself in climbing up and descending down a very thorny *Babul* tree on which he took shelter. This is the story of a brave *shikari* and his two green horn assistants.

As I wanted a shot gun at a reasonably cheap price, I thought of buying one from the *malkhana*, i.e. armoury of Rajshahi District which had a small stock of confiscated firearms. Annada Shankar Roy, ICS, was the District Magistrate of Rajshahi who had come to our mess as an invited guest in the past and I had a nodding acquaintance. I wrote to him about my intention to buy a confiscated gun from the *malkhana* and got a reply stating that I was welcome to visit the armoury and choose any gun I liked. He would pass necessary instructions to SP who, on his part, would instruct the Reserve Inspector of Police to do the needful. I went to Rajshahi, saw S.P. who asked me to go to the Police armoury and ordered his officer to help me in all respects. There were few guns in good order. There was, however, a Norwegian self-loading gun but nobody knew about its working and none had offered to buy it during annual or periodical sale of confiscated fire arms as the gun was not in working condition. I chose the gun and both I and the Inspector went to the D.M. who inspected the gun and ordered its sale to me for a paltry sum of Rs 15 as I was gambling on the purchase of a gun which was not working. He was kind enough to issue a license on the spot on payment of the requisite fee and I returned triumphantly with a license and a gun to the mess. There were 12 bore shot gun cartridges in the mess and we decided to test the gun. I did not like to load and fire the gun from my shoulder nor did any of the British boys who were generally bolder than I was. It was decided to load the gun with two cartridges, tie it on the verandah railing and pull the trigger with a long string from a distance. This operation was carried out and the gun fired but did not reload the second cartridge nor did the barrel burst. Thereafter I was bold enough to fire the gun again from my shoulder. It fired one cartridge without reloading. I decided to take it to a gun shop in Calcutta and get it repaired. This I did by taking it to Calcutta. First I took the gun to Ashootosh Daw & Co. who pleaded their inability to help. I went to a few other Indian gun dealers who all failed. I then took it to the well known British arms dealer Rodda & Co. They kept the gun and later informed me that they could not repair the defect. The defect was, however, rectified by Manton & Co. another reputed gun shop which charged Rs 30 for the job. So I possessed a self loading gun which fired five shots but still it sometimes missed loading each time and then I had to do loading by pulling the reloading mechanism by hand.

During my stay in the college after I thought that I had learnt motor car driving sufficiently well I thought of taking out a driving license from Rajshahi district. For this purpose I made an application to the District Magistrate and was told to undergo a driving test which would be held in Rajshahi Town by the Deputy Superintendent of Police, Rajshahi. I drove the old mess bus which had no brakes and in which the steering wheel would operate only after a false turn of 180 degrees. On my way out I could not stop the bus and knocked against a railway crossing barrier gate. However, as I managed to slow down the bus there was no damage to the vehicle's body. Somehow I drove the rickety bus a distance of 16 miles without any more mishap and reached the office of the Superintendent of Police, Rajshahi. One Sri Basudev Kabiraj, DSP, boarded the bus and asked me to drive through the town. I drove the bus through the town well enough but at one sharp turn I could not manouvre the steering wheel quickly enough and as a result one front wheel fell into a roadside drain. The bus had to be pulled out by a few men and the DSP asked me to appear in another test after undergoing further training. I returned to the mess. There was the college Doctor, a perfect Anglo Indian gentleman, who had a Chevrolet car. I requested him to allow me to drive the vehicle a couple of days and also to allow me to appear in the next test with his vehicle. He was gracious enough to allow me. I drove the vehicle around and it was easy because the vehicle had its brakes, steering mechanism and everything else in proper shape. On the day fixed for the second test I drove the vehicle with the Doctor's driver at my side and an orderly and appeared in a test which was held by the same Deputy Superintendent of Police. He asked me to drive through the town and also tested my theoretical knowledge of a motor car mechanism and was satisfied that I could drive the vehicle well and had enough working knowledge of car mechanism. He recommended issue of a driving license to me. I deposited the requisite fee and returned to the mess. Eventually, the driving license came and I was glad to have it. I profusely thanked the Doctor for his kindness. Later when I used to go to Calcutta I used to hire a Morris Ten Sedan car from a friendly automobile workshop on Dharmtala Street on a hire charge of Rs 10 per day but had to bear expenses on account of petrol and engine oil. I used to drive with my mother and elder brother and visit Bhatpara at a distance of about 26-28 miles where my maternal uncle and several aunts lived. We used to spend the day and return in the evening. Petrol was priced at Re one and 2 paise per gallon on which a rebate of an anna was given so that each gallon, i.e. 4.5 litres of petrol cost 15 annas and a half in the later 1930s. At the time of writing these memoirs petrol is being sold at Rs 27.70 per litre.

Before our departure for District Training a new batch of British trainees arrived consisting of three British young men named Frank Carman, Paul Barnes and Hughes-Hughes, the last being of Assam Cadre. Frank Carman was an upright, God fearing Christian Scientist, Paul Barnes was jovial and of normal temperament and behaviour. Paul Barnes went as a trainee in Berhampore under R. Banerjee after I left. Hughes-Hughes was a friendly man but was somewhat of a braggart and when he was asked to learn something he used to say that he had already acquired sufficient knowledge and experience in the particular matter and had nothing more to learn. He had many falls from the horse while riding and I told him to be more careful but he replied that he was born on the saddle, meaning that he had become an experienced rider even in his infancy. He used to go out with golf clubs and started to learn striking golf balls in the parade ground on Sundays and Thursdays when the ground was free of other games. I saw him driving the balls which were going in all directions. Sometimes he missed the ball completely or cut it. I asked him to buy a book and learn how to play golf or wait till he got a teacher. He told me that he was born with a golf bag to which I quipped that it must have been very painful for his mother and all my colleagues burst out laughing.

Before the trainees dispersed, there was a ragging session but I did not take part. However, one night I found myself on the mattress hoisted by four colleagues while I was asleep and they were trying to take me to a small pond and throw me therein. I, however, slithered out of the mattress and threatened them with playing dirtier tricks on some of them if they tried again.

Indoor Classes—Instructors staff consisted of the Chief Law Instructor who was a senior Police Inspector; there were other Law Instructors and other instructors were a Hindi Instructor who was a Bengalee teacher recruited from outside. Accownts Instructors were civilian accountants. They took classes not only of the officer trainees but also of sub-inspector cadets as well as constables under training. I suppose the course was the same for both the officer trainees and cadet Sub-inspector in the subjects of Law and Hindi or Bengali but the sub-inspector cadets were not trained in accounts syllabi to the same extent as the officer trainees. Bengalee officers had to learn Hindi and Hindi speaking officers had to learn Bengali. And the British and Irish officers had to learn both the languages, i.e. Bengali and Hindi.

Law books consisted of the Indian Penal Code, Criminal Procedure Code, Railway Act, Highway Act, Arms Act, Public Vehicles Act, Ferries Act and many other minor Acts. Accounts books consisted of Fundamental Rules, Civil Code, Treasury Rules etc. The Hindi Instructor was teaching Hindi mostly verbally although some of us bought Hindi books to be able to read, write and speak in Hindi and translate English into Hindi or Hindi into English which expertise was necessary because most of the recruits in the rank of the constabulary were mostly Hindi speaking men from Bihar and U.P. The Principal did not take any classes but paid occasional visits and he had his own office to attend to and deal with matters of administration, overall accounts of the Institution and correspondence with a number of officers, namely the I.G. and D.I.G. of Police, Accountant General of West Bengal, the District Magistrate and the Superintendent of the district of Rajshahi.

Outdoor Training—Outdoor training was imparted to learn drill as well as to be able to act as a commander of a section, platoon and a company and move them in proper marching order. the Instructors were mostly Havildars and Subedars but the Chief Drill Instructor was one Khan Shahib Meher Ali Khan who had a very commanding personality and a deep tenor voice which could carry his words right across the entire parade ground. There were P.T. Instructors who were mostly Havildars and Naiks and there was also a riding Master who was a retired JCO of the Army. In my year he was a Sikh gentleman who had very good manners and knew his job well.

The officer trainees had to undertake one weekly night round by turn who had to go around the premises of the campus, namely, to check if the sentries who were in-charge of armoury and magazines, i.e. ammunition depot were alert, that all trainees were in their barracks and checked that nobody was loitering around nor were there any trespassers. Besides, the officer trainee was also expected to carry out day time inspection of the barracks, kitchen, stables, latrines and urinals to ensure that they were properly maintained and were in a clean condition.

Games—Outdoor games such as Polo and Hockey which were compulsory and were taught, especially the former. Cricket and Tennis were played but not taught but some seniors used to instruct the ignorant on rules of the games and help new trainees to learn the same but most of the trainees had in their early student life played the games. At least I had played cricket, tennis and done horse riding but had not played polo or billiards. Billiards was the only indoor game which most officer trainees played in the mess in spare time i.e. before or after lunch on sundays and holidays and in the evening before dinner.

Mess life—In the mess Wednesday night was important when the Principal and his wife mostly attended the dinner and there often would be outside guests, both ladies and gentlemen. We had guests in the person of senior officers of the District of Rajshahi in which Sardah was situated. They were the District Magistrate, Superintendent of Police, the Executive Engineer and some English Clergy men. Occasionally the Range DIG used to come down from his HQ at Jalpaiguri. In my time he was one E.B. Jones, a handsome dignified bachelor policeman, who was known as "Angry Jones" because of his temper and strictness. We also had Sir Robert Neil who was the then Home Member in the Govt. of Bengal and was later appointed as the Governor of Assam. He came to the mess on the eve of his joining as the Governor of Assam. One frequent visitor was one couple named 'Hills'. The husband was an officer of the Midnapur Zamindari Company and they lived in a nearby village close to the mess. Mrs. Hill who must have been very handsome in her younger days but had become plump when I saw her during my training. She used to joke with and tease the British trainees and one of my colleagues William had become a favourite of hers and had often been invited to go and stay in the house of the Hills. Becuase of the mess night on Wednesday there was no parade next morning. It was a formal dinner on the mess night and usually all present had to wear mess-kit with black boots and rowels. They had to drink a toast to His Majesty, King George the Fifth of England who was also 'the Emperor of India'. I remember that during our training King George the Fifth died and we had to wear a black arm band whether on parade or in civil clothes or in mess kit for a month in order to express our formal grief and perhaps loyalty to the Crown. As we had to drink a toast with wine wishing good health to the King Emperor and the Principal used to say gentlemen 'the King Emperor' and we used to stand up and repeat 'The King Emperor' and drink the toast at the end of the dinner on the guest night. As Bery and I were teetotallers we approached the Principal with our problem and he at once replied that we could drink the toast with soft drink or even water.

On some Sundays and holidays we had visitors who stayed for lunch and there was game of billiards. Hill played both polo and billards and was good at polo. Later the Principal's wife Mrs. Taylor joined her husband and she took to horse riding and started playing polo alongside her husband and the trainees. After her joining, the officers had more frequent invitations to have lunch or dinner at the Principal's house and all these were enjoyable events even for Indian officers who found certain things not to their traditional liking but could enjoy if they had no complex. In the Principal's house there used to be some indoor games like 'hunting the slipper', 'Charade' etc.

I remember one occasion in which a British officer cadet named Chitham who did not know much about drinks tried to be smart in a laughable way. In the Principal's house we were invited one evening to have dinner and drinks. The Principal's wife was serving drinks and she had served one round of drinks of our choice to all of us. At the time of the second round when she approached her husband he said 'same darling' meaning the previous drink we had been served with and when she approached Chitham he also said 'the same darling' and she burst out laughing and so did others. Although an Englishman the same British trainee made another faux-pas by using the word 'Sod' not knowing 'Sod' may often be used as an obscene word which meant a sodomist. Although I never used the word, I myself was not aware of the meaning of a 'four letters word' used in the novel Lady Chatterley's Lover. As this word was being very often used by some British officers one day I enquired of the senior most cadet namely, William, after the other cadets had left about the meaning of the word and he was surprised that I did not know. He further enquired if I had never indulged in the act which was meant by the word. However I came to learn what the word 'Fuck' meant and started admonishing others whenever they used the word which was done too often.

During training we got two chances to appear in written examinations in law and accounts which were held in Calcutta and both Bery and myself looked forward to this event because that provided us an opportunity to travel to Calcutta and be with our family members at Government expense and also got daily allowance at double the rate, i.e. Rs. 15/- per day which sum of money was adequate to stay in a reasonably good hotel like Spencer's and to cover expenses on taxi fare in those good old days.

Settlement training—There was another important event like 'Settlement training'. This was a very important part of the officers' training. This was undertaken both for the purposes of knowing the laws of rural land ownership, records maintained in Government offices and also to determine ownership of land in private hands as well as owned by the Government and included land, tanks, hillocks, river and all other water bodies. This knowledge was necessary because in police service one had to deal with land disputes, trespass, riots, illegal reaping of harvest as well as crimes leading to assault and murder over land disputes. The second purpose was to give an opportunity to the trainees to know village life and fend for themselves by setting up a temporary mess house, appointing cooks, sweepers and other staff and stay in a small tent. During the settlement training each trainee had to stay in a small double fly tent and the ground was covered with straw and a *durree.* There was an extension of the outer fly which served as a bath-cum-toilet room. All the furniture for living a camp life had to be arranged or bought by the trainee himself, namely, a folding camp cot, bedding including a mosquito net, blankets, bed sheets, skeleton camp furniture like a folding chair and a small table, preferably folding, a bath tub and a commode.

Each police probationer was coupled with a trainee ICS officer to form a team. For police probationers the training lasted 2 months to learn settlement work. During our time settlement work was going on in Balurghat subdivision in Dinajpur district. In the first month the camp had all i.e., IP and ICS trainees together. Each police trainee was coupled with an ICS trainee and I had Mriganka Mouli Basu, ICS, as my mate. In the second month each couple went to a village to do actual settlement work. Mriganka was a quiet man of conservative tastes and did not like riding nor did he take easily to European life style. We had also visitors in the person of the Director of Land Records who was one B.B. Mukherjee, who was the father of one P.B. Mukherjee who became Judge and later Chief Justice of the Calcutta High Court. His youngest son Sabyasachi Mukherjee became the Chief Justice of India. We had also a visit by one Mr. Saxby who was the Member of the Board of Revenue and was the Head of the Department of Land. Land Survey and Land Revenue. During this first month we played hockey and did horse riding frequently.

In the second month of settlement training the groups dispersed and tried to do actual work by writing khatians, parchas and check the measurements of land holdings including water bodies. In the first month we had the settlement officer in the person of one Bell, ICS, who was a friendly chap keen on teaching us the right things. During this period I often indulged in shooting feathered game. I remember that I had done very good duck shooting in a large nearby jheel within a few miles of our settlement camp where I used to go on horse back and carry my gun and cartridges. I do not remember if the gun belonged to the mess or was my own. I remember a funny incident when in a large field from which crops had been harvested and farmers including women were busy in weeding out roots of the crops already harvested and there was clear vision all round. I had an urgent call of nature to evacuate my bowel but there was no place nor any bushes to conceal myself where I could relieve myself. Having no other means available I spotted a large tree in the field and I climbed the tree and went up pretty high from where sitting on two branches I relieved myself and used toilet paper to clean myself and climbed down after wearing my trousers, I had been carrying a bottle of water to drink with which I cleaned my hands. Another incident I remember which occurred during the joint camp namely, that I had learned shooting wild games before I joined the police and once or twice I went out to shoot jackals which were annoying us at night by their loud howlings. There was an ICS officer named Hatch-Barnwell (Junior) with whom I did not have good relationship because he was uppish and tried to pose himself as important agent of the British Raj. After one night's sound of firing next morning he threatened me saying that if I used the gun again at night he would pull down my tent. I answered back saying that if he did so I would not only pull down his tent but also pee on it. After this I fired the gun next night but later I refrained from shooting jackals although their disturbing howls and visits to forage near the camp kitchen and bins of food remains kept us awoke. Actually before this incident another significant incident occurred in the common dining tent during the joint camp. I had just bought Jawaharlal Nehru's Book of autobiography and was reading out some paragraphs of the book to Bery. Hatch-Barnwell was present and asked me to shut the 'bloody book'. I answered back saying that I shall not and intended to read aloud instead of sotto voce and make him hear. He left the table in disgust.

In order to prevent rain water coming inside the tent we had to dig a trench around each tent below the periphery of the outer fly and provide an outlet so that no rain water could flow inside the tent. In order to prevent snakes slithering inside the tent, I also sprayed carbolic acid around out of a newly bought bottle. Now I doubt if the smell of phenol i.e. carbolic acid is actually repugnant to snakes or the acid prevents snakes from going over a ground sprayed with the acid.

This settlement camp for trainees used to be held in Winter months, namely, from December to March which were pleasant and a Police officer's training ended in two months' time i.e. end of January. ICS officers had to however stay for another two months' because in their job in the district they were the principal land and revenue officers and had to supervise the work of subordinate officers. The gazatted officers in the provincial services, namely, Dy. Magistrates and Munsiffs on probation also joined the settlement camp and their training lasted four months. Our camp was set up in a large fallow land a few miles away from the subdivisional town of Balurghat by the side of the river Atrai. After training in settlement work we returned to the PTC mess and took the horse and syce by train. After return we prepared ourselves to leave the Training College to be posted to districts. I remember that William and Jameson decided to ride back to the college and arrived two days later, dust covered, sun tanned and famished. Their goods came by train.

Before leaving the P.T.C. we had to pass our drill examination and horse riding with the Principal himself as the examiner in both of which I succeeded in the first attempt. The Principal later told me that although I made mistakes in commanding a company (i.e. a number of platoons in various formation) but I kept a brave face and issued commands to rectify the mistakes. He was therefore pleased to declare me 'passed'.

We completed our training in the college and were ready to leave. And the important part of the training in the college was to make the non-Indian officers acquire rudimentary knowledge about India, Indian ways of life of the towns and villages and above all to live and survive the drastic climatic change in living environment and difference in food habits and availability of food staff taken in the British Isles and India. The other important part was orientation of the Indian officers in the British way of life. The college establishment was organised and run like a British Regimental mess. Every Indian was keen to adapt himself to the daily routine and the manner of living expeccted of the inmates of the the mess. Members of the staff and servants were also trained for the purpose. Rulers usually set the pattern of living for others around them to emulate the British Raj and PTC was no exception. Imitation of their way of life was taken as a mark of distinction. It was not difficult to acquire a veneer of westernisation which apparently was what was expected. On the other hand the British officers also acquired skin deep Indianism but some liked to live almost like upper class Indians.

We all had to be put through district training lasting for another six to eight months to be trained in all the important aspects of district police work. The reason was that all IP officers' substantive posting was in the post of a Superintendent of police to be in charge of police work of a district. I was posted to be trained in the district of Murshidabad with head quarters at Berhampore.

2

Learning Basics of a New Career

For district training I was posted to Murshidabad with its headquarters at Berhampore which was built by the East India Company as a cantonment where the then Muslim ruler Siraj-ud-Doula had his capital of the province of Bengal at Lalbagh at a distance of about 14 kms from Berhampore Town.

Berhampore Town was built by the East India Company to accommodate troops and their officers as well as some civil administrative offices and officers residences. There were a number of barracks on two sides of a big field known as the Barrack Square. On the other two sides there were official residential houses of high civil officials on one side and offices of the District Administration, treasury, police armoury etc. on the other side. Some barrack quarters were at my time also allotted to some high officials like the Superintendent of Police, the Superintending Engineer of Irrigation and Waterways, the Superintendent of the Berhampore Central Jail and junior officers like Assistant Magistrate and Assistant Superintendents like me. The individual bungalows were occupied by the District Magistrate, the District Judge, the Civil Surgeon. There was a District Club and also a big tank known as Laldighi in the town which still exists.

At the time I was posted in Berhampore the town had an excellent social atmosphere amongst the District officials with all the officers being Indians. M.K. Kripalani, ICS, a bachelor was the District Magistrate, K.K. Hajara, ICS, was the District Judge, Captain A.K. Gupta, IMS, was the Civil Surgeon, R. Banerjee, IP, was the District Superintendent of Police, Man Singh and Sunny Gupta were the Superintending and Executive Engineers of the Irrigation Department, both being appointees of the Secretary of State for India in London. One Girija Datta, an officer of Bengal Police of Dy. SP's rank who was the Superintendent of the Berhampore Central Jail, Aga Hilaly, ICS, was an Assistant Magistrate under training and myself an IP officer was the Assistant Superintendent of Police under training. I could not get any accommodation in the bungalows or officer's residence in the Barrack square and had to rent a small flat in nearby Gorabazar. Later, I moved into the residential accommodation of Aga Hilaly after he was posted out.

All the senior officers were well known and well reputed and were very sociable and hospitable. There were frequent small parties at least once a month, if not once a fortnight, by turn in each officer's house where most of us were invited and used to have good food and enjoy admirable hospitality. M.K. Kripalani and A.K. Gupta were bachelors but still they entertained regularly. Two young officers who were bachelors namely Hilaly and myself could seldom reciprocate this hospitality of our seniors and we could only invite people to tea after arranging to bring cakes and pastries from Calcutta and preparing other dishes like sandwiches, *samosas* at home or buying sweets locally.

I was very lucky to have R.N. Banerjee, an IP officer promoted from the post of a directly recruited Dy. SP. He knew his work thoroughly and could train me not only in official work but also in social manners and etiquette. Moreover, he took a liking to me and felt elated and satisfied that for the first time a direct IP officer had been posted as a trainee under him. He and his family treated me as a member of their family. Gradually I was treated as a younger brother and his wife treated me as a '*devar*' (husband's younger brother) and all the sons and daughters called me 'uncle' and in course of time we developed genuine mutual love, respect and affection for each other. I came closer to this family than any of Banerjee's own brothers. In course of time I became known to all his near relatives. After I came to occupy the position of a member of the SP's family, the children and their cousins called me '*Kakababu*', i.e. 'Dear uncle' and for the children of the family '*Kakababu*' was I and no one else. I used to go to SP's house on all days except when I went to other officers' residence in course of social visits. Aga Hilaly was also a regular visitor to K.K. Hajara's residence in the evening and was liked by the Hajara couple who had not had any children. Later Aga Hilary became the Principal Foreign Secretary of Pakistan. Aziz who was my District Magistrate in Rajshahi had earlier become the Principal Foreign Secretary of Pakistan and later the Minister in Charge foreign affiairs. Actually all the Muslim ICS and IP officers earlier posted in Bengal rose to be high ranking officers in Pakistan.

My first training was to be in a police station for two months and I joined the nearest PS namely Beldanga PS and had to rent a house of 3 rooms. As I wanted a cook-cum-bearer I replied to an advertisement put in by 'Cooks & Bearers Club' in the *Statesman,* Calcutta. The club sent 2–3 names with their biodata and I selected one resident of Orissa on the basis of his bio-data. As we had been cautioned to get antecedents of a new household appointee checked I obtained details of this candidate's residence and parentage and wrote to the O/C of the PS concerned. After a few weeks came the reply that the appointee had been arrested thrice in the past and had been jailed twice for stealing in the houses of his former employers. I confronted my employee who admitted having been in jail twice. I dismissed him and wrote back to the 'Cooks & Bearers Club' that they should not have such people on their panel, not to speak of recommending them for employment. Later with the help of a gentleman employed in Beldanga Sugar Mill, who was a distant relative of the SP, I appointed a local man who served me for two months.

In the police station I had to know all about registers and documents maintained therein and had to write all of them for a few days. I had to record First Information Reports of a few cognizable criminal cases also. The registers and documents were all maintained according to the rules in a book titled Police Regulations, Bengal which was like a Bible of the Police in Bengal. It was a masterpiece prepared in the earlier days of the British *Raj* and consisted of 3 volumes. The first volume contained all the rules and regulations, the second volume contained mainly model reports and list of documents to be maintained in each police station and all other police offices and the third volume was an elaborate index in which the subject was referred to under different probable titles. I had to undertake complete investigation of two criminal cases reported at the *Thana* (police station). I chose to investigate one case of burglary and one case of rioting and completed investigation including writing of case diaries with the help of the officer-in-charge and making entries in the village crime note book, (in short VCNB), etc. The village crime note book was a very important record in the police station and was maintained in five volumes with a supplementary one. I took great interest in reading the past entries and also made entries in the way of training for checking correct entries during my future inspections of the police stations under my control as the Sub-divisional Police Officer and the Suprintendent of Police in a district.

The next phase of training consisted of a stint of a month's attachment to the Circle Inspector's office in Jangipur. Not being able to rent independent accommodation I stayed in a room of the local PWD inspection bungalow. The Circle Inspector used to train me in the duties of a Circle Inspector and teach me as how to maintain registers and documents which were kept according to the Police Regulations, Bengal. He also asked me to accompany him during his tour of inspection and supervision of important cases. Under the Inspector's guidance I had to undertake thorough inspection of a police station in his circle in the same way as he did. The Inspector accompanied me and was present while I did my inspection and recorded notes in the inspection book of the police station inspected.

The third phase of training took me to the Reserve Office in the District Headquarters at Berhampur which was functioning under a Police Inspector who was an Anglo-Indian gentleman at the time. The Reserve Office maintained account of the Reserve Police Force consisting of *Subedars* and Sub-Inspectors, *Havildars* and Head Constables, *Naiks* and Constables and of the entire police force in the Armed Branch of the District Police. There were also the armoury and ammunition depot of the armed police and extra weapons and ammunitions for use of other units namely the police stations and town outposts. In those days police used Muskets, i.e. 303 rifles which had been in long use of the Army and had become unserviceable. They were made serviceable again by grinding out the rifling inside and making them smooth for single shot guns of .410 bore. Special ammunition was manufactured for use of these weapons. The *thana* police used to be supplied with these muskets which did not have long-range nor could be fired rapidly so that least damage or injuries could be inflicted on those who were fired on. The special armed police of the district (SAF) used rifles with magazines taking 9 cartridges besides one in the chamber. The SAF utilised as armed men to guard treasuries in Sadar and the Subdivisions, the police armoury and the ammunition depots or any other place which required armed police guards. Contingents were also sent out to help the *thana* police in case of widespread troubles, rioting, etc. The Reserve Inspector was also responsible for supervising weekly drill in muster parade which was attended by SP and all available officers. There was an unarmed wing called Reserve Office in charge of an Inspector or Senior Sub-Inspector of Police who was responsible for keeping disposition of the district police force in different units and put up records for posting and transfer of all officers of and below the rank of an Inspector within the district. This office had also to put all the armed and unarmed policemen through the rifle and musket firing course once a year and the unarmed police posted in police stations, town outposts once in two years and the Reserve Inspector or his subordinate Sub-Inspector had to arrange to take the force, the target frames and papers, chairs and tables to the firing range which was usually situated out of the town in a less populated area. The personal guards both in plain clothes as well as officers' orderlies who may have to carry revolvers to guard the officer and the police officers, both of gazetted and the non-gazetted ranks, had to be put through a course of revolver firing once a year. The Superintendent of Police or his Additional Assistant or Deputy Superintendent was supposed to supervise such firing as often as practicable. In the course of training I attended and supervised such firing practice several times and always took the opportunity to practise with my personal revolver. I had bought one Webley & Scott revolver of .38 bore as a personal weapon. In course of training in each branch, the Superintendent of Police used to have a discussion with me about progress of my training and questioned me on some points. Next part of the training was to learn work of the Intelligence Branch Office in the district which was usually situated in another building. I got training under the Inspector and came to know the documents and registers to be maintained as well as the functions of the Department and how the officers went about in the matter of collection of intelligence. This branch was mostly concerned with gathering of political, terrorist and labour intelligence and hardly took any part in collection of criminal intelligence.

Last part of the training was in general police work which the Superintendent of Police assisted by his Addl. SP and/or Dy. SP had to do in his day to day work in the District Police Office. This training first consisted of learning the general outlines of an SP's work and also of details of registers, documents, returns, files etc. which the SP's office had to maintain or had to send to higher offices. An important part of SP's work was to prepare the budget, control expenditure and maintain accounts as per orders and instructions contained in government published books and maintenance of daily cash book showing income and expenditure of each day. Money was always drawn from the local Treasury or the State Bank of India within the budget provision. There were occasional receipts of money from other sources like fees for lending the Police Band Party, special posting of police force to benefit individuals, clubs and societies but such money was always deposited to the credit of the government in the treasury or the Bank and could not be mixed with the budgetary provisions of the district nor spent for any purpose. Superintendent, R.N. Banerjee, used to do accounts work in the office chamber of his residence in the afternoon and I was ordered to attend. He was very thorough in checking and used coloured pencils to mark every item for different kinds of checks. I had only to watch and occasionally put queries which he answered and explained lucidly. After lunch I often felt drowsy having actually nothing to do but to observe and learn. I still remember with shame that I had once dozed off for a few seconds and woke up with a start and apologised. The SP told me in an affectionate indulgent tone that he had noticed it and was quietly smiling. Work of Accounts I learnt under R.N. Banerjee stood me in good stead throughout my service life and even later in my private profession in post service life.

Besides officialdom and its social life, there was a vigorous social life amongst the officers and elitist public. Murshidabad was the capital of the last Muslim rulers of Bengal and the royal residential town was known as Lalbagh which contained the royal palace and other buildings connected with a reigning *Nawab* (King). In the district there were many *zamindar*s (landlords) and big affluent business families dating back to the time of the last Muslim rulers and early days of the East India Company. The British also conferred *zamindaries* on a number of affluent Hindus who were loyal to the British and did not have much love for their former Muslim rulers. In Murshidabad, the descendants of the *Nawab* were also staying and living a quiet life. The palace was a must for sight seers, historians and archaeologists. Among important members of the public were the *Maharaja* (Nandis) of Cossimbazar where the East India Company had their *Kuthis,* i.e. principal trading centre, Junior *Raja* of Cossimbazar (another Raj family), *Raja* of Azimganj, the town being the home of a number of rich Jain and non-Bengalee business families. The premier prince was the *Nawab* of Murshidabad followed by the *Maharaja* of Lalgola, Lalgola being the terminal station of the Eastern Bengal Railway on the river Padma across which lay the district of Rajshahi. Most of these personages were also members of the District Club of which only Class I officers of the government, *raja*s, *Maharajas*, big *zamindar*s, eminent lawyers and physicians, heads of some Government departments could become members. The elitist public of Murshidabad were sociable and very hospitable.

The affluent public often had social ceremonies like weddings, ceremony of first giving solid food to a male child and religious ceremonies like rituals of wearing of the holy thread by the Brahmins and Kshatriya were also held. Important officials were invariably invited to attend and were served good food and wholesome entertainments like magic shows, musical soirees etc. My SP was very popular amongst the public and was never left out from the list of invitees. He invariably saw to it that his favourite ASP, i.e. myself was also invited on these occasions. Among other senior officers Hajaras were also popular.

My SP often took me to accompany him in his Chevrolet car to go on tour of inspection of an office or supervision of investigation into a serious criminal case like a dacoity, robbery, murder or rioting. I was always glad to accompany him to be able to get out of the town and moreover to earn a small sum of money as TA which amounted to a daily allowance of a princely sum of Rs 6.

While I was in Berhampur, a serious case of molesting a young housewife occurred. In this case wife of a junior officer who rebuked her newly appointed servant was molested and seriously injured by the servant who pushed the handle of a palm-leaf fan into her private parts thus injuring her with serious bleeding wounds. She was profusely bleeding and was taken to the local hospital for treatment. The husband came to SP and related the brief details in tearful eyes. SP assured him of catching the culprit who had fled the town and ensuring that justice would be done. He ordered First Information Report to be recorded on the crime and sent out an alert notice to all neighbouring police stations and despatched some police officers from the head quarters. I am glad to say that the culprit was arrested in the afternoon of the same day at an outstation ferry and was brought to headquarters. SP saw the culprit and left it to his subordinate officers to administer a little physical punishment before putting him in the *thana* lock up and sending him up as an undertrial prisoner next day to the court. I cannot but record here that while R.N. Banerjee was SP, Howrah, a case of misappropriation of a large sum of money namely Rs 60,000 occurred in Howrah Town and the owner who was well-known to SP and myself (I was Addl. SP) came to SP and sought his help. R.N. Banerjee assured him of catching the culprit and recovering the money and fortune again smiled on him. Howrah Police caught the culprit at Howrah Station and recovered the entire sum of stolen money. Later I shall recount my stint of a year with R.N. Banerjee in 1945-46 in Howrah.

Berhampore town had a District Club. It was customary for all Class I officers to become members of the club and after being duly proposed and seconded I was elected to be a member. The club had a tennis court, a squash court, a billiards room and a small library. Most of the officer members played tennis and some billiards. I remember that District Magistrate Kripalani, the District Judge Hajara, Civil Surgeon Captain Gupta, SP and myself were regular tennis players besides a few others. Kripalani was the best player and I was not too bad due to my playing the game in my college days and in the Training College in Sardah. In billiards also I attained a tolerably good standard having played the game regularly in Sardah PTC mess. As Kripalani was fond of tennis and would not miss the game if he could help, he often sent words to me asking me to attend. As I was also fond of the game and somewhat proficient I joined Kripalani as often as I could. As a matter of fact I played tennis throughout my police life wherever I could find a tennis court and exception was Howrah which did not have a District Club.

In Berhampore I used to go out duck shooting with my gun and managed to bag ducks from large tanks on a few occasions. SP was also interested but the most interested was Kumar Dhirendra Narayan Roy of Lalgola, grandson of the *Maharaja*. Before I joined the Police I went to the *Sundarban*s on a *shikar* trip and the local gun dealer Motilal Bhunja who used to sell guns and cartridges had a 4 bore duck gun. While in Berhampore I remembered about the gun and its potentialities and managed to induce him to sell the gun to me. Cartridges had specially to be made and Manton & Co. of Calcutta made these cartridges for me. They were huge things compared to 12 bore cartridges.

During my stay in Berhampore, Kumar Dhirendra Narayan Roy, in consultation with the District Magistrate and the Superintendent of Police invited Sir Khwaja Nazimuddin, the then Home Minister of Bengal and Sir Azizul Huque, Chairman of the Legislative Assembly to come to Lalgola for a day as his guests for a day's duck shooting on the Padma char land. The two high dignitaries agreed and Kumar Sahib invited me and the SP. We reached the palace in the afternoon by SP's car and stayed in the palace. Kumar *Sahib* discussed plans of operation for the next day when we shall form two or three parties, mostly two shikaries together. SP was attached to Sir Khwaja Nazimuddin and I was attached to Sir Azizul Huque. I took my self-loading 12 bore shot gun as well as the 4 bore duck gun which could be handled by two men acting in unison. Sir Azizul and I tried our best to approach the birds which consisted of a large variety of ducks and geese like teals, pochards, mallard and Siberian geese white and grey but we had to walk in knee deep muddy embankment and we had no cover and were visible to the birds. The ducks would move away to a distance outside our gun range. Sir Azizul therefore decided to use the 4 bore duck gun which had double the range of a 12 bore gun. I offered to act as the support and advised him to put barrel of the gun on my shoulder and to fire by putting the butt on his own shoulder. He did not agree as he feared the vicious backkick might cause a broken collar bone. It was, however, sporting of him to act as the support and I volunteered to fire the gun. In doing so he had to go forward into deeper mud. I fired two shots from two different positions and one small bird fell. We were somewhat unsporting in the sense that we were firing at sitting ducks and geese because the birds were flying over water at a much longer distance. Incidentally the gun was so heavy that there was hardly any recoil not to speak of a vicious recoil. However, Sir Azizul was fed up with acting as the support with the heavy gun barrel on his shoulder and going more than kneedeep into soft mud. We, therefore, decided to continue our efforts with the 12 bore shot guns and failed. We continued our exercise till lunch break when we decided to call it a day. Sir Khwaja Nazimuddin and SP's team could not also bag any bird. Only Kumar Dhirendra Narayan, a veteran and experienced duck shooter of the char area, came back with a Siberian goose. It was decided to have goose roast at dinner which we all partook of. This occasion, however, gave me an opportunity to be closely known to two important members of the Muslim League Ministry which formed the Government in Bengal and I managed to keep up my acquaintance with Sir Nazimuddin for many years to come. Sir Azizul died sometime later due to a sudden heart attack. Both the persons were found polite, generous and considerate. Nazimuddin developed a little affection for me because in subsequent years he allowed me to use his own official two and five seater planes to reach me to my place of posting in Barisal and Dacca.

Soon my training was completed and I got an order of my posting as the Sub-divisional Police Officer, Netrokona, which was one of the four subdivisions of the district of Mymansing. Netrokona was at the farthest north-east corner of Bengal bordering on Assam. I prepared myself to join my post and arranged to send my household goods like furniture and crockery cutlery by train. I myself spent a few days of my joining time to enjoy dinners and luncheons given by my senior colleagues in Berhampore and the remaining few days with my mother and brothers in Calcutta. Before I proceed with the tale of my life in the police, I would make a brief reference to my earlier years.

3

Ancestral Tales—Birth of a Life Long Nationalist

Born in a Bengali Brahmin family of West Bengal, I am a progeny in the eleventh generation of my forefather, one Gadadhar Mishra, who migrated to Bengal from Kanyakubja, i.e., Kanouj in UP. I belonged to the subclass Vaidik amongst the three subclasses of Brahmins. Vaidik Brahmins were so named because they all devoted themselves to the study of the Vedas, Upanishads, six branches of classical Hindu philosophy and ran 'tols' and schools to teach Sanskrit grammar, literature and books on the Hindu religion. They also performed Pujas and administered 'Deeksha' or initiation ceremony into religious life and became religious Gurus or preceptors. People of this community were seldom affluent except when some disciples donated large tracts of farm land to their Gurus out of love and respect which sometime helped them to acquire a considerable wealth. But then again this affluence did not last long as such properties became divided and sub-divided amongst heirs of the original donee. Gadadhar Mishra first settled in Bhatpara 25 miles north of Calcutta and one of his direct descendants shifted to a village named Ariadaha in the outskirts of Calcutta. My great grandfather, although living a conservative religious life of a devout Brahmin, indulged in certain unnecessary luxuries like having luxury boats to cruise along the river Bhagirathi on the bank of which Ariadaha was situated. He got the handle parts of the boat's rudder and oars covered with silver sheets. He also spent money in charities and thus reduced the family fortunes. On his death my grandfather who was a sober worldly wise man paid back debts of his father, expanded the *zamindary* to about 2000 *bighas* of land in the district of Midnapore. He decided to move to Calcutta and bought a house with a large compound and a small tank the total area being 27 cottahs, i.e. 1.5 acres. He bought 3 other houses, two in Burrabazar area and the third one in Bhowanipore. The two houses in Bhowanipore were situated in very respectable localities in which well known advocates, barristers, High Court judges and *Zamindars* resided. My grandfather moved from Ariadaha to Calcutta with his wife, two sons and four daughters. My father was the younger son and was admitted into Hindu School to get English education. He passed his entrance examination and later continued his studies for higher education in the Intermediate classes. My father lost his mother, i.e. my grandmother early and the two brothers had often to cook the family food if the sisters were absent or were not allowed to cook food during menstrual periods. In this connection I cannot help relating a funny incident. My father was appearing in his intermediate final examination but he had to cook his own food everyday to be able to leave early enough for the examination hall which was in central Calcutta. One day he noticed that he had not cleaned his hand thoroughly and noticed that part of the hand was covered with soot of a cooking pot. As such he considered his hand not clean enough to continue to write and the answer paper remained incomplete. He gave up his studies after my grandfather died and he and his elder brother continued to concentrate on consolidating the inherited family fortunes.

Zamindari work consisted mainly of renting out land and collecting rent in the form of cash or paddy and that did not fully engage the two brothers and as such they decided to embark upon a trading enterprise. In those days there were no motor cars and the only means of decent conveyance was horsedrawn carriages. Bullock carts and palanquins carried by men were also used as inferior means of conveyance. There was only one firm, named Hart Brothers which sold imported Australian and large sized local bred horses. My uncle and my father decided to start a business in buying and importing good carriage horses. Horses were imported from New South Wales in Australia and were known as Walers. They rented two stables both situated on the Dharamtala Street now known as Lenin Sarani, one such stable was at the site where Wachel Molla & Co later built their departmental stores. Hart Bros had their business premises also on the Dharamtala Street and the building had a white statuette of a horse on its top. The business went on for several years and very distinguished citizens of Calcutta were customers of Bhattacharyya Brothers. Once the Lieutenant Governor of Bengal himself came to see the horses in the stable and my father had to receive him and to shake hands with him. Later I learnt from him that he moved about rather cautiously so as to prevent his right palm which had become unclean by shaking hands with a beef eating Englishman from touching any part of his body. He gave out the reason that the Lieutenant Governor who was an Englishman ate beef with fork and knife and did not wash hands after a meal and as such his own hand had become polluted by shaking hands and he was not at ease till he washed his hands. It was another episode of the stern conservatism although mentally he was a liberal in many ways. The family had a landau carriage for its own use to which were harnessed two Waler horses. There was a telephone connection at the residence as well at the two stables. The joint family of my father and his elder brother were living a more or less happy affluent life till tragedy struck in the form of my uncle dying of tetanus infection. There is a belief that horse dung has tetanus germs in it and one has to be careful when dealing with horses. My uncle most probably acquired an infection of tetanus and succumbed to it.

This tragedy was followed by another of far greater dimension. An epidemic of Glanders which only occurs in horses like foot and mouth disease amongst cattle. One after another horse caught infection and began to die. I heard from my mother recount the tales of those horrible days when the telephone would ring at all hours of the day and night and the stable keeper would announce death of one horse after another. The family faced financial disaster because a good number of horses were bought either on credit or with loan taken from the bank or private moneylenders. The creditors pressed for payment and the family had to make distress sale of their residential house as well as four other houses in the town. Still all the debt could not perhaps be paid. My father and his eldest nephew tried to save the *zamindari* by transferring a major portion to a supposedly reliable family friend as a *benamdar* who later proved to be dishonest and asserted the *benami* sale of the *Zamindari* land as true and got himself declared as the real owner of the land by dint of actual purchase. Thus, the family was financially ruined. My father moved into a rented house and so did my cousins. The cardinal mistake was not to insure the valuable livestock and they failed to do so because of lack of business acumen and experience and insuring live stock was not a usual practice.

Although my father came of a family who lived on land and never undertook any business activities, still he had somehow or other, developed a keen desire to undertake business ventures. After failing in trading in horses, he started a small business in coach building in a portion of a large vacant land adjacent to our rented residential house. This venture also failed because of lack of capital which gradually eroded on account of taking out the profit as well as part of the capital to meet expenses of running the family, spending on children's education and in weddings of daughters. This business was wound up during my early childhood. I still remember having seen a few half built and nearly fully built carriages which remained unsold in the carriage shop. The family had a very faithful 'Good Friday Man' in the person of one Gangaram Singh who stayed with us for many many years. He was our escort in our childhood.

After the carriage making shop closed my father embarked on brick making in kilns and stocking kerosene oil as a wholesale dealer. These ventures also failed as there were none to supervise the operations though my eldest brother who was a college student at that time tried his best to help. The last business venture he indulged in was in timber, i.e. buying timber logs and converting them into planks and rafters but he did not succeed on this either for one reason or another. I remember the sawmen from Sindh or Gujarat who worked manually to saw large timber logs in the compound of our rented residential house.

We, four brothers and two sisters, were living with parents. The sisters got married off and we brothers used to go regularly to schools and colleges. It was also customary for the boys to have a stint in a *Pathsala* which was run by one Nibaran Pandit but we soon left the *pathsala* and got admitted in High Schools. In 1920 we moved from the rented house into a small house built on a lane branching out from Haris Mukherjee Road. We lived for many years in this house which was in a locality of

Bhawanipore, where lived many well-known people like Sir Ashutosh Mukherjee, Justice Sir Charu Chandra Ghosh, Justice Sir Chandra Madhab Ghosh, Justice Dwarik Chakravorty. Adjacent was Harish Park, named after the memory of the well known patriotic writer Haris Ch. Mukherjee who grew in prominence with such luminaries as Madhusudan Dutta, Ishwar Chandra Vidyasagar, Prince Dwarkanath Tagore who were then the champions of the glorious Bengal renaissance.

Our rented house as well as the one built by my father had two schools in the vicinity. One was South Suburban School founded in 1874 and Mitra Institution built much later. Almost all boys of local families studied in South Suburban School as did Sir Ashutosh Mukherjee, my father and many others. I was admitted to the South Suburban School at the lowest class which was known as the ninth class. There were nine classes and one had to appear in the Matriculation (school leaving) examination after studying a year in the first class and passing the test examination. My eldest brother passed the M.A. examination in English, second eldest brother became M.A. B.L. and the third eldest and I became graduates. There were two long vacations one in early summer in May and June after which was held the half yearly examination and the second one was during the Durga Puja in September and October after which the annual promotion examination was held albeit a couple of months later. Before the school closed for summer vacation, the school held classes in the morning for about 4-5 weeks to avoid summer heat. These few weeks used to be the most enjoyable for middle class students who used to go half an hour earlier and used to play games like kabadi, gadi etc. or play on the swing or seesaw balancing board in the adjacent Haris Park.

During my school days, we played a number of games mostly outdoor. Playing football was a regular pastime and we played the game with school mates and local friends in a part of the *Maidan* and often in a big field known as Porabazar or Scorched Market. This field was a property of the Port Trust of Calcutta then known as Port Commissioners and was the venue of many fairs and exhibitions. Over the years several of them were burnt down due to outbreak of fire for one reason or other. After fire broke out in many more exhibitions the field acquired the name Porabazar, i.e. the Burnt Market. During the vacation period as well as on Sundays and holidays we used to play *Marbles, Danda Goli, Thieves and the Police* as well as *Lattoo* which was a top or a spinning toy with a groove round the tapering side and around which was wound a strong piece of string with which it could be thrown on ground or even put on one's palm with a rotating motion. The wooden top had a projecting iron nail on which it whirled. We held competitive games in *Danda Goli* and marbles but the most interesting was a game known as Russo-Japanese war in which one old top was put on the ground along a line and two lines were drawn on each side some distance away. There were players on both sides and each player got one shot to move the target to one's side beyond the second marking line on its own side. Whichever side could take the target in its own area first won the game. For the purpose of playing soccer more seriously I enrolled myself as a member of a club known Elysium Club. The Club was situated in a lane nearby and it had its playground where soccer and cricket were played according to the season. This club took part in several tournaments organised for boys and I took part as a team member.

I have a happy memory of my school days except for the first few weeks of my admission. In the lowest class there were some older students who made vulgar gestures and used obscene language meaning of which was not clear to me nor to many other students who were brought up in a cleaner atmosphere. They also used to write obscene words on the walls of the toilet rooms. Mentally I used to feel disturbed, almost tormented, although they did not manage to drag me in their fold. I soon began to learn my lessons and started doing comparatively well in the examinations. In the upper classes the competition became confined to three students including myself each of whom stood first in his section and sometimes topped the list in the whole class. I also topped the list of students who passed the Matriculation examination.

Looking back I now realise how good education was denied to the students in the lowest classes for which incompetent and half educated teachers took the classes and taught subjects. Although the school was half English medium in the sense that except in Bengali and Sanskrit, answers had to be written in

English in the class and in the yearly and half yearly examinations. The teachers could not pronounce English words correctly nor could the teachers in history and geography correctly pronounce historical and geographical names spelt in English. We learnt wrong pronunciation and it was difficult for us to rectify our erroneous habit in later years when we began to feel ashamed of our wrong pronunciation. Students, however, learnt to write correct English having had to master contents of two books on English grammar authored by Rowe & Webb and Nestfield besides studying a book of English idioms by Mcmordie. I had difficulty to correct myself and to succeed in correct pronunciation in later years, especially after I joined the Police service when I stayed in a mess with the British boys who were my colleagues.

The school had a large compound with trees in a part of which drill classes were held by the Drill Master who was an ex-army man with a strict sense of discipline. Students played or strolled about in the compound during half-an-hour break for midday meal or tiffin. While I was a student in the lower classes. my two elder brothers who were three and five years older were students in three and five classes higher than mine. We all brothers won prizes for doing well in some subjects in the annual examination. It was a practice to allow students who did well to sit in the front benches close to the teacher's desk and platform. I occupied such a bench for 7 years till I passed out of the school. Three insignificant incidents still stick out in my memory. One day in the geography class a student was asked to point out India in a map of Asia. He searched fervently all over the map and failed to point out. Sitting close to him I whispered that India was on the back of the map and he turned the map to find India and received a few strokes of the cane. After the class he was furious with me and I apologised profusely and told him that I could not imagine that he would believe my absurd suggestion. On another occasion I bought a slab of caramel which we called chocolate in those days and it was imported from England. When I was about to eat, a fellow student came up to me and said that the caramel was prepared with the breast milk of English prostitutes and was an impure thing for a Brahmin to eat. I believed him and he took the slab and merrily ate it. The third incident occurred during an annual examination. A number of students never learnt to read the Devnagri script in which Sanskrit text books were written and memorised English or Bengali translation of important paragraphs beginning with specific words. One close friend had secreted with him translations of the Sanskrit text smuggled into the examination hall but did not know where from to begin or where to end because he could not read or understand the questions written in Devnagri script. He sought my help with tearful eyes and I had to read out the beginning and the end of each question to enable him to put the translation of the passage in English from the smuggled answer paper.

When I entered the school Sir Ashutosh Mookerjee was the President of the School Committee and used to preside over the annual prize giving ceremony and distribute prizes. Later Sir Pravash Ch. Mitter became the President and distributed the prizes till I left the school. The two most memorable prize giving ceremonies occurred during my school days. On one occasion Mahatma Gandhi came and joined the ceremony. He was clad in a short Dhoti of *khaddar* (home spun and woven cloth) and had no garment on his upper body. That was my first glimpse of the Mahatma in flesh and blood. We students were overwhelmed with joy. He was given an ovation by all present who shouted 'Gandhiji ki Jai' (victory to Mr Gandhi). He silenced us and spoke a few words about need to be conscious about working for the country's freedom and lead a life of student with rectitude. A couple of years later poet Kazi Nazrul Islam came to a prize distribution ceremony and he recited one of his patriotic poems. We were simply enthralled. I do not still know who was responsible for bringing these two eminent sons of India to our prize distribution ceremony especially because the then President of the school Sir Pravas Ch. Mitter was known to be close to the British *Raj*. There was one great difference in the attitude of the students and their parents of my days and those in present times.

During the nine years of my school life in the 20's national movement to achieve freedom from the British rule started at the clarion call of Mahatma Gandhi who had come to India from South Africa and electrified the people of India with a strong national fervour. The earliest occasion still existing in my memory was my attendance and presence in the Bengal Provincial Conference which was held under a big *pandal* in a field near our rented house and almost adjacent to a corner of which was my father's coach building workshop. I do not remember who attended but there were several public leaders and the main theme was to try to achieve self rule, if not complete freedom, for the country. In the 1920s there were numerous public meetings held and almost all of them were held in Harish Park within less than 100 yards of our residential house. My father did not, so far as I remember, attend but we all four brothers attended and listened to the speeches of the political leaders. Bhowanipore in South Calcutta could boast of several prominent Congress leaders like Chittaranjan Das, Subhas Chandra Bose and his brother Sarat Chandra Bose, Jatindra Mohan Sengupta, Santosh Basu and many others. There used to be many meetings which were attended by outside national leaders of eminence like Mahatma Gandhi, Jawaharlal Nehru, Maulana Muhammed Ali and Shaukat Ali known as Ali Brothers, Urmila Devi, Basanti Devi, Jinnah never came. In some meetings members of the audience burnt foreign goods and there were bonfire of English made shirts and *punjabis.* I remember my eldest brother coming home bare bodied after he burnt his shirt and *genji.* We all started wearing *khadi* clothes, namely *dhoti*, shirt or *punjabis.* Father bought a charka for us and we joined spinning classes which were held in the compound of a local primary school. There was a cotton wool tree (*karpas* tree) in our residential house compound which yielded cotton wool and we brothers were delighted to use that cotton to spin yarn. The spun yarn was not sufficient to weave even a handkerchief. We gave away our yarn spun to a central pool which sent the yarn to a Khadi Bhandar (store) which had its own spinning and weaving sections. *Hartals* or *bandhs* were declared very often for one reason or other and on these days we did not go to the school or college. The streets were patrolled by the police in police van and military armoured cars which often became targets of brickbats thrown at them. I remember having thrown such missiles on several occasions. Such acts were mostly committed by young men and boys at the entrance of narrow streets or lanes who kept watch over the police and ran inside whenever the police got down from a vehicle to chase or to beat them up. There was great excitement when Lord Simon came to India as the Head of a Mission for dialogue with the national leaders mostly belonging to the National Congress. In the 20's and early 30's the freedom movement was strong in Bengal. Although talks were held in Delhi, there were simultaneous agitations in Calcutta with posters all over the places asking Lord Simon to go back without holding any meeting in India. These slogans were shouted orally as well as displayed on posters, placards and wall writings.

In this period, terrorism often became a tool in the hands of a small section of nationalists who thought that besides Gandhiji's non-violent non-cooperation movement, there was need to resort to violence to terrorise the British government and to punish some British and Indian officers who meted out brutal treatment to freedom fighters. The object of terrorism was not only to create an atmosphere of terror in the civil administration but also to kill wrongdoers and high officials of the *Raj* in order to bring the administration to a standstill. Terrorism had started in the beginning of the twentieth century especially during the years of partition of Bengal at the time of Lord Curzon's Vice-royalty. The most famous case was Alipore Bomb case in later years in which Barin Ghosh, his brother Arabinda Ghosh and many others were made accused in a charge of an attempt to wage war against the British *Raj*. Chittaranjan Das, who was a young Barrister-at-law was one of the defence counsels and he managed to get Arabinda Ghosh acquitted by the trial court. Several others were found guilty and sentenced. In the short span of 3–4 years many acts of terrorism occurred in late 20's and early 30's in Bengal, some of them resulted in success and some in failure. Three District Magistrates of Midnapore were killed. Simpson, IG of Prisons was killed in his office in the Writers' Buildings, Calcutta, one IG of Police named Lowman was badly wounded in a Dacca shooting. During a convocation meeting of the Calcutta University in the senate Hall attempts were made on the life of Sir John Anderson, Governor of Bengal, on Watson, the editor of the pro-British newspaper named *The Statesman* and many others. Prominent amongst the terrorists were Binoy Bose, Badal Gupta and Dinesh

Dutta who killed the IG of Prisons. Two committed suicide but the third one was caught alive and awarded the capital sentence which was carried out. There were young women among the terrorists and names of Suniti and Shanti Ghosh and Bina Das can be cited who operated in Calcutta and whose names readily come to my mind. The most important event was the successful terrorist attack on the European Club and police armoury in the town of Chittagong which resulted in loss of European lives and looting of rifles and revolvers from the armoury. Several terrorists were killed during assault and later there was a continuous fight between the police and armymen on one side and the terrorists on the other who had escaped into the hills and forests of Chittagong hill tracts but some terrorists were killed and some were captured. One young female student Pritilata sacrified her life by leading the assault on the Club. There was another young girl named Kalpana Dutt who later married S.M. Joshi, a communist leader and lived many years as a political worker. The mastermind behind planning and execution of the terrorist operation was one Surya Sen who was known as "Masterda" and managed to escape. The police, however, managed to capture several leading terrorists like Ananta Singha, Ganesh Ghosh and others who stood trial and were sentenced to transportation for life or long terms of imprisonment. Surya sen was later captured, tried and sentenced to death. These events electrified young people, many of whom formed small terrorist groups and began to learn the art of bomb making. They also learnt the art of attack and defence with *lathis* and daggers. I was in one such group and planned to throw bombs at the Europeans who were only admitted to be on the first floor of Firpo's restaurant on Chowringhee Road which could be easily attacked with bombs from a double decker bus passing along the Chowringhee Road. From the upper deck of a double decker bus bombs could easily be thrown into the restaurant. As the restaurant was peopled with European women and children we did not have the heart to carry out the plan. We had no seasoned leader to guide us and we could not plan any successful outrage. I had joined two clubs. One was meant for body building by undergoing physical exercises to develop one's body to become strong and muscular. One practised on parallel bar and rings, with dumbbells, lifting weight and skipping. I had joined this club at young age and had good results in making my thin body strong and somewhat muscular. In the other club I used to learn *lathi* and dagger play both for attack and defence. One evening I received a blow on my nose from an opponent's *lathi* and started to bleed profusely. I was made to apply ice and continued to do so for 3 hours till about 10 p.m. for fear of being detected with the injury and being severely remonstrated by my parents if I returned home with the injury. Ice had done wonders. Not only bleeding stopped but there was no swelling or pain later. Subsequently I had, however, a dent in the nasal bone which lasted all my life. It was a habit of mine and my friends to go to shows of physical prowess, muscles display and control and body building as well as boxing on the state. I remember two well-known boxers of the day named Phani Mitra and P.L. Roy whose display we watched from the auditorium. As a result I also decided to learn boxing and after procuring two old pairs of gloves I and a couple of other friends started to learn boxing at home without any training. There was a friend who was a better performer than I was and I started reading books and made up my mind one day to give him a knock out. I remember that day I myself received such a blow instead of giving a blow to my opponent that I fell down nearly unconscious. Later I also joined a wrestling club and learnt wrestling from an *Ustad,* i.e. 'an expert' but smearing body with loose earth and a lot of rough handling by the '*Ustad*' did not suit me and I had to give up both wrestling and boxing and started playing tennis in the college ground. In the Punjab also daring acts of terrorism occurred and in one case Bhagat Singh, Sukhdev and Rajguru took part, got caught and were convicted and faced capital punishment. There were many others but writing from memory, I cannot recollect the names.

At the same time, the Congress leaders, especially Jawaharlal Nehru, condemned all acts of terrorism not only because such acts were against the principle of Gandhiji's non-violent movement but he also thought them to be futile and these acts would not achieve any tangible success. Moreover, hundreds of young men would pay severe penalty as price for a small success. As we all revered Gandhiji and all National leaders, Jawaharlal's constant reprimands and condemnation depressed our small group and we nearly gave up our plans of violent action. Still being the leader of the group I and a friend decided to see Jawaharlal to make him desist from condemning us even if he could not appreciate or encourage such acts. I and a co-worker decided to see him during one of his visits to Calcutta but it was nearly impossible to see him in the midst of his busy schedule. After making two futile attempts in the forenoon and afternoon on the penultimate day of his stay in Calcutta we gate-crashed and forced ourselves in Jawaharlal's presence when he was staying in Dr D.N. Moitra's residence in Bhowanipore. He got very angry but agreed to listen to us. We told him that we had formed a small terrorist group and planned action but his condemnation had raised serious doubts in the minds of most of the group and asked him to stop such condemnation. He told us that we were fools and day dreamers and would just shed our blood in vain. For a drop of British blood, dozens of terrorists would die and our efforts would only bring pain and hardship to us and our families and the society at large. He advised us to abandon our erroneous path and join the main stream of national movement. We openly expressed our dissent and had the temerity of using words of threat to a leader whom we worshipped. On communicating result of our conversation with Nehru, our group almost decided to abandon their plans of killing innocent civilians. In his autobiography Nehru has described this incident in detail on pages 316 of the 1947 reprinted edition of John Lane The Bodley Head, London as reproduced below.

"On my last evening in Calcutta, a little before I was due to go to the station for my departure, two young men called on me. They were very young, about twenty, with pale, nervous faces and brilliant eyes. I did not know who they were, but soon I guessed their errand. They were very angry with me for my propaganda against terroristic violence. They said that it was producing a bad effect on young men, and they could not tolerate my intrusion in this way. We had a little argument; it was a hurried one, for the time for my departure was at hand. I am afraid our voices and our tempers rose, and I told them some hard things; and as I left them, they warned me finally that if I continued to misbehave in the future they would deal with me as they had dealt with others.

And so I left Calcutta, and as I lay in my berth in the train that night I was long haunted by the excited faces of these two boys. Full of life and nervous energy they were; what good material if only they turned the right way! I was sorry that I had dealt with them hurriedly and rather brusquely, and wished I had had the chance of long conversation with them. Perhaps I could have convinced them to apply their bright young lives to other ways, ways of serving India and freedom, in which there was no lack of opportunity for daring and self-sacrifice. Often I have thought of them in these after-years. I never found out their names, nor did I have any other trace of them; and I wonder, sometimes, if they are dead or in some cell in the Andaman Islands."

At this time Gandhiji started Salt *Satyagraha* and the movement spread to Bengal. Besides he declared the campaign of boycotting liquor shops and embarked on the Salt *Satyagraha* in the form of violating the law that no one could extract salt from the sea water or any other source except a licensed person or establishment which had to pay license fee and tax on the salt extracted. Gandhiji also declared *satyagraha* on liquor shops because liquor consumption was ruining poor people in health and wealth.

There was no sea near Calcutta but salt *satyagraha* was launched in Kalikapur which was at a distance of 12–15 miles from Calcutta. There was a large shallow salt lake and on the shallow banks salt accumulated as a result of drying up of water by solar heat. Most *satyagrahis* of Calcutta and some leaders flocked there and nominally broke the law. There were several possé of policemen under junior officers who would chase the *satyagrahis* or beat them up. As the *satyagrahis* were far too widely scattered the police could not effectively prevent them nor could they assault all the violators of the law. I took part in taking salt in small bags and brought it home. No policemen chased or assaulted the group I was in.

More effective were our efforts to prevent people from buying liquor. There were several country liquor shops in Bhowanipore. I organised a dozen of my local *'para'* friends who were all nationalist-minded and started boycotting two liquor shops within a distance of a mile or two of our residence. There was no coercion but would-be shoppers were persuaded not to enter or buy liquor. One liquor shop was in the red light area and the women resented our efforts and told us to leave the area as their clientele were not venturing to visit the area and they would starve. We had no reply to give and being raw youths we could not always understand how their livelihood would be effected. We undertook the work in batches on alternate days. One morning I learnt that three of my coworkers had been arrested by the police and put in the lock up. The guardians blamed me and I myself felt embarrassed that the police did not carry out raids on any of the days I was present and as the leader I should have courted arrest first. For the next few days I went everyday but the police did not come. The movement came to a halt when government of India agreed to allow individuals to make salt for their own need. After this salt *satyagraha* active freedom movement ceased for a while till Gandhiji launched his 'Quit-India' movement in 1942 with the slogan 'Do or Die' *(Karenge ya Marenge)* when I had already been serving in the Police service. This I shall refer to in an appropriate place.

Struggle was still carried on by the terrorists and their groups, dozens of the former were convicted and hanged, some were shot-dead in combats. Hundreds were in jail after being tried in court or awaiting trial and the rest were detained under special laws enacted for the purpose of dealing with terrorist or other types of violent freedom struggle. In the 30's an important event took place. A *Swadeshi Mela* or a National Fair was held on a moderate scale and my father asked us to hire a stall to propagate sale of a medicine he prepared to cure threadworm in men, women and children. My elder brother ran the stall and earned some money by selling the medicine. I became a volunteer in the mela to help the organisers either to man the gates or to control crowds. The crowd was much smaller than in present times because the population of Calcutta was much smaller. The most memorable aspect of the mela was *yatra* performance every day and on many days the noted musician nationalist Mukanda Das was the star performer. He sang many inspiring nationalist songs which we learnt and repeated at home or in the club. I also became a member of a local club which was the haunt of nationalists or students who wanted to spread ideas of freedom and fight against the British. The Club had a good library which offered many historical or topical books giving authentic records of early British atrocities in the days of the East India Company and their minions Debi Singh, Chait Singh and other. I benefited a lot in historical knowledge of comparatively modern times by reading these books borrowed from the library. Many of the books were authored by the noted historian and sociologist Benoy Kumar Sarkar who wrote both in English and Bengali. I had also special interest in dance and ballet shows and my eldest brother and I rarely missed any such shows. I attended Rabindra Nath Tagore's Gitinatya performance on two occasions, Uday Shankar's performance on one occasion, and ballet performance by teams from Java and Iran besides performance by European groups names of which I do not remember now.

At this time I read a lot of literatures and books on terrorism and freedom fighting activities in other countries. Books on the Russian revolution to soften the autocratic rule in the Czarist regime, details of the French Revolution and terrorist activities in Ireland to end the British Rule were all read. I concentrated more on books on Irish struggle, especially activities of Sinn Fein, Michael Collins and his colleagues. I also read the entire book 'Pather Dabi' by Sarat Chandra Chattopadhya, a proscribed book at the time. All this reading I did while sitting in the Reading Room of the Imperial Library, now renamed 'The National Library'.

I wrote a long article in Bengali giving details of Irish terrorism and struggle for Independence making special mention of Michael Collins and his co-revolutioneries. It emphasised on the atrocities perpetrated by the special British regiment known as Black-and-Tans. The Irish revolutionaries finally managed to free the greater part of Ireland but like in India the country was left divided in two countries, the larger one was named Ireland and the smaller one Ulster or Northern Ireland because the Protestant minorities opposed independence of the whole country to be free from British sovereignty. The hostilities between the Irish people and Northerners are still raging just like between India and Pakistan with the difference that Ireland is insisting on incorporating Ulster in the rest of the country.

The article was meant to be published in a well-known monthly magazine to urge the terrorist organisations in India indirectly to carry on the armed struggle against the British rule by terrorist means. I personally handed over the envelope containing the article to the somewhat nationalistic monthly magazine 'Prabasi' edited by Ramananda Chatterjee but the article was not published. Might be the Editor considered the article to be too bold or to be unfit for publication.

In the summer of 1932 I went to Shantiniketan to attend Gurudeva Rabindranath's birthday celebrations. But that year 25th *Baisakh* was a day of storm and rain and no outdoor celebrations could be held. I was a guest in the house of a college classmate of mine, named Samiran Chatterjee, who had matriculated from Shantiniketan. He was known practically to all the teachers and students as well as Gurudev himself. I attended indoor functions where I could see and listen to Gurudeva to my heart's content but I did not get an opportunity to speak to him or to Dr Amiya Chakravorty who was acting as his secretary. I came to meet Santidev Ghosh, who was a popular and prominent student of Shantiniketan and was having a hand or a say in almost all matters. Another incident occurred on that evening namely one student who was called 'NUTUDI' was getting married and there was limited feasting on that occasion. I do not know the full name of the lady till today. But she was also a popular figure in the campus. I made acquaintances with some visiting young men and almost became a friend of one young man of the well known family of Nahars of the Indian Mirron Street, Calcutta. The family was staunchly Congressee and produced several Congress leaders, one of whom named Bijoy Singh Nahar was a very well known nationalist who became a Minister in West Bengal after Independence.

I had just completed my I.Sc. studies and been entering the outskirts of the wonderful world of science as an Honours student of B.Sc. course. At this period my inborn belief in God as one who could be pleased by worship or angered by blashphemy got shaken. I read a lot of books on popular science especially the two volumes by Sir John Arthur Thompson titled 'The Outlines of Science' and several books by Sir James Jeans. I was so much shaken in my age old belief that I conceived the idea of seeing Gurudeva Rabindra Nath Tagore who was a firm believer in God and revealed his belief in many ways in all his writings of prose and poetry. I sought an interview through the good offices of my friend Samiran who approached Dr Amiya Chakravorty and actually got an appointment for me—a young student who had just appeared in his I.Sc. examination of the Calcutta University. Samiran came down to Calcutta and informed me that I was lucky and Gurudeva agreed to see me. On the appointed day and time both Samiran and I went to Gurudeva's Jorasanko house. Samiran went in first and reminded Gurudeva about his appointment with me which he had in his universal graciousness granted me and got his permission to take me in. Samiran ushered me in and left. I saluted the poet by touching his feet and he asked me to sit on a stool. He was wearing silk gown of amber (*Gerua*) colour and was relaxing in an easy chair. He opened his eyes to see me and enquired why I wanted to see him. I explained my dilemma that new study of science had been shaking my inborn believe in an almighty benevolent God and I wanted my age old previous belief to be restored in course of discussion with him. I questioned him how could he believe so firmly and strongly in an almighty benevolent God when nobody could see him and most people could not even feel his presence whereas science could explain most of the happenings on this earth, in the solar system and in the universe. I was told that science could not explain the most important thing how the universe was born and how the physical, chemical and gravitational forces came into being. I countered the argument by saying that these were inherent in the universe which did not require a God to create them or create the different causes and circumstances which regulate them. It was surprising that he was patient with me and did not dismiss me outright. He went on to say that he felt the existense of the omnipotent God every minute and everywhere. It was unfortunate that I was deprived of the happiness in feeling God's presence, etc. At this stage I became agitated and became somewhat inpertinent and said that his God headedness as expressed in his writings was probably a contrivance to capture the Indian mind both of the Hindus and Muslims who were mostly religious in nature and belief. This impertinent remark shook the poet and he opened his eyes wide and sat up from his reclining position and went on to confirm his deep and sincere belief in God and asked me to read books on philosophy and literature, i.e. other than on science to get back my old belief. I left saying that I had greatly benefited and consoled by my conversation with him and thanked him for being so gracious to a mere ignorant boy, etc. Till today I do not know how a Nobel Laureate of Rabindranath's stature had so much patience with and tolerated so much impertinence from a boy 18 years old. Frankly speaking I became agnostic afterwards and in course of more than 69 years I have lived after that interview my belief in God coincides with that of the great scientist Albert Einstien who thought 'Science without religion is lame but religion without science is blind'. Also certain it is that a conviction akin to religious feeling of the rationality or intelligibility of the world lies behind all scientific work of a high order. This firm belief bound with a deep feeling in a superior mind that reveals itself in the world of experience represents by conception of God. In common parlance this may be described as pantheistic.

During the years I studied to become a college graduate, there were no important political movements and the 1930s were years of worldwide depression. Government of India ceased to recruit any officers in most All India Service posts except in the Indian Civil Service and Indian (Imperial) Police which were controlled by the Secretary of States for India in London. There was, however, recruitment of commissioned officers in the three armed forces, i.e. the Army, the Navy and the recently formed Air Force. I appeared for the joint entrance examination in 1932 held in New Delhi. In spite of securing the second place in the list of candidates who appeared in the written examination I failed to get qualifying marks in the interview for which 400 marks were allotted and as such I failed to get into the armed forces.

I passed my B.Sc. examination and got admitted into the post-graduate M.Sc. class in physics. In our student days we did not bother much about our career or future plans of livelihood, nor did our parents. The opposite is the situation today for students and young men and women and career building takes priority over all other things in life. Two of my elder brothers were employed, the eldest being in West Bengal Civil Service and another brother had started his practice as a lawyer in the District Civil Courts of Alipore and later joined the State Judicial Service. My eldest brother used to think of helping me to build a career and wanted me to study medicine as well as to appear either in the competitive examination for the ICS or the IP service. He was posted outside Calcutta and sent me money to get admitted as a medical student in the Calcutta Medical College. I went to the Medical College to see what kind of student life I would have and entered some class rooms and also a room where the students dissected dead bodies. In the latter case the horrible stench was so repulsive that I gave up the idea on the grounds that if at all I should have joined as a medical student after passing the I.Sc. examination instead of losing two years and secondly I did not like the medical student's life as a whole. So I decided to appear in competitive examinations.

I got question papers of the previous two years of the ICS and IP competitive examinations and studied them. I found that I was not well versed in English literature and the classics to be able to succeed in the ICS examination. Regarding IP examination, I found that the questions were of the Pass and Honours standard of my B.Sc. examination and without knowing English classics I should be able to do reasonably well in the IP examination. With that idea I went to a good tailor in Calcutta and orderd a good 3 piece suit of good quality fabric for me. I rememberd that in the military entrance examination, most other candidates were better dressed than I was and I must have lost marks on account of not appearing in smart well-tailored clothes.

I appeared in the IP examination of 1935 which was held in several local centres. The good thing about this examination was that medical fitness test was held before one was allowed to deposit fees for the written examination. I passed the medical test and prepared myself for the competitive examination in a desultory manner; whereas I and all students studied hard for our university examination but most of us took the competitive examination lightly. My examination centre was in the Presidency College in Calcutta and Prof B.M. Sen, the then Principal of the college, was the principal invigilator. The notable thing in the examination hall was that no body tried to seek help from his fellow examinees who could not also think of helping any one. After the written examination, I was called for the interview which carried 200 marks. I did fairly well at the interview but rather poorly in the written papers, and was almost sure that I would not succeed. While I continued with my post graduate studies having been promoted from the fifth to the sixth year class, I began preparing myself for the next IP examination for a second time.

Then on a Sunday the English newspaper we subscribed to published results of the 1935 IP examination and I was surprised and delighted that I was declared as having succeeded in getting one of the two posts reserved for Bengal. The other successful candidate was one Harbanslal Bery. I told my family members and rushed to my cousins' house where my eldest brother had gone to and showed him the newspaper. He was overjoyed and I was grateful to him for advising me to appear in one of the two examinations in which successful candidates were appointed by the Secretary of State for India in London.

Perhaps a week later I received an official letter from the office of the Inspector General Police, Bengal, intimating my appointment as a probationer in the IP Cadre in West Bengal and asking me to appear before the Assistant Inspector General in the IG's Office. I did not attach much importance and appeared before him dressed in my English clothes. There was also the other successful candidate Harbanslal Bery. He was much smarter and seemed to be nicely dolled up. We saw the AIG, one Mr Hardwick. He first took us to see the IG of Police, Mr Farmer and also the Home Member Sir Robert Reid. Hardwick told us that we are going to see Sir John Anderson, Governor of Bengal the same afternoon and asked me to have a haircut. I apologised for my uncut hair and went to the nearest barber's shop Youd & Co within a stone's throw of the Government House. A gentleman of Jewish origin ran the shop. He gave me a hair cut and charged the princely sum of one rupee, which was the highest sum, I had till then paid for a haircut.

We were taken to make a courtesy call on the Governor Sir John Anderson. I went in after Bery and the Governor shook hands, congratulated me for succeeding in joining a prestigious and useful service and wished me a good career. We were taken back to the AIG's office when the AIG told us to come again to his office next day and see him so that he could tell us what uniforms, clothes and other articles each one of us should buy and take when joining the Police Training College, Sardah, where we would undergo training for 15 months or so. On the next day we were supplied with the list. I bought summer and winter suits, shoes and other essential items. The unusual items were riding breeches of woollen whip cord, top boots with spurs, mess kit consisting of a short white jacket and black woollen trousers with silk tape lining on the sides and Wellington boots with rowels. The AIG also told us where to buy the goods namely breeches, mess kits, buttons, sword, etc. from the Army & Navy Stores and all leather goods from Morrison & Cottle, a small shop making and selling shoes and boots on the Chowringhee owned by an Englishman. Morrison & Cottle took measurements and supplied the leather goods by delivering them at my residence with a bill for payment. I was surprised at their heartwarming treatment to an unknown Indian customer and trust reposed in him for making payment of a couple of hundred rupees later. Army & Navy stores did not take any part of the price as advance but delivered items on cash payment. I got civilian and khaki clothes made by Ghulam Mahammed & Sons situated on the Chowringhee Road at the crossing of Lindsay Street. I also bought suitcases and a long steel box known as Kit box which would contain all items of uniform, leather goods, boot and a sword in a scabbard. The sword bore the emblem of a crown with two letters IP carved on the hilt. Thus prepared I left to join my training in the Police Training College.

When my name appeared as the only successful Bengali candidate in the whole of India, a number of aspirants came to my residence to seek advice. I told them that I had not done well in the written examination but perhaps others had done worse;

in short I was foolish but perhaps other competitors were greater fools. I lost 15 marks deducted for bad hand writing but still there was a small difference with the next examinee, one Pranab Kumar Sen, who succeeded in getting into the service next year. I was lucky to have the difference to enable me to be successful in 1935. I have already described my life as a trainee in the first chapter of this book.

4

First Independent Charge of a Sub-division

I mentioned earlier that I joined as the Subdivisional Police Officer, at Netrokona, a subdivision of the district of Mymansing, now in Bangladesh, which was formed out of the north-eastern area of Bengal bordering on Assam. It was with a very heavy heart that I left Berhampore with its very friendly atmosphere in which I received abundant hospitality and affection from most of the official and non-official families of the local aristocracy which was perhaps the largest in Bengal.

Netrokona town was on the railway map of the Assam Bengal Railway. I travelled by rail and also sent my household goods and furniture by railway goods train. The local Police officers received me and I occupied a one-storeyed bungalow, one of the two best residential government buildings in the town of Netrokona. The other adjacent bungalow was occupied by Karunaketan Sen, ICS, who was the Subdivisional Officer on whom I called as a matter of obligatory courtesy. Both Karunaketan and his wife Mrs Sudha Sen were very friendly and assured me of all help in my official and domestic life. Karunaketan Sen was two years my senior in the university and was well known to all youngmen as a brilliant student who always stood first in all the university examinations from the Matriculation to his graduateship. I had frequent invitations to tea and dinner from the Sen family though I was not in a position to reciprocate their hospitality as frequently.

My stay was for a few months only. I remember that there was a case of small rioting in the town or its vicinity and Sen attached a lot of importance and decided to accompany me to look into the incident, its origin and repercussion as well as to devise steps to prevent recurrence. I accompanied him and it was a very educative and profitable experience for me. He did a very thorough job of his study and supervision. I was impressed because he did the whole thing systematically and thoroughly. The exercise was a great improvement over the superficial or haphazard way I learnt to supervise investigation into a criminal case during my training. I saw the Sens' practically every evening and played the game of word making. Mrs Sen was very well educated having served long as a teacher in a Girls' high school in Kurseong in the district of Darjeeling. Sen was posted as the SDO in Kurseong, got to know Mrs Sen who was then Miss Sudha Roychoudhury and they got married. Later I learnt that Sen had during his training in the UK liked an English girl and wanted to marry her. The girl came to India to see what kind of life she would live in India and saw Sen's father. I learnt that Sen's father had great objection to his son marrying a foreigner and implored Sen to desist from the idea and Sen decided to obey his father.

My short stay in Netrokona as the SDPO was uneventful but still I shall mention a few events. One day I received a small gift of a few mangoes and other fruits and a few sweets from the Maharaja of Susang of Durgapur which was at a place in the north of the sub-division bordering on the Garo Hills in Assam. Two well dressed messengers delivered the small gift on a plate covered with decorated woven fabric I estimated that the total value of the gift was about Rs 70-80, i.e. much more than what the government service conduct rules permit a gift to be accepted. The upper limit was Rs twenty only. I took two mangoes and two sweets and returned the remaining items with a letter of thanks and profuse apology over my inability to accept the valuable gift. In course of my duties I had to visit Mymansing town which was the headquarters of the district. Two things occurred during my first visit. First I was ticked off by the Superintendent of Police for refusing to accept the small gift from the Maharaja of Susang and thus insulting him. I was taken aback and took pains to explain my reasons for refusal. SP pointed out that the Maharaja of Susang was the premier *Zamindar* in the district and he usually sent small gifts to most newly posted government officers in the subdivision and in the District Headquarters. Government had already permitted the officers to accept such a gift on the first occasion. I replied that I did not know and would have acted differently if I was warned beforehand. I was also ticked off for having my woollen socks with a narrow strip of fold at the top. In those days shorts or half pants were worn almost always by the Police officers during day time and trousers were worn on night duty to prevent mosquitoe from bites. I expressed my regrets and told him that I was buying the woollen socks from reputed shops but all of them shrank a good deal after washing. However, I promised to try other brands. Soon after I read an advertisement in the newspaper that one knitwear shop was selling socks, sweaters and other woollen goods which were shrink proof. I have forgotten the name of the shop which was on a street named St. Mark's Road in Bangalore in the native state of Mysore. I received two pairs of socks which were made with soft khaki wool of very good quality and I continued to buy the woollen socks from this shop till khaki trousers replaced half pants. The SP used to call officers for the annual or periodical conferences. I had to attend and stay in Mymansing town for a few days. During such stay, I was allowed to visit and avail of the facilities of the District Club. As I was fond of tennis I used to go to the club to play tennis in the afternoon. After the game most players, both ladies and gentlemen, used to sit by the side of the tennis lawns and gossip for half an hour or so. One evening I heard a young Briton mention the poor education we Indians received in our schools and universities and he cited a couple of instances and added that most Indians were ignorant and foolish. I got furious at this generalisation and blurted out that all countries had students who did not benefit fully from education imparted in schools and colleges. I got a reply from an English woman player that it was not so in England. I then asked her to hear stories of actual incidents which my colleague K.K. Sen, ICS, SDO, Netrokona had related to me. He told me that on reaching UK he got himself admitted into the London School of Economics. After a few days one fellow student enquired of him if he had colleges and universities in India to which query Sen replied that he had come from the Calcutta Zoo (Zoological garden) to join the School of Economics for postgraduate studies. On another occasion Sen was travelling by train when a British fellow traveller who on learning that

Sen was from Calcutta in India, enquired if Calcutta was in Bombay and Sen said no. Then the traveller enquired if Calcutta was in Baroda and Sen replied in the negative and told him that Calcatta was in Eastern India, nowhere near Bombay or Baroda. Sen was however curious to know why his fellow traveller mentioned these two names and learnt that the gentleman knew names of only two places in India because his father served as a Railway guard in the then Bombay-Baroda Railway which connected the two cities bearing these names. The British gentleman was not as lucky as I was when a visitor told me that he had his business premises in Bangalore town and I enquired if it was on St Mark's Road. He was dumb founded and enquired how could I possibly know that his business premises was actually on St Mark's Road and if I was a thought reader. I, however, put him at ease saying that the only street name of Bangalore city I knew was St Mark's road and consequently I could only name that one street. Going back to the main story of the particular evening in the club, I noticed that all English men and women suddenly felt a chill and giving this as an excuse all left. I did not certainly endear myself to the British community. Sudhangshu Halder, ICS, who was Additional Judge in the District told me that I was tactless in relating the incidents of the English peoples ignorance but his very smart wife congratulated me for being able to give a fitting reply to the rudeness of the Britishers who tried to prove that we Indians were all fools and ignorant. Later I received congratulations from K.K. Sen and his wife whom I told about the episode on return to Netrokona.

On return from the District Headquarters, I wrote another letter to the Maharaja of Susang again apolosing for my inability to accept the entire gift and promised to make good my default by paying a visit to him and being his guest provided he agreed. Soon a reply came cordially inviting me to be his guest and stay as long as I liked. Soon an opportunity came when I had to visit Durgapur Police Station in which jurisdiction the Maharaja's palace was situated. I stayed there for two days and saw the Maharaja and became friendly with his sons one of whom Dr Surjit Sinha was a well known educationist and later became the Vice Chancellor of Jadavpur

University. The family had beautiful guns and rifles and the members were known to have gone far and wide all over India on shooting expeditions. There were two elephants in the *Raj* Estate one of which was offered to me to go to the Garo Hills. Garo Hills forests had a particular fascination for me after I had seen the cine picture 'Mukti' featuring late actor Pramathes Barua and actress late Kanan Devi. It was a moonlit night and I wondered into the bordering forests of Garo Hills and tried to feel like the actor. The area was in Bagmara forest beat near the border with Bengal. Although I roamed for hours at night, I did not see any game but I felt animals escaping through the undergrowth. I shall have occasions to refer to the Garo Hills again because in later years I paid as many as four visits with the idea of shooting big game including elephants. Another day still sticks in my memory. Durgapur PS could be reached by rail upto Jaria Jangal and then one had to travel several miles on mud road. During the monsoon Sen and I had once gone to Durgapur PS on some official work. During the return journey there was a heavy shower and even the hired jeep we travelled in got stuck. Both Sen, I and our orderlies had to get down into the muddy road to push the jeep out of very muddy patches. The going was so slow that it seemed that we would never reach the rail head.

During my posting in Netrokona, an Irish officer, named James Jameson, was posted as SDPO, Jamalpur, another subdivision in the same district and I learnt that while trying to shoot a leopard he got badly mauled and was rushed to the Presidency General Hospital, now known as Seth Sukhlal Karnani Hospital in Calcutta. I paid a visit and found that Jameson was out of danger. One major Murray, IMS was treating him. In those days Britishers and Anglo-Indians were only admitted and treated in the PG Hospital.

Before I close this chapter of my posting in Netrokona I may state that Mymansing was the largest district in India, slightly larger in size than the country of Belgium in Europe and had four outlying subdivisions named Netrokona, Tangail, Jamalpur and Kishorganj besides the Sadar Subdivision of Mymansing. During this period another incident occurred. I was taken by some one to see a girl of a well reputed family for the purpose of marriage which did not take place. The curious thing is that after many years I married another girl who was this other woman's niece, i.e. sister's daughter and the Mymansing girl and her husband naturally became close to me and my wife after my marriage. I got a transfer order to act as an Assistant Superintendent of Police, Headquarters in Rajshahi. I was delighted to move from a remote nearly unknown town to a well known town in Central Bengal which was also perhaps the fourth largest town after Calcutta, Dacca and Mymansing in the then Bengal. I took leave of Netrokona with a glad heart except that I knew I would miss the friendly company and hospitality of Sen and his good wife Sudha.

5

Work and Social Life in a District Headquarter

In Rajshahi town I had a nice one storeyed residential house with a tank and a large compound with many trees. Besides there were servants' quarters, a stable and a motor garage. I got a horse from Rabindra Chandra Datta, ICS, whom I had come to know and who I understood had a horse which he wanted to dispose of. I got the horse from him and do not remember whether he took a small sum of money as its price or made a gift of it. I used to ride the horse along the Padma embankment for pleasure and used the horse to go out to supervise criminal cases in the neighbourhood.

The Superintendent of Police was one Hirendra Nath Gupta, a very senior IP officer and the District Magistrate was one Johnson, ICS. Saibal Kumar Gupta, a senior ICS officer, was the District Judge. One Major A.R. Ardeshir, IMS, was the Civil Surgeon. He and his wife used to frequent the club and Ardeshir played both tennis and billiards in the club with us. Later Major Ardeshir got several promotions and retired after attaining the rank of a Major General. I happened to be his guest for one day in Poona, now Pune, in a later year. Major Ardeshir was posted out and Dr Satya Charan Sen joined as the Civil Surgeon. Mr S.K. Gupta was transferred and one Mr Kulada Charan Das Gupta joined as the District Judge. Das Gupta became the first ICS Chief Justice in the Calcutta High Court which had the tradition of having a lawyer as the Chief Justice. Das Gupta was also promoted to be a Judge in the Supreme Court in post-Independence years. Major and Mrs Ardeshir were a very loving couple and would crack occasional jokes at each other and also at others. One evening Major and I were playing carolina in the billiards room. In the game of carolina there were coloured balls and a coloured ball had to be put into the designated pocket of its own. Major Ardeshir pocketted a ball and uttered satisfaction by saying 'There you are'. I shouted back that it was in a wrong hole. Mrs Ardeshir who was sitting on a high bench to watch our play quipped "That's what I told my husband on our wedding night" and the Major lovingly remonstrated saying "Don't be naughty darling." Besides there were Executive Engineer of PWD, a cheerful English bachelor who had a nice small Morris Nine motor car and used to give me occasional rides therein. H.N. Gupta had a charming hospitable wife in Shantilata and had a number of children. Sen the Civil Surgeon and his wife with their children constituted a nice family. I enjoyed immense hospitality from Gupta and his wife and Dr Sen and his wife, the latter treating me almost like a son. The PWD Engineer was soon replaced by one Tarapada Marik with whom and whose family I became very friendly and I enjoyed frequent hospitality from them in the form of meals and riding in their big Fiat car in moonlit nights.

My residential house had no electricity and electric installation was sanctioned and ordered by the government. This was done during my stay. One Anil Behari Sen was the Assistant Engineer (Electrical) and he used to come to supervise the electrical work of installation and sometimes have a cup of tea with me. He held a Class II gazetted post in the state government but seemed to be cut for 2 or 3 steps above that post. Later I learnt that he was in the United Kingdom for several years and got his engineering degree from Glasgow University. He had recently married and I decided to call on him and his wife who were staying in a rented house in the town. Mrs Sen was beautiful and charming and I and the family soon became good friends. We often exchanged hospitality and our friendship was a long lasting relationship of love and mutual help. We remained friends throughout our life. Unfortunately Sen died in 1993. I came to know his parents and close relatives who were in Barisal, District Bakarganj where I got posted twice. I see Mrs Sen even now when she comes to Calcutta or I go to Delhi. Incidentally Sen joined the central government engineering service and was posted in Delhi. Dr Sen and his family members and Mr Marik and his family members and I remained friends for many years even after Independence and saw each other in Calcutta which, after Independence became the place of posting of majority of officers in the service of the truncated state of West Bengal.

In the town I also met a lady who as a girl was a playmate of mine when I was a child. In my childhood days, one day we quarrelled and she mildly rebuked me. I was furious and called her a mare because she had a longish face. As we were lipsing abuses in English and I had not yet learnt my English grammar properly. I said, 'You is a mare'. She knew better English and said that I did not know correct English which should be 'You are a mare'. I protested saying that I meant her only and the verb should be singular, i.e. 'is' instead of 'are'. This controversy went on for some time till a gentleman who was standing by told me that the word 'you' is plural and the verb should be 'are'. That silenced me. In Rajshahi I told a brother officer about the episode and he had a good laugh and added that the gentleman was more keen to correct the boy's bad English rather than bad manners in abusing a girl playmate. However, the lady was a relative of Mariks and joined our private parties in Rajshahi. She was a good singer and regaled us with songs of Rabindra Nath Tagore.

In Rajshahi there were two English bachelors and some Protestant missionary ladies who were members of the Club and played tennis and other indoor games. In those days there were reasonably frequent invitations to tea and occasional dinner parties given to close friends. It was almost customary to serve cakes and pastries and I used to buy these whenever I visited Calcutta. On return I used to throw small tea parties either in the club or at my residence. Sometimes one of the lady missionaries used to bail me out by making cakes for my tea parties.

While the Maharaja of Natore seldom came to the club, Raja of Dighapatia, a place near Natore, was a regular visitor and played tennis. He was also friendly and hospitable. I went to see him in Dighapatia and there were two brothers named Sukuls who were also big *Zamindars* and friendly and hospitable.

Certain incidents occurred which deserve to be related herein. Soon after I joined the then IG of Police, one A.D. Gordon, later knighted wrote a DO letter to all IP officers in the state stressing on the need to do our duty and on taking planned steps to serve the public for whom the Police existed. Towards the end of his DO letter he invited comments and suggestions. I took the letter seriously, read and reread it and took pains to make a few suggestions which were perhaps a little critical of the Police Administration which were also indirectly related to minor defects in the District Police Administration. I got a letter of thanks from the AIG. A few weeks later Gupta, SP, called me and enquired if I had sent a letter in reply to IGP's and I admitted. He told me in a roundabout way that I was a fool to take Gordon's letter seriously and to believe that he really wanted criticism and suggestions. Actually Gordon did not expect a reply from a young ASP and certainly not a critical appreciation of existing police administration. As a matter of fact my SP had been warned to keep a watch over his young officer (i.e., me) with 'way ward thoughts'. I expressed surprise over this hypocrisy of Gordon and apologised for my foolhardiness.

The second incident was my capture of a medium sized crocodile alive. Although born in a vegetarian Brahmin family I had developed passion for *shikar*, more for quadrupeds than for feathered game which most other officers were fond of.

There were 'jheels' i.e. large shallow water bodies in the district and there were small and medium sized crocodiles which lived mostly on fish but were not of the Gharial type, i.e. entirely fish eating types which had long saw toothed snouts. Words came to me that two crocodiles had been spotted in a jheel at a distance of a few miles from the town and I could perhaps shoot them. I went with my shotgun or perhaps a new .423 Mauser rifle I bought from a Calcutta gun dealer. I was accompanied by my orderly whose name I still remember to be one Ram Baran Singh, who was a police constable. Having no car or a motor cycle, both of us rode our bi-cycles and reached the jheel. I could not see the crocodiles which could always be spotted because they usually float at a safe distance and keep their snouts above the water surface to breathe. A crowd of villagers gathered round me and made suggestions about what to do in the circumstances. From amongst the crowd, one villager came forward and told me that he knew one crocodile den or lair which was approachable from the bank and the crocodile might be in its nest. A crocodile always had its den which was dug into the bank having its entrance and exit hole at the water's edge. I went to the spot and saw that it was actually a crocodile's den because a croc's paw marks could be seen. The villagers wanted me to shoot the animal when it came out but it was not known if it would come out in daytime or during my stay there. Then an idea struck me. A few months back I had seen a picture titled "Bring 'em Back Alive" with one Frank Buck as the main hero. The film showed how in Africa he actually caught different animals including snakes, crocodiles, leopards and lions, some with a noose, some in a strong net or making the animal fall into a pit. A large heavy animal like an elephant, rhinoceros or buffalo was not captured.

On the spot I chalked out a plan and told the villagers to help me to catch the animal alive if it was inside the den. Some of them were aghast and refused to help me and to get into trouble with a crocodile but a few agreed to carry out my plan in the preliminary stages. I got a few bamboo sticks and closed the mouth of the den hole at the water's edge by driving stakes deep into the ground to prevent the croc from getting out and this it did by walking back with the tail first. I then guessed what direction the hole of the den, which was in the shape of an underground tunnel, had taken. I got a villager to dig into the likely place where the tunnel would pass through. In the first instance we drew blank but the tunnel was there. I choose a spot at further distance into the land from the first one. This time we dug and then found the existence of a tunnel below and could see the tail of the animal. I made a third hole and found the earth slightly moving and knew it was a spot on the back of the animal. Then I knew that it will be very difficult to bring the animal out although it was easy to kill it by putting a few bullets into the animal but that would frustrate all my plans to be a mini Frank Buck of India. I decided to dig a sloping hole further inland which joined with the tunnel. My idea was to bring out the animal through this path and catch it with a noose of a strong rope. I got the rope from a villager's cattle shed and put the noose at the expected path of exit. I prodded the animal with a stick but it would not move nor come out. Then I conceived of lighting a couple of jute sticks and placing the burning sticks on the croc's back. Before prodding the animal I had put my orderly assisted by two villagers with one end of the rope in their hand and myself assisted by two villagers with the other end. I asked a villager to apply the burning jute sticks to the back of the animal. Soon the croc tried to move away from the heat and seeing an opening came out through it roaring. The four villagers ran and scattered but I asked my orderly not to panic and hold the rope fast. The animal came out fast but it had the noose on its neck and we two were jerked forward till the whole body of the crock appeared. The croc roared and thrashed its tail but my orderly and I did not relax. On seeing that we two had managed to put the noose and the croc had only a little space to manouvre four or five villagers came to help us. With the rope pulled taut the animal could only move the lower part of its body and thrashed its tail and opened its vicious jaws to snap at anything it could find. Then I remembered what Frank Buck had done on such an occasion and asked a villager to bring me a sturdy tree branch from which a small branch forked out. I preferred a branch of a *Babul* tree which was one of the strongest wood growing everywhere. They brought one such branch and one 'dao' (an axe). I got it cut in a 'Y' shape to make a fork in the shape of a sling handle but the handle was kept long. I took the forked branch and managed to put it on the tail and held it fast to the ground. I ordered a medium sized bamboo pole to be brought and asked a villager to tie the tail with strong strings to the pole which reached up to the head of the animal on the other side. After carrying out this operation, I had to deal with the croc's mouth which was opening and roaring full throated baring its frightening teeth. I went from behind and managed to put the fork on its snout and held it fast to the ground. I asked two villagers to help me to hold the head down and mouth shut and used a piece of rope to tie its jaws so that it could not open its mouth. Thereafter I tied the pole along the length of the croc, fastened the nooze into a tight knot and put the animal into a helpless posture. The question now arose how to transport the animal to Rajshahi town at a distance of 5–6 miles. There were no motor cars or motor trucks and a bullock cart was the only solution. It meant we had to accompany the bullok cart walk on foot and push our bicycle back rather tediously. We had been to the jheel at 10 am and it was 3 pm already and we had no food. I decided that we would carry the croc on one bicycle by tying the pole with the crocodile on the horizontal rod of one cycle. I asked my orderly to do so after assuring him that I had a gun and there would be no danger. The orderly who had witnessed the whole operation trusted me and my skill and agreed. So we started for the town with the croc tied to the pole and travelled back to the town, drawing small knots of people following us from different villages. After reaching my bungalow I put the animal in the shade of a tree and decided to eat our luncheon. A little later I decided to untie the croc from the pole and let it loose in the tank in the bungalow compound but did not free it completely. I kept the long rope tied on its neck depression intact. When I took the croc to the tank it was eager to get into the water and I let it go by tying one end of the rope to a strong peg driven deep into the ground. At first the croc would not move nor open its mouth or move its tail. When taken to the water edge it had to be prodded to come to life, i.e. to behave as a live crocodile and it slid into the water. News soon spread and all my colleagues and their family members came to see a live crocodile caught by me and brought to the town without causing any injury by gun shot.

That day I passed the night quietly but from the next day I was worried over food to be given to crocodile. I knew there were a few fish in the tank but not enough to enable the croc to catch and feed on them. If the croc could not catch and eat fish it would die of starvation and I would be responsible. I ordered purchase of a few chicken and duck eggs and kept them at the water's edge near the peg hoping that the crocodile which was moving about would come up to the peg and eat the eggs. I left the eggs at night and protected them from marauding crows with a screen over them so that any one at ground level could see the eggs but not birds flying or sitting on a tree. Next morning I got up early and inspected the site and saw all the eggs intact to my great disappointment. Thereafter I bought some live fish from the local bazar and let them loose into the tank. As the day was a Sunday, my friends and colleagues again came to see the crocodile. Some ladies saw the eggs and mourned over the fact that I had caught a pregnant female crocodile which had laid eggs and rebuked me for my cruelty. I kept silent for some time and later told them the facts when all burst out into laughter.

However, the question of feeding the crocodile continued to worry me. One day the Raja of Dighapatia came and saw the crocodile which willy nilly had to put its snout above the water to breathe. I told him of my worry over feeding the crocodile and he volunteered to take it to his palace which had a brick cement built tank which was once used as a large lily pond and display of coloured fish. I agreed and again brought the crocodile out of water, made it immobile and put it in the Raja's car on its open luggage carrier. After a week or so, I went to Dighapatia and learnt that the crocodile had managed to climb out of water one night and moved about in the closed courtyard occasionally thrashing its tail at the closed doors. There were bed rooms and living rooms round the fish pond and the womenfolk insisted on the Raja taking steps to kill or to remove the animal. Raja had given me assurance that he would not kill the animal and had finally released it in a nearby jheel after writing a short history of its capture, life in captivity for a few days and its final release into its natural habitat. He had put the paper in a properly sealed copper cylindrical capsule which he tied to the tail of the croc with a wire by piercing a fin on the tail. That is the long story of my second memorable episode.

Gupta SP decided to go on leave and one Muslim SP officer Abul Hasnat was to be his successor. I decided to arrange a farewell party and did so at the police lines. All officials, many club members and local dignitaries and local junior officers were invited. I gave a nice short speech which I delivered extempore but which I wrote down earlier and more or less committed to heart. A few others spoke and bade goodbye to Gupta. The District Magistrate who presided over asked Gupta to speak but Gupta was jittery and nervous and rose to thank the organiser and plumped down on his chair profusely sweating. He was a great conversationalist in private talks but was mortally afraid to open his mouth in a public gathering. All of us had tea and I accompanied him and his family by train as far as my jurisdiction lay and bade a sad goodbye.

The third episode was in respect of the local club affairs. The club was in a bad financial condition and it was decided at a meeting of the members to ask for voluntary donations. One Aziz Ahmed, ICS, was the new DM and also the President of the club. We suggested that each member should donate Rs 200 to boost up the club's finance. Nobody spoke but I got up and said that there were rich people like Rajas, Maharajas and *Zamindars* who were members of the Club and well paid senior officials like the District Magistrate and the District Judge as well as low paid officers like myself and there must be some rationale in fixing the quantum of donation which should be more or less proportionate to the members' income. Aziz Ahmed argued otherwise but I stuck to my point and advocated my stand. Most of the members agreed with me but Ahmed took it as a defeat at the hands of a junior officer, got red in the face and grudgingly agreed to fix the sums of donation as per my formula. I do not now remember how much I paid and how much did Ahmed paid.

Abul Hasnat, new SP was a keen tennis player and was a sexologist. We took interest in planning and trapping criminals. Abul Hasnat had a lot of sense of humour and we carried on nicely as long I worked as ASP Headquarters. We used to play tennis and plan for trapping criminals. The most important thing that happened was a complaint from a local businessman that the O/C of Atrai PS was demanding a sum of Rs 500 in order to investigate a criminal case properly and to arrest the accused persons. Otherwise he would not do anything. The businessman thought that the sum demanded was too large for a police officer for doing his duty and sought SP's intervention. SP entrusted me to handle the case and catch the offending O/C flagrante delicto.

In those days there was no vigilance department nor was the Special Police Establishment Act enacted to check corruption. It was simply a case of corruption u/s 161 IPC. The merchant was told to fix the time and date of paying the money but he was warned not to accede to the police officers' request to pay him in the premises of the police station which I could not approach or go into without alerting the O/C or his colleagues. A few days later the merchant came and produced fifty Rs 10 notes which were signed on the back by SP. The meeting was to take place after dusk on the bank of the river Atrai and I could see the transaction by hiding myself in a boat. We hired two boats after getting down at the nearest railway station and I placed my boat at a little distance from the merchant's boat. I had also a powerful torchlight with me. On reaching the *ghat* of the PS the merchant sent words through a man of his that he was ready to meet O/C and was waiting in his boat at the ghat. I could see a lone figure coming out of the *thana* premises with a lantern and could recognise the O/C whom I knew. The merchant went out of his boat and met the O/C on the river bank which was wet and a little muddy or sandy. I saw the two talking for a while and the merchant extending his hand and the O/C extending his own in the posture of taking something from merchant's hands. My boat was at a mere distance of 20–25 feet and in complete darkness. I flashed out my torchlight and walked up to the spot where the two men stood. I saw a small bundle of paper drop on the wet ground. I identified myself and told the O/C that he had been trying to extort money for doing duty and I had seen him accept the money. The O/C started trembling and did not say anything in his defence. I picked up the notes which, when counted, amounted to a sum of Rs 500 and the SP's signature was on the back. I went to the *thana* premises and told the story to the ASI present and got a seizure list prepared by the ASI who signed the list and so did the merchant. I made a general diary entry and left the place. The O/C was suspended. The local Inspector was entrusted with the investigation of the case and he submitted a chargesheet against the O/C to stand trial in the Magistrates' Court in Rajshahi u/s 161 IPC. There were headlines flashed in the newspapers and some members of the public congratulated me and the SP for our efforts to root out corruption.

Eventually the trial started in a case u/s 161 between The State (Crown) *vs* the accused. The public prosecutor opened the case and examined all the main witnesses namely the merchant, the SP and myself. The accused had brought up one Baroda Pain, one of the very best criminal lawyers practising in Howrah Courts. All the witnesses were examined by the Public Prosecutor and cross-examined by the Defense lawyer. The most important and crucial evidence was mine and I gave straightforward and truthful evidence. Then began Baroda Pain's cross-examination on every point in my deposition-in-chief. The cross-examination was in such minute details that I became bored and slightly annoyed as nearly two hours had elapsed since I stood in the witness box. The court also advised the Defense lawyer to conclude his cross-examination. Baroda Pain told me that he would put his last question and expected me a highly placed idealistic young officer to tell the truth without leaving a shadow of doubt. He asked me if I saw the notes fall from the hand of the accused person on the ground which I later picked up. He further clarified and questioned if I had seen the currency notes fall from the hands of the accused or those of the merchant. I said they must have been dropped from the hands of the accused who had extended his hands as if to take something. He questioned if I actually saw the notes in the hands of the accused and saw him drop them on the ground. I could not truthfully state that I did so because the merchant had his back to me and the accused faced me but the hands of the accused were not in my view because of wrong stance of the merchant. I could not therefore swear that the notes were actually in the hands of the accused who later dropped them. Baroda Pain suggested if I could hear the conversation of the two men and I replied in the negative. He suggested that the accused had actually refused to take the money and the merchant had dropped the notes at the feet of the accused when he faced failure and in order to save his face. To the defence lawyer's suggestion if there was no remote possibility of such a thing happening I could not truthfully deny because I did not see the notes being dropped by the accused person. After getting all depositions and completing cross-examinations the public prosecutor summed up the prosecution case and it looked strong and unrebuttable. But then Baroda Pain's wizardry came into play. He admitted all the points which the prosecution had tried to prove but put emphasis on one point namely that the merchant had himself dropped the notes when the accused refused to accept them and the main witness to the drama, i.e. myself could not vouchsafe that the bundle of notes were seen in the hands of the accused and that he was seen to drop them. He pleaded with the court that if there was the smallest chink in the chain of evidence and there was any shadow of doubt about the guilt of the accused, he could not be convicted. Actually the court accepted this argument and gave the accused benefit of doubt and held the accused not guilty and acquitted him. I was not sorry for the O/C being found not guilty and being acquitted as he was a good man and a good performer as a police officer. The entire Bar congratulated Baroda Pain who came out with flying colours. Later when I was posted to Howrah I saw him and reminded him of the story and had a good laugh over my defeat. He told me that he was almost certain that the accused was guilty but his profession demanded that he rescued him from a foolish predicament. He appreciated my extreme truthfulness but the last advice he gave was that I need not have been so scrupulous in my statement and might have stated that actually I saw the notes in the hand of the accused who dropped them on the ground. While I was posted in Rajshahi, my SP Abul Hasnat showed a lot of interest in checking crime of theft and burglary in Rajshahi town and encouraged me to organise raids, intensive police patrol in different areas and to recruit veteran thieves and burglars as secret agents. In the last act I succeeded in recruiting two veteran burglars who helped me to catch a few veteran criminals in their act of committing burglary. Later I found that a few unknown new persons got into my net and I suspected that my secret agents were working as "agent provocateurs" and I abandoned my operations.

I concentrated on intensive patrol in crime affected areas of Rajshahi town by leading a batch of 25–30 town constables, a section of armed police and took an Armed Inspector or Sub-inspector, two police sub-inspectors and a few head constables to form a formidable contingent. The plan was to surround different parts of the town and search all lanes and bye lanes for criminals for about an hour. Then we moved on to another selected area and a signal was given by sounding a bugle at night so that the contingent could surround the new area and conduct the search. On the first night we did not succeed in catching any thief or burglar and let off some persons arrested on suspicion after interrogating them. To my disappointment, three thefts and burglaries occurred in other areas. This operation of surrounding an area by surprise and searching for criminals continued for two more days. On the second day no burglary occurred in any area and I was pleased. On the third day four burglaries occurred in areas during the time when such an area was not surrounded and combing searches were not carried out. I realised that the burglars were more clever than we were and refused to go out of business by the remote chance of being caught in the police net. I abandoned the operations and town patrol reverted back to the old system of disc or lane ticket systems.

One day SP got a pucca information about dacoity which would be committed in a rich *jotdar,* i.e. a village *zamindar's* house in a village several miles away. Fortunately the village was connected by rail. SP took a contingent of armed police of two sections strong, i.e. about 20 men. He asked me to accompany him and we set out after dusk. We reached the village on foot by walking a mile from the railway station and left the main force behind. SP, myself and a subedar entered the village, met the Head of the family whose house was to be robbed and took him into confidence about the probability of a dacoity being committed in his house and about our identity and mission, i.e. to capture the dacoits flagrante delicto. We asked him to take and introduce us to the owners of the surrounding houses where our police force would be stationed. We all took our positions in the cattle sheds or in Dhenki ghar, i.e. where paddy was husked to make rice. We were bitten by mosquitoes and we had to tolerate all the hardship in order to achieve the grand success of catching a dacoits' gang in their actual act. In the first few hours we were alert and on tenter hooks lest we failed to catch all the culprits. Hours passed and we became mentally and bodily fatigued but we did not fall asleep because the mosquitoes were very active and kept us wide awake. At last dawn appeared and at 5 a.m. we gave up all hopes of capturing the dacoits and were keen to return to headquarters. We were expecting visits by the residents of the village and offer of cups of tea. But there was silence of the desert prevailing all around. I went to SP and we went out to see why there was no noise of waking up, cry of the infants or any other sound except of the lowing cattle and crowing cocks. We went to all the huts in the small village and found that there were no resident men or women. Men, women and children had all left, some locking their rooms. We searched for the villagers but saw no one except a few men standing in a field at a distance. We saw two *chowkidars* coming towards us and we identified ourselves and told them about our mission. To our dismay we learnt that the householder who was supposed to be the victim did not believe us and took us to be a very well-armed and well organised gang of dacoits who could not possibly be resisted by the combined strength of all villagers in the neighbourhood as each of us numbering 20-22 people was either armed with a revolver or a gun. We all came out and told the *chowkidar*s to call the villagers back as it was then broad day light and the *chowkidars* also admitted that they got information about the dacoits gang taking charge of the village but were helpless to come to their rescue or to call up the local police station. Thus, our first venture to capture dacoits ended in a fiasco.

The last episode I remember with amusement is the occasion when the then IG of Police, Sir Archibald Douglas Gordan paid a visit lasting 3 days to the district to undertake annual inspection. In those days it was customary and almost obligatory for the IG of Police to carry out local inspection of half the districts in the state every year. Gordon had a reputation of being an efficient and hard working police officer and we all tried our best to keep the police office, the police lines, DIB office clean, spick and span. We worked hard to bring all registers and papers uptodate and some were swept under the carpet. SP said that we would not be able to please the IG with our work alone but should take recourse to other means like entertainment, supply of good food at the circuit house where he stayed and charge less than market prices for victuals supplied. SP and DM invited IG to sumptuous dinners and SP also coaxed the local club authorities to throw a large well attended tea party. We had cakes, pastries and patties brought up from Calcutta and ladies of the local Christian mission helped in making sandwiches of different kind and they played hostess on behalf of the Police. Gordon loved to play tennis and so did SP and I. We made up three players and required a fourth man. We got one of the two missionery gentlemen to make up a foursome of a doubles team.

SP, my partner and I won the first set. In the second set we seemed to struggle but actually slackened and allowed Gordon and partner to win 6-4. In the third set we again seemed to struggle hard but lost the set miserably at 6-1. This went on for 2 days and the subterfuge was repeated but taking defeat in different order. At the end of two days Gordon told us that we played very good tennis in spite of having lost the match on both the days. The inspection was over and the District got good inspection report from IG Gordon.

Soon after I got my transfer order and got posted to work as the Subdivisional Police Officer (SDPO) in Brahmanberia, a subdivision of the district of Tipperah. I was sorry to leave Rajshahi where the official colleagues were very kind and hospitable and a good district town with many amenities. However, I did remember that an ASP's normal posting is to be in charge of police work in a subdivision till he is promoted to the next higher rank of Superintendent of Police to work as an SP or an Additional SP in a district or a DC of Police in Calcutta. My successor was one Prasad Kr. Bose, a direct Deputy SP who joined and took charge from me. Prasad and I were close and loving friends since our boyhood. Bose had got married a few months back and took his wife along.

6

Drums of World War II—Quit India Movement The Great Bengal Famine of 1943

I joined Brahmanberia which was linked by rail of the East Bengal Railway (EBR) and then by Assam Bengal Railway (ABR) in the easternmost districts of Bengal. One had to cross the Jumna which was the name of the Bramhaputra in the lower Bengal. One boarded a steamer at Serajgunj and disembarked at Jagannathganj. One could travel by train from Rajshahi to Serajgunj and from Jagannathgunj to Brahmanberia by train. In Brahmanberia the SDPO had a nice one storeyed brickbuilt house which had two bed rooms, a drawing room, a living (sitting room) besides a small office, kitchen and servants' quarters. The bungalow was situated in the so-called civil lines where only civilian officers had their residence and was nearly out of bounds for the public between dusk and dawn. There was one Kucchari bari of Sankrail Estate which belonged to my old friend Raja of Cossimbazar, Kamala Ranjan Roy, of my Murshidabad days. The small town had a lot of educated gentlemen and also a good club. Somehow or other the club and most town people were more fond of the SDPO than of the SDO and the SDPO was usually the President of the club, although it was customary for the principal civil officer to be the President, namely, the District Magistrate in a District club and SDO in a subdivisional club, unless the district town was also the seat of the Divisional Commissioner who would generally become the President of the District club but he often declined to do so.

There were several families like Bardhans, Sahas and a few Muslim families who wielded social power and controlled the club. The club had arrangements to play cards, table tennis and tennis on a grass court which was playable only during winter and dry summer season. The club had also a radio set operated on car battery. As it was the year of 1939, which saw the beginning of the World War II the radio gave details of news about fighting and mostly about successes of the German Army overrunning countries in Europe and held a captive audience. It was surprising how practically every Hindu delighted at the success of each German campaign and almost wished the allied powers defeated hoping that this would release India from the British bondage. The thrill of listening to the radio continued till 1942. One Muslim gentleman named Jamaluddin was very attached to the two senior officers, i.e. SDO and SDPO and tried to induce us to nominate him for a government title like Khan Bahadur or Khan Sahib. In the district town of Comilla there was one Syedul Huque who was the chief of the District Muslim League and he also aspired to acquire a title. Both I and SDO recommended Jamaluddin each year for a Khan Bahadurship but after two years he was honoured with the title of Khan Sahib. Syedul Huque being a staunch Muslim League chief however got Khan Bahadur's title, Bengal then having a Muslim League Ministry. Although Jamaluddin was extremely delighted, his happiness was not full to the brim because Syedul Huque bagged a higher title. Jamaluddin was not a Muslim League supporter and was loved by both Hindus and Muslims. There was one Abinash Bhattacharyya who grew all kinds of lemons with exotic aroma which he presented to high officials and important visitors.

Japan had joined the war on the German side and had already occupied a large part of China, Phillippines, Laos, Cambodia, Dutch East Indies and Burma. There was a large flow of Indian refugees who were residents in Burma and had to flee for their lives because of looting, arson and other atrocities committed by the Burmese who looked upon the Indians as foreigners and took the advantage of the fall of the British Sovereign power to commit all types of atrocities. There was no British Rule in Burma and Japanese control of the whole country was fully established after Malay and Singapore and Rangoon were captured. Singapore's fall was a great blow to British prestige and morale because Singapore was made a fortress with a number of 18" guns facing the sea and any naval battle would have been disastrous for the enemy. But the Japanese were better strategists and captured Singapore by surreptitious advance through the jungles overland on the north and a large number of British and Indian troops became Prisoners of War. Referring to the overland routes of the refugees from Burma, through the Arakan Hill on to Chittagong Hill Tracts became a nightmare for the fleeing Indians who died by hundreds and lost all their belongings due to looting by different local tribes en route to India. Soon it became apparent that India lay open to easy attacks by the Japanese especially their bombers and fighters which could take off from nearby bases in Burma. During my tenure in Brahmanberia there were two days of air raid by Japanese planes which dropped a few bombs on or near Akhaura Rail junction. I had to go to inspect the damage, help the distressed and to send reports to the higher authorities. I found that only a few bombs had been dropped and the target was the important railway station at Akhaura which connected Chittagong, Noakhali, Comilla and Chandpur. The bombs missed the railway station and the yard and fell on villages nearby. As it was a day light bombing there was hardly any explanation for missing the main target. Two or three persons died and several became wounded. Several houses were damaged. The bombs were small in size but the power of high explosives was very apparent because several GI sheet roofs had been blown off and fell at distance of scores of yards away. The SDO and I and all other officers organised relief and treatment of the injured. The Japanese bombers made a peculiar humming noise when flying and we could know when these bombers flew over the subdivision. Bombs were not always dropped in our area even if the planes flew over it. It may be that they overflew our sky when going out for or returning from a bombing mission elsewhere.

A very unfortunate episode came out in the course of handling the Indian refugees coming out of Burma. One senior ICS officer S. Ghosh was appointed the Administrator and Coordinator of the refugees, to arrange their accommodation, give them money for subsistance because they had left everything behind. Ghosh handled crores of rupees without keeping an account but perhaps for the first time in history of Bengal a senior ICS officer proved to be acting dishonestly. It seems Ghosh had misappropriated lakhs of rupees amounting to not less than one crore. This fact was not detected till he tried to buy 3 valuable immovable properties in Calcutta including Royal Insurance Company building in Dalhousie Square. The special police establishment which was formed to deal with corruption during the war years took up investigation and submitted chargesheet. The trial lasted and the final judgement was given convicting and sentencing Ghosh to a jail imprisonment of several years. A large fine was also imposed which Ghosh was not in a position to pay and the properties he bought were seized and confiscated by the government. After several years Ghosh came out of prison and offered to pay the fine imposed on him and wanted to get back his properties because his properties had risen considerably in value. Although I am not sure about the result of his efforts but I think he did not succeed in his venture to get back his properties.

During the war I had to go to Calcutta and stayed with my old boss R.N. Banerjee who was then SP, Howrah. During my stay there was night bombing in Howrah and I could not resist the temptation to go out and take up a position at a height from where I could see the Japanese planes and their bombing. Against good advice of the officers I went upto the roof top of the three storeyed barrack building which was the highest in Shibpore area and could see the Japanese planes and could also get a rough idea where the bombs were dropped. The newly built cantilever Howrah Bridge seemed to be the target as well as some parts in Dalhousie square area. I could also see the machine gun fire from the Japanese planes which were visible because it was a bright moonlit night. What was however surprising was that so far as I remember no anti-aircraft gun fire was directed at the invading planes nor do I remember any fighter aircraft going up to attack the bombers. It was almost obvious that government had not enough resources to defend Calcutta or perhaps eastern India. Next morning I went out and learnt that bombs were targeted at the bridge and some were dropped in Bentinck Street and Hatibagan areas. The bombs missed the bridge and those dropped in the town fell on the street and side walks and did little damage to the buildings nearby. The 15 inches thick baffle walls built with bricks and cement mortar which we used to think as useless proved sturdy enough to stop all splinters. Some casualties occurred in Hatibagan and Kidderpore dock area but damages were negligible. The government in its wisdom had dug trenches and those people who were in the open took shelter therein. There was a well organised ARP which went into action to give first aid to the injured and to remove more serious cases to the hospitals.

I returned to my subdivision and soon the Congress party decided to break the law prohibiting processions, meetings and congregations during the period when the Indian National Congress launched 'Quit India' movement. I requisitioned a vehicle from headquarters, mustered policemen from outside and remained on alert. One afternoon, a group of local Congress workers under the local Congress leader assembled at a prominent place in the town near the market place and tried to hold a meeting. We had already promulgated an order u/s 144 Cr.P.C. prohibiting assembly of five or more persons. I asked them to disperse as they were violating the law but they refused. I ordered the arrest of about 8–10 Congressmen including all the leaders and asked them to climb into the vehicle which all of them quietly did and were driven to the Court and produced before the SDO. I do not remember if the arrested men were released on personal bonds or were treated as undertrial prisoners and kept in jail overnight. I remember that all of them came out next day. The Congress leaders could not behave in a more gentlemanly or nonviolent way than what this group did. Before their arrest they told the others at the meeting to carry on but others felt disheartened at the arrest of their leaders. There was no doubt that the Congress only organised a token violation of the law to defy the British regime in response to the call of the Mahatma. There was no further demonstration or agitation in the town or anywhere in the subdivision during the 'Quit India' movement.

Soon after I got an order of posting as SDPO, Chandpur, another subdivision of the district of Tipperah. Chandpur was much more important than Brahmanberia. Chandpur was an important river port and was one of the terminal points of Chandpur-Goalunds steamer route to cross the Jumna to take the train to Calcutta and rest of the country.

In Chandpur the SDO was one S.K. Dehlavi, ICS, who was married to a French lady. We became instant friends and worked together wherever needed and there was no rivalry between us. During this period government of India adopted the policy of denial i.e. withdrawing all river crafts from South Bengal, especially the Eastern districts of the province. The result was that there was scarcity of rice in the upper and western parts of the province due to failure to move food stocks from the rice bowls of Bengal like Bakharganj, Noakhali, Tripura, Khulna, etc. This created a famine condition which the government failed to foresee or were callous not to take remedial steps to prevent by arranging movement of rice from surplus districts to other districts. I have forgotten to mention that the denial policy was to deprive Japanese Army from penetrating into Bengal by water transport in case they succeeded in landing troops on the sea coast. The result was a horrible condition of famine during which an estimated 30,00,000 people died and there were shrieks of the starving men, women and children shouting for a little rice or gruel or whatever substance they could get to eat. In the district we did not realise the extent of the tragedy and death due to starvation which occurred mostly in Calcutta and western districts of the province. However, the Japanese did not come by sea and entered the easternmost state of Manipur by overland route. I do not think the Japanese were serious to invade India. In the years before the Great Bengal famine of 1943, i.e. 1942 Mahatma Gandhi launched 'Quit India' movement and some attributed the callousness of the British government to a policy of retribution against the Indian masses large sections of which took part in the 1942 movement. So far as Bengal was concerned, lacs of Muslims who did not largely take part in the political movement of 'Quit India' died as a result of denial policy of the government. It was certainly one of the largest 'man-made famines' wholly preventible with foresight and by taking positive steps by the government and its agencies in the right direction. At this time Dehlavi got into trouble being implicated in a criminal case of causing simple hurt to a local lawyer who was hit in his leg by a pellet when Dehlavi was trying to shoot a dove with his airgun. He had to compromise the case by paying a compensation of Rs 1,000 to the victim complainant.

In Chandpur we took very stringent steps to enforce price control. Rice was selling at Rs three and annas four per maund. I remember a big and very respectable Muslim merchant being arrested for selling the rice at Rs three and annas six. He pleaded with tearful eyes to let him go after he promised never to violate the law. Both Dehlavi and I were young foolish idealists and were not moved by his plea that his salesman had made the mistake and sent him up for standing prosecution. There were several other cases of worse violations and we sent up the culprits if such cases came to our notice and we could get proper evidence.

It was in the months after Mahatma Gandhi launched 'Quit India' movement that there was a case of fire in a local Christian church and the police recorded an FIR of an arson case and took up investigation under supervision of both the Circle Inspector and myself. As the church had no apparent enemy we concentrated our efforts to find out if the local Congress workers and their sympathisers had a hand in the arson case. Although suspicion fell on the Congress workers or their sympathisers but however much we tried we could not get any evidence to prove or even reasonably suspect the Congress workers. I did not allow mere imagination to play and to put the blame on the Congress. Because of its special importance the case was made a 'Special Report' case and progress reports went to the IG of Police and the Range DIG of Police, S.G. Taylor, who was my principal in the Police Training College. A few days later I got a letter from the Range DIG that the Police should have succeeded in detecting the culprits and adequate attention might be paid to the investigation of the important case. Actually the DIG was disappointed that I did not hold the Congress workers responsible for the arson nor did the police arrest any one without any ground whatsoever except that there were Congress workers in the town. We concentrated our efforts and tried to get inside information. To my regret I replied to the Range DIG's letter stating that investigation of the case was receiving as much attention as it deserved. Later my SP told me that my reply had displeased the DIG and advised me not to write such blunt or truthful replies. I should have written that I was acting on the wise orders of the DIG and would be making utmost efforts. As we had already made our utmost efforts, I could not lie in my reply. Whatever be the reasons my work in Chandpur did not satisfy the government and I was transferred back to work as SDPO, Brahmanberia. I was happy to be back amongst friends and gentlemen who also welcomed me with open arms.

It was at this time as the President of the local club I was approached to make the clay tennis court into a concrete court suitable for playing tennis the year round. I made a small extra contribution of money and approached the club members and the local merchants who all donated money to make a concrete tennis court which was declared open by me on an auspicious day. A marble tablet was also put in the slab of cement stating the date of opening the new tennis court by D.G. Bhattacharyya, SDPO. Thereafter, there was renewed activity in the club. It was 1943 when the tide of the World War was at its worst after Japan joined the Central Axis powers and conquered and occupied large chunks of littoral China, Korea, all the countries in south-east Asia including the Phillippines, Dutch East Indies, French Indo-China and Burma Siam, however, was spared for reasons I did not come to know. The Japanese were also at the doorstep of India and set foot in Manipur. The District Magistrate and all Subdivisional officers who were in charge of the District and Subdivisional treasuries received secret instructions to destroy all papers and currency which would be left after sending out as much money into the treasuries in the interior districts, i.e. in the western parts of Bengal. SP and SDPO's were told to assist in the operation of destruction. In Brahmanberi most of the Hindu gentry were anti-British and fervently prayed for defeat of the British so that India would become independent. As my old nationalistic feelings of the past had not died down, some disloyal and treasonable thoughts crossed my mind. I started thinking if I should cross over to the Japanese if they actually came to Brahmanberia. I know I would not have done this stupid treasonable act but such thoughts continued to creep up in my mind.

The British organised themselves and began to plan to launch counterattacks and snatch back Burma from the Japanese and the famous General 'Stilwell' made a name for himself by constructing a new road to Burma through the hills and jungles and actually leading his troops later to drive the Japanese out of Burma. American Generals and troops also played an important vital role in the Pacific War and it was left to General MacArthur to accept surrender of Japan a few days after atom bombs were dropped on the cities of Hiroshima and Nagasaki, two industrial towns in Japan. Thus, the war in Pacific theatre ended but many of the countries under French and Dutch occupation declared themselves independent. Out of French Indo-China three countries emerged namely Laos, Vietnam and Cambodia and the Dutch territories known as Dutch East India became Indonesia. Much later India, Burma, Ceylon, Malaya and Borneo which were in the British Empire became independent. Most of the countries enlarged themselves in territory but India was torn asunder to become India, Pakistan, Nepal and Bhutan. Division of India into Hindustan and Pakistan both in the northwest and east spelt disaster on the great subcontinent. After the Second World War it was of no benefit to any of the European Powers to keep their colonies in Asian and African countries in their empire and be responsible for their defence and security. After the war most of the countries which had foreign territories under their domination became weak both politically and economically and handed power to the important local political parties. These powers were the British, French and Dutch in Asia and also two other countries, Portugal and Belgium in Africa. Although Portugal was not involved in the War it also gave up its territories in Africa and India on account of local political agitation which often took violent turns.

During my stay in Brahmanberia one unforgettable thing happened. The very well known Sitar Maestro Baba Alauddin Khan who was born in a village in Brahmanberia subdivision wanted to visit his native village. Some intrepid gentlemen welcomed his visit but wanted him to come with the entire troupe of dancers and musicians under Uday Shankar to give a performance in Brahmanberia which deserved to see his performance and the troupe of which he was the master musician.

He managed to induce Uday Shankar who gave us details of the size and shape of the stage and the manner in which it was to be built for safety of the dancers. The best cinema hall of the locality belonging to one Banik family was chosen as the venue and a stage was built according to the instructions received by us. The troupe members arrived a day or two earlier. Baba Alauddin Khan was taken to his native village and was greatly pleased. Members of the troupe were accommodated in the local government bungalows and some private houses where they were given whatever comfort was available in a distant subdivisional town in those days of the early 1940s. The show was performed in a fully packed house but many had to be disappointed. We requested Baba Alauddin and Uday Shankar to repeat the performance and they agreed. The show was repeated on the second day. In those days Uday Shankar had his old team with Mademoiselle Simkie, Zohra sisters and others. Smt. Amala Shankar was in the troupe although she had not yet married Uday Shankar. All profits after meeting expenses were handed over to the troupe on whom we showered our praise and gratitude. As one of the principal government officers and the president of the local club I came in close contact with Uday Shankar, Baba Alauddin Khan and important members of the Shankar troupe.

During my first tenure in Brahmanberia I had gone on a month's leave and decided to visit Peshawar and Khyber Pass. After reaching Delhi I found that I had only come halfway and had as long a rail journey to cover as I had already undertaken. I decided to spend my leave in Mussourie, a very nice hill station in North UP. I stayed in one of the two best hotels, namely, Savoy which was more or less in the centre of the town. There were many important personages staying in that hotel in the person of Raja's, Maharaja's, Nawab's and a number of high officials. Of the former I remember names of the Maharaja of Patiala and Nawab of Rampur and amongst the high officials were three senior ICS officers, C.M. Trivedi, Chief Secretary of Central Provinces, N.M. Ayyer, a Divisional Commissioner of Bihar and another senior officer of CP Cadre named Chandra who was the Dewan of a well-known native state. They were all accompanied by their good wives. I met also P.C. Chakravorty, a senior Engineer of Bengal Nagpur Railways and his wife at whose table I used to sit in the dining room. All these officers soon took to me and I also liked their company. The senior ICS officers used to pull my leg all the time although very affectionately. Mrs Chakravorty was often oblivious of her surroundings and used to indulge in sweet loud laughter which reverberated throughout the dining hall and other diners would look up at her. There were one Aaron Arakie, a Jewish gentleman and his handsome wife and sister-in-law from Calcutta, whom and whose brothers I came to know much better after Independence when I came to live as a neighbour of theirs in Calcutta.

The cynosure of all residents in the hotel was Lieutenant Bhagat who had won the Victoria Cross in the Second World War and was also the first Indian to do so in that war. He later went on to become a Lieutenant General and was chairman of DVC after retirement.

After my holiday was over I kept myself in close touch with the Chakravorty's who stayed in Calcutta and by correspondence with Trivedi and Ayyar. Later Trivedi became the War Secretary in the Government of India and was knighted to become Sir Chandulal. He was invited to my wedding and acknowledged my invitation by sending a decent wedding gift. Even earlier I had been invited to have a meal with him in Delhi where I spent a few weeks of holiday in 1995. Ayyer later became the Chief Commissioner of the Andamans and Nicobar Islands and also visited my residence after Independence. His wife used to pull his leg by calling him the biggest liar and jokingly said he was born in a liars' hamper. Mrs Ayyer herself was a daughter of a senior ICS officer.

Sometime later I received a letter from Sir Chandulal Trivedi to enquire how I was and I replied that I was allright except that I was compelled to increase the length of the leg of my trousers because my one leg had become longer by relentless pulling by three senior ICS officers while I was in their company in Mussourie.

Soon after I got promoted to the senior rank and posted out to serve as an Additional Superintendent of Police in the district of Bakarganj with the town of Barisal as the district headquarters town. On joining I found that I was one of the two Addl. SP's, the other being a senior promoted IP officer named Anath Nath Gongulee. I was allowed to occupy the government. bungalow which was an excellent one with a spacious lawn and ground for growing flowers and vegetables. Gongulee, a bachelor, preferred to stay in a hired house in the town with his nephew and nieces and I was delighted to have the better building as my residence. One Mr Price was the SP and one B. Dey, ICS, was the District Judge. I do not remember who the District Magistrate was. There was a good District Club which had all the government officers of the Indian (Imperial) service as members and also the European officials of the local Inland Steamer Companies like IGN and RSN. The local Chief Engineer of the steamer company was a very nice Englishman with whom I became very friendly and whom I came to have dealings with after Independence when he became the General Manager of the Hooghly Docking & Engineering Co., Howrah. The Club had a nice bar, a library, billiards table and tennis courts. I was only interested in tennis and billiards. In all the District Clubs card playing was an important and popular indoor game and Barisal Club was no exception. From my college days I tried hard to learn playing Contract Bridge and had even bought books and a device called "Bridge self Teacher". However, much I willed, I could not concentrate on the game nor could develop any interest. I was occasionally cursed for my inability to play the game and to make up a team of four.

I grew a very nice vegetable and flower garden in the compound. I especially remember one thing namely that I could grow beautiful zinnias and gerberas in the monsoon. I had a lawn mower and I took pleasure in helping the gardener (*mali*) in mowing the lawn. The town had not much motorable roads and a bicycle would suffice to carry a touring officer to all the places in the town and suburbs. SP had a motor car but he had little opportunity to use it. It was customary for young police officers to take part in sports with the lower ranks, i.e. constables, *Havildar*s and *Subedars.* I used to play soccer with the policemen and one day I snapped a bone and fell like a log on the playground. The local surgeon bandaged me up and prescribed a period of rest. I had what is called a "Pot's fracture" in which the smaller bone of the leg broke and the outer round bone at the ankle had also cracked. The surgeon did a good job and fitted me with a shoe strengthened by two thin steel flats driven into the plaster bandage. He, however, advised me to consult a specialist surgeon in Calcutta after six weeks or more. With the shoe fitted I could easily ride and drive a bicycle and could travel by public service steamer or by the government steam launches 2 or 3 of which were in the district especially for the senior district officials to go on official tour. I was in charge of what was known as South Zone comprising the police stations in the sub-divisions of Firozpur and Patuakhali, the latter stretching on to the Bay of Bengal. On the western side was the district of Khulna divided by a very wide river named Baleswar.

In the meantime Gongulee got transferred and his successor was one M.A.H. Maswood, a Muslim IP officer who was a year senior to me with whom I was in the Training College for a few overlapping months. I applied for leave on the ground of the weakness I was feeling and was granted leave for a month but no successor was posted and Maswood was asked to take charge of my zone. Like me Maswood was a bachelor and he asked me to allow him to stay with me both sharing expenses of running the household. As I expected posting back to Barisal after expiry of leave, I left everything as it was and only locked my almirahs of clothes. I repeatedly requested Maswood to look after my personal and household articles carefully and ensure that they were not stolen or damaged. He assured me that he would do so.

I went to Delhi and spent almost the entire leave in Delhi. As it was the year's end, Delhi was in festive mood in spite of the war going on but tide of the war was turning in favour of the Allied Forces. This time I met a number of old and new friends some of whom were rich and greatly fun-loving and were members of important clubs in Delhi. In their company I visited two important clubs where we held big parties during the Christmas week and on the eve of the New Year's day we had dinner and dance at some well known restaurants and in the clubs. I managed to get good accommodation in Pataudi house on reasonable charge and stayed comfortably in a central place where other occupants were all high civil and military officers.

At the end of my leave I returned to Barisal and occupied my old rooms in the bungalow. On checking the book shelves and some other almirahs, I was shocked to find that most of the books had lost their covers, became loose or were even torn. My stock of extra buttons which I got from each tailor whenever I got new suits made had all been used up and many other household items bore marks of scratches and damage. I enquired of Maswood how all this happened in spite of his presence and he told me that his nieces (i.e. sister's children) had come and stayed with him during my absence and committed all the mischief. He could not control them partly out of affection and partly out of his not giving serious attention to my request. In any event, I could not do anything in the matter nor kick up a row with my old friend and a senior colleague. A few months later I got transferred to work as Addl. SP, Howrah.

7

War Time and Social Life

In Howrah I had my old boss Raghbendra Banerjee who was working as SP for more than five years in the same post. Banerjee was popular and had excellent relationship with the District Magistrate who was one K.A.L. Hill, ICS. Banerjee was particularly very popular in the District and hundreds of industrialists and well-known traders used to come and see him to make his acquaintance and to seek his favours.

Howrah had no government quarter nor a fixed rented house to serve as the Addl. SP's residence. I rented a house in the interior of the town in unhealthy surroundings and stayed for a while. After a good deal of efforts I could rent a small flat on Dobson Road. It was near the offices, courts and residence of the high district officials. Still I was not happy and continued to search for better accommodation. An opportunity came when one Arthur Hughes, ICS, a bachelor and almost a saintly person agreed to share his rented house with me and I moved in. The house had two small bed rooms, a dining room and a huge central hall, unusually large enough where one could hold big parties. I do not remember the exact process of development but I gradually became a socialite and was having many guests in the house and was being a guest in other houses and parties. The war was still going on and street lights had their black cylindrical cover and our cars had their special hoods. I had an ARP car for my exclusive use and was very happy over it. I used to go out to Calcutta in the evenings whenever I could manage and the Calcutta Club of which I intended to become a member held special attraction. I made many new friends but two require special mention, namely, R.K. Sarkar and his charming wife Tara Sarkar and Prem and his wife Shakuntala Bhatia. We remained life-long friends. R.K. Sarkar joined Dunlop as the Chief Publicity Officer and Tara Sarkar held a talk in English for children in the All India Radio. Prem Bhatia was a journalist and joined as the Public Relations or Publicity Officer of the Government of Bengal, Prem Bhatia left his job and went to Delhi. He became a well-known journalist in the country and later came close to Jawaharlal Nehru after Independence and became our Ambassador in Kenya and perhaps also in another country. After his stint with government he became an editor of at least two important newspapers, published in North India.

Howrah Town comprising of three police stations of Shibpore, Howrah and Golabari constituted a congested ever active industrial town mostly of mechanical and engineering works. The biggest was Burn & Co. Ltd. which had perpetual labour trouble. Besides there were the Hooghly Docking and Engineering Works, Port Engineering Works, Guest Keen & Williams Ltd., Shalimar Works and small ship building works and hundreds of other steel, iron and cast iron works. The first four had British managers and other senior officers but their presence did not prevent labour trouble or clashes between the authorities and labour leaders. One Shibdas Banerjee was an important labour leader. He was a gentleman to the bone and was always reasonable. Howrah town was surrounded by such police stations as Sankrail, Bowriah, Mali Panchghorah, Bally which were all fully industrialised and contained many jute, cotton and oil mills. These were controlled mostly by Marwari Industrialists and famous Industrial Houses like Goenkas, Jatias, Jalans, Jains and Singhanias were in control. These people used to come to SP for help or assurance of help in times of trouble. The European managed mill authorities more or less approached the British IG or the Home Secretary direct and the latter used to pass on the message to SP, DM. They and their junior colleagues who had no option but to rush out to help the mill authorities. Burn & Co. was a regular nuisance having trouble in one shop or another perpetually and kept the police busy for the whole year. A very serious riot broke out in Port Engineering Works in Shibpore where the British manager and his British assistants were severely assaulted and some received grievous injuries. SP had to rush out with a force and I accompanied him. We were amazed to find that the workshop was in a shambles and most of the officers who were severely hurt by steel and iron materials being used as missiles and thrown at them had to be rushed to the hospital. Police pickets were posted and some of the available rioters and their leaders were arrested and a criminal case was started.

In Howrah town there were many labour lines in which labourers and their families stayed. In some of the labour lines usually called coolie lines, only employees of a big industrial unit lived and in some there were mixed population, i.e. workers employed in two or more mills or industrial units. Often there were quarrels and fights which were tackled by the local police. One day about noon we got information that all the people of two coolie lines had come out and started fighting each other mostly by wielding *lathis*. SP ordered a squad of policemen armed with guns or rifles to report to the area from the Shibpore Police Lines which was at some distance from the venue of the fight which was in Howrah PS area. Both Hill (DM) and Banerjee (SP) decided to go and asked me to accompany them. When we arrived we found that the two sides were wielding *lathis* and were doing more jockeying than actual fighting. I had taken about 10 constables with *lathis* and two with guns from Howrah P.S. to accompany us. I decided to warn the fighting crowd and planned to attack and disperse them with whatever small force we had. DM and SP warned me that I would fail but I assured them that a determined *lathi*-charge would succeed and I shall lead the force. Moreover I had two constables with guns and I and my orderly had a revolver each. DM and SP cautioned me against being rash and foolhardy and getting myself and the police force under me overwhelmed by the mob to get hurt and routed. I replied that I was sure I would succeed and sought their permission to launch the attack. I am sorry to write down that both DM and SP asked me to wait till they got inside a mill through a small wicket gate fixed in the big steel gate for safety and left me, a young police officer, to handle the situation which they considered dangerous. After I saw both DM and SP disappear and to be in a safe shelter behind a strong steel gate I warned the two armed constables to keep their weapons in ready position but never to open fire without my order. I and my orderly drew out our revolvers out of the holsters. I warned the rioters to disperse and without giving them much time to decide I ordered a determined rushing *lathi*charge and the fighting crowd of both sides dispersed like chaff in the wind. I did not anticipate to achieve complete success with such ease and so quickly. I searched for the rioters in the two labour lines but they were not to be seen and most living cubicles were closed by being bolted from inside. I knew they would not come out again. I left a sub-inspector and the police force to be in the area to prevent trouble flaring up again and prepared to leave. I went to where DM and SP had taken shelter and knocked at the gate. There were many questions from inside before the two faces appeared through the wicket gate. On being assured that the rioters had dispersed they came out and congratulated me and went back to their own offices. I stayed back and the small armed contingent appeared. I posted half of them and sent the others back as well as the Police force of Howrah PS. I had taken along with me in case they might be needed elsewhere.

Raghabendra Banerjee stayed more than 5 years as SP, Howrah and in course of such a long period came to know people worth knowing in all walks of life in the district and they loved and respected him. He was always willing to give legitimate help who sought such help.

Banerjee conceived of an 'Idea', somewhat grandiose for a policeman, to start a Boys' Vocational Training Centre and also a small hostel for a few trainees. He informed the government of his scheme and got their approval. He went round and selected some plots of land which contained a longish jheel or waterbody and approached the owners to gift the land. He had already registered a society under the name and title of 'Howrah Homes' which became a society with independent entity. He got himself, some government officials and influential local people and a couple of owners of the plot of land to form the Executive Body. As he and also his good wife who hailed from Uttarpara Raj Family were very religious minded. Banerjee also made provision for setting up a temple of a god of Hindu Pantheon by the side of the tank. His Excellency R.G. Casey, Governor of Bengal laid the foundation of the Homes and later also attended the opening ceremony of the Homes starting its work of vocational training. The Homes were a great success and a number of young men joined for being trained. Qualified teachers were appointed but the expenses were more than what income could be earned and after Independence the authorities were compelled to hand over the Homes to the Government of West Bengal. The Temple and its land, however, remained private properties with the Trustees responsible for running it, i.e. holding *Pujas* and religious ceremonies. Reference to this episode will be incomplete if I do not make special mention of Casey and his wife. R.G. Casey was an Australian and he was appointed as the Governor of West Bengal. He was an efficient administrator and was popular in the province. Mrs Casey was a very beautiful unassuming lady who was also popular and liked and loved by all who came in close contact with her. Before leaving Bengal R.G. Casey was knighted and he left as Sir Richard Gordon Casey. R.G. Casey went back to Australia and became the Foreign Minister in the Australian government. Later he was appointed the Governor General of Australia and was raised to the peerage.

The war ended and we were happy to see bright lights on the streets and remove car lamp hoods to be able to drive at a normal speed in the streets. ARP was offering to sell cars which their previous owners did not want back due to rough use by the ARP department on bad roads in Howrah. I was offered a car and I bought one Vauxall 14, the first motor car I actually owned. Ownership of my car gave me free movements especially for my journeys to and back from Calcutta. But I had to undertake a lot of repairs to the car and got the engine rebored and overhauled. During my stay in Howrah I came closer to one Suresh Sinha who had a small two room flat on Garcha Lane in Ballygunge. In 1944 he married a young girl of Maldah town, named Namita, who was good looking but had not the polish and sophistication of a city girl. Sinha wanted his wife to be a modern society girl and he requested me to help his wife. He also wanted to move in high society and in this matter I could also help him.

In Howrah I started throwing dinner and cocktail parties and had many new and old friends who came in couples. Alcoholic drinks were still reasonably priced and I offered such drinks freely to my guests while I was a teetotaller myself. I had a radiogram and bought dance records and had a lot of dancing in the big hall which was sometimes decorated with flower bouquets fixed on the wall. Arthur Hughes and Banerjee family used to be invited while the former made a brief appearance at the start of the party and the latter did not like to join young group of merry makers.

These parties were mostly held at an interval of two months but more frequently in winter. I had quite a large circle of friends and acquaintances which consisted of both Bengalees and Non-Bengalees including Punjabis, Parsis. In course of throwing these parties I made a mistake by inviting friendly senior police officers including AIG of Police, some special superintendents and once the IG of Police and his wife. I suspect that although only selected people of good social status were invited, the higher Police officers did not like witnessing a young Indian officer throwing cocktail parties where only foreign liquor like Scotch Whisky, Gordon's Gin, was served and soon after I got my order of transfer to Dacca to serve as Addl. SP.

I got my transfer order in early 1946 and I was on joining time when the notorious Calcutta riots broke out on the 14th and 15th August of 1946 between the Hindus and the Muslims of Calcutta. Riots were started by the Muslims of Calcutta on the slogan "Larke Lenge Pakistan" when they were returning from a Muslim League meeting in Calcutta maidan. The riots were widespread and occurred not only in areas of mixed Hindu and Muslim population but innocent peaceful Hindus living in Muslim majority areas were killed and so were innocent peace loving Muslims in Hindu majority areas. Women and children were not spared. Although I was not on duty but still I toured some affected areas and found that the senior police officers and all their subordinates had been thoroughly communalised and Hindu police officers allowed killing of Muslims without hindrance and so did Muslim police officers about Hindus being killed. I had seen officers of one community going to the scene of carnage, inspect the dead bodies and expressing satisfaction if the corpses belonged to the other community. I had seen even a High Court Judge haranguing men of his own community to kill members of the other community. I was amazed at the communal frenzy which had gripped the police officers and all sections of the two communities in all spheres of life. No doubt there were exceptions where thoughtful compassionate Hindus and Muslims tried to protect lives of people of the opposite community. Hardwick was the Police Commissioner and he hardly moved out of his office, Surhawardy was the Chief Minister and he became ineffective. Burrow was the Governor of Bengal. I am surprised why the Police Commissioner, the Chief Secretary, the Chief Minister and above all the Governor did not call out the Army but preferred to remain callous and indifferent witnesses to the terrible but avoidable carnage of innocent citizens of Calcutta. At least 30,000 people were killed before the Army was called out on the third day and they imposed day and night curfew and controlled the rioting within 40 hours. I consider this rioting to be a great blot on the British Administration and I pronounce this judgement from personal experience, visits to places of rioting and complete indifference of the highest authorities in the Civil Administration.

8

Problems of Communal Strife

I left Calcutta on the fourth day in the midst of a curfew bound city and reached Dacca. I joined as one of the three Addl. SP's, two others were Frank Carman and another Addl. SP whose name I do not remember. One Leslie was the SP. I had a nice two storeyed *pucca* house in Ramna area, which was a posh area mostly lived in by officers and some rich Hindus and Muslims. After the riots Surhawardy was replaced by Sir Khwaja Nazimuddin as the Chief Minister and my Chandpur SDO S.K. Dehlavi became his official private secretary.

Dacca district was divided into two police administrative zones and I was in charge of one zone. Another Addl. SP was in charge of the other zone while the third Addl. SP was designated as Addl. SP, HQ and was in charge of HQ administration to help SP. Although communal riots of August 1946 in Calcutta had not reached Dacca in a tidal wave form but small waves and ripples did reach Dacca especially Dacca town. Moreover, the town had a notoriety of numerous small communal incidents from before which later erupted into more frequent incidents of a more violent nature. Formerly stray incidents used to occur in which one or two people were killed in hostile localities and Hindus of Kansari (Brassmith) community took active part in killing Muslims but killer Muslims retaliated whenever an opportunity presented itself.

A Police Control Room was set up which was manned by Addl. SPs during day and night, i.e. 24 hours, each Addl. SP manning the control room for 8 hours. There were vehicles and two or three squads of armed policemen always ready to go out whenever news of any disturbance came to the Control Room. Such news were about actual killing, preparation of attack, arson, and looting. If the incident was serious the Addl. SP in charge would himself go out and for lesser incidents he would send an

Inspector or Sub-inspector with a section or half of armed police squad and they would first try to prevent killing, looting and arson and then make preliminary investigation to detect and arrest the culprits and leave some policemen to augment the local police patrol. As a matter of fact there were police patrols in all mixed localities in the town, each patrol party consisted of 4 armed constables, mostly from the District Armed Police. Lest there be any trouble, four constables of the same community were posted together and divided into two parties for the purpose of patrolling and given strict instructions to perform duty and invariably introduced an element of surprise by back tracking over the same route. In spite of all these precautions, we noticed that whenever a Hindu was killed in one locality a Muslim was invariably killed in another locality mostly on the same day. We used to hold the patrol responsible and the team had always a ready answer that they were at the other end of the road or in an adjoining locality. We could not prove that the killing, looting or arson took place in their presence. We later discovered that some policemen left a place to keep the ground clear for the criminals to do the killing knowing that the incident would occur. It was also discovered that a Hindu was killed in the area where a team of Muslim constables patrolled and vice versa. Later we constituted the team with two constables of two different communities, i.e. one Hindu and one Muslim but they refused such an arrangement on the ground they would feel unsafe as the constable of the other community might desert him to be killed by members of the other community. So we composed each team of four constables each with two Hindus and two Muslims and two constables of one community will remain together. By this arrangement we thought we could ensure security of both communities in an area.

During my duty hours, I went out on many occasions, especially to prevent apprehended attack or to ensure safety of residents in a locality or to help the Fire Brigade to operate under police protection. It was customary for people of one community to prevent the Fire Brigade for saving the properties of the other community. The intense hatred between the communities can be gauged from an insignificant incident which was witnessed by me. When I was basking in the goodwill of the

Muslim community, I was one day invited by the Nawab Bahadur of Dacca and went to his palace to have tea. On our way we saw Nawab Bahadur's young grand child preparing small earthen balls and drying them in the sun with a 'Batul', a type of bow used as a sling lying beside him. The Nawab enquired what he was doing and the child replied that he was preparing shots to kill the Hindus. The Nawab became ashamed and told the child not to utter such naughty words.

I shall, however, mention four occasions in which I had to open fire. The first was an information received at the control room that a boatful of armed men were heading for a village to commit murder and arson. I went out with a posse of armed constables and reached the high-bank of a narrow river. True to information, a boatful of armed men was sailing up the river, I shouted to them to turn the boat back and not to proceed but they did not listen even when we threatened to open fire to stop their further advance in the direction of the village they wanted to attack. I could not make out whether the men in the boat were Hindus or Muslims as it was dusk but they did not pay heed to my orders repeated by the junior officers. As *lathi* charge or use of tear gas was impractical I ordered opening of fire by a few selected men and a volley of shots say a half dozen was fired. One guide who knew the assailants tried to prevent the armed constable from opening fire again so as to minimise death and injury and he in his efforts went in front of one gunman and shouted to the boatmen to go back. He did so when a gunman opened fire again and it happened that this particular gunman's rifle bullet pierced his cheeks and went through. Fortunately the man had opened his mouth wide and no part of the bone structure or the gums or teeth was injured. As I saw the assailants boat turning back, I took the injured man in my jeep car and rushed him to the emergency ward of the local government hospital. I offered to donate blood if required or to arrange other donors but the surgeon-in-charge said that the injury was not serious and the wound would soon heal up after proper dressing and stitching and that no blood transfusion was necessary. This was a very comfortable information because I felt deeply moved that one who tried to help the police should be a victim also. I used to go to the hospital to see him. We did not know if our bullets hit any of the would-be rioters in the boat because they did not make any report of any death or injury. Next day we made enquiries in the suspect village in pursuance of a criminal case started by me but the villagers reported that none had gone out to take part in the intended rioting witnessed by us the previous evening. Under the rules the Divisional Commissioner had to hold a departmental magisterial enquiry into justification or otherwise of police firing ordered by a police officer of SP's rank. Sometime later news about the second case of apprehended attack came to me that a public bus carrying passengers most of whom were Muslims would be attacked by a Hindu mob when it would pass along the route through a Hindu locality. I took two armed constables, my orderly guard and boarded the bus and ordered it to proceed. True to information given to the police, we saw a small crowd of Hindu rioters who were armed with swords and daggers but could not attack the passengers who were travelling in the bus unless and until the bus stopped. A part of the riotous crowd started throwing stones to stop the bus and smashed the glass window panes. I did not have a chance to warn the crowd but opened one round of fire with my German Luger pistol and asked the driver not to stop. The bus went through without any attack. After reaching it to a safe area, I telephoned for a jeep car to be sent to me with a small police party. We returned along the same route and seeing a police car with armed police-men the riotous crowd dispersed but at the spot I found a strapping young man aged about 28-30 years old lying dead on the road. I found that my pistol bullet had hit him on the head and killed him on the spot. The hit was wholly accidental because the bus was running over a bad road with potholes and the passengers inside including myself were almost jogging up and down whether seated or standing. I did not and could not take aim but just fired one shot in the exercise of my power as a police officer to defend life and property. It was sheer bad luck that the bullet hit anybody, especially the young man, on the head and killed him. I arranged to have the body taken away for a post mortem examination.

Many highly placed members of the public, both Hindus and Muslims were residents of Dacca town. Nawab Bahadur of Dacca and Mr Shahabuddin, brother of Sir Khwaja Nazimuddin, deserve special mention. During the days of sporadic rioting and regular killing and especially after the Great Calcutta killing of August 1946, all citizens were keen to cultivate acquaintance and friendship of the police officers and I was not an exception. I came to know most of the dignitaries worth knowing and was occasionally invited to have tea with them. After the first incident several Hindu leaders came and appreciated my successful action. After the second incident I was congratulated by the Muslim leaders for saving lives of a busload of Muslims.

The third instance of facing a riotous mob occurred in the old city. I received a telephone call from the Vice Principal of Jagannath College that a mob had surrounded two Muslims and would kill them. The two had taken shelter in the verandah of his residence and the mob was being persuaded by him not to attack and kill two innocent people, especially who had taken shelter in his house. He, however, told me that he thought his appeal would not change the determination of the mob and he sought police help. As I was in my residence I could not get any armed police party to accompany me and I rushed out accompanied by my orderly armed with a police .38 bore revolver and I with my Luger Pistol. I reached the Vice Principal's house and got all information from him and saw the two terror-stricken Muslims who had come from outside Dacca city and did not know that they had entered a Hindu locality. They fell at my feet praying to save them and I assured them that I would try my best but I had not the manpower. I appealed to the mob surrounding the Vice Principal's house but they would not listen. I warned them that I would use whatever force I could and would open fire. They had seen only two policemen who had no rifles nor stenguns and would not be able to stop them. The mob was gradually advancing and I knew that if I allowed them to come too near we two policemen would be overrun and overwhelmed and the two Muslims would be killed. I issued a warning and fired one round with my pistol while the orderly stood by with a revolver in hand. This firing made the mob stop advancing and sound of firing brought out the Vice Principal who was my friend also. He heard what I had done so far and realised that the situation was grave and would turn into an ugly tragic incident resulting in my shooting some people down and then getting killed after being overrun and the two Muslims would also get killed. My friend was very intelligent, cool headed and tactful. He approached the mob and first enquired if any one was hurt and was relieved to know that none received any bullet injury. He then explained that he knew me well and I was a conscientious police officer and had done my duty. If they persisted and went nearer some people would surely get killed and perhaps the mob would also kill me and my orderly and the two Muslims. He harangued them to understand that killing of innocent citizens of another community was neither a bold patriotic act nor would it solve the communal problems or even stop stray killings in Dacca. Fortunately for all of us my friend's appeal aroused good sense amongst the mob which agreed to disperse. My friend invited me into his house and the orderly and the two Muslims also entered his house. We stood at the gate. I telephoned to the control room to ask for a contingent of armed police to come to the site as soon as practicable and take me, my orderly as well as the two Muslims to a place of safety. One van came with several policemen under a junior officer into which I put the two Muslims and I and my orderly drove away in my jeep car escorted by the van. Again I got congratulations from the Muslim leaders and from the DIG of Police and the Divisional Commissioner who wrote (as I found out several years later) Mr Bhattacharyya always responded quickly to a situation and did not allow grass to grow under his feet for any reasons whatsoever. The Divisional Commissioner was in a position to write this because he held the statutory enquiry into all cases of firing by me or by the policemen under my command.

In the mean time besides many cases of stray killing, there were instances of mob violence by members of one community on the houses of residents of another community resulting in the murder of several men, women and children and looting of the houses of those killed. We could prevent such incidents if we could get prior information but there were few telephones in localities where ordinary or poor people lived. The police seldom got prior information and could not play an active role to prevent. Some victims were saved due to co-operation and humaneness of some members of the attacking community or help received from members of their own community who reached to their rescue from a nearby village or part of the same village.

I remember once visiting a Hindu house which was attacked but the household had two guns and the attackers would not dare to go into the house or approach it near enough to set it on fire by pouring petrol or kerosene. The attackers told the householders to surrender the guns by throwing them outside and they would do no harm and only take away the guns and cartridges. After resisting this dangerous proposal for some time the residents eventually threw out the two guns and cartridges. After taking the guns and loading them the mob entered the house and killed everyone found inside—men, women and children. I went with a force of armed men and inspected the site and made preliminary investigation result of which has been described hereinbefore. The police also tried to get information about the culprits whom they could hardly find out or know their identity. Imposition of curfew and posting of a small contingent of armed police were the usual steps taken temporarily. I remember this incident especially because on entering a room on the ground floor I slipped and fell on the bloody floor. I found that I had stepped on several severed fingers which acted as roller bearings. The scene was the ghastliest I had come across except during the 1946 riots in Calcutta.

There was another case in which during my control room duty hours at night I got information that a Hindu mob had attacked a Muslim village and had been burning the deserted huts. I went out with a few armed constables and reached the village. I saw huts burning and saw people approaching the burning huts. I thought that the Hindu mob was still trying to set fire to the remaining huts. There was, however, no evidence of murder and I decided that instead of opening fire with a rifle by a constable I would fire one blind shot with my Luger pistol. All ran away. We went in and did not find anybody. After lodging an FIR I went to the site next morning and learnt that a Muslim young man who was trying to save some properties from inside the burning huts and was thought to be a Hindu rioter by me when I opened fire, was hit. It was dark except flickering light from distant burning huts and I could not see the sights of the pistol and actually took a blind shot. Unfortunately for the young man and me, the bullet hit the young man's thigh. He was treated but unfortunately died. Like in all other cases of opening fire by me or under my order, the Divisional Commissioner exonerated me and held that I had acted bonafide and rightly exercised the right of private defence.

However, the local Muslim leaders who were full of praise for me so long realised that I was too active a policeman and my quick reaction had resulted in death of several Muslims as against one Hindu. They informed members of the Muslim League Party in power and I was transferred to join as Addl. SP Bakarganj for the second time. I may mention that the two other Addl. SP's in charge of the Control Room had, as far as I remember, no occasion to open fire or they managed to scare away the riotous mob before being forced to open fire. I was not sorry to leave Dacca where I was sick of having to face killing of human beings and witness damage to valuable properties everyday and organising quick measures to prevent such occurrences, most often futile attempts because the police reached the places too late. But preventive patrols did have some good effects and did not allow more such incidents to occur.

Dacca was the second largest city in Bengal and was the seat of education, culture, literary and political activities in East Bengal. It had a university, a number of colleges and good hospitals well staffed with teachers and doctors. It had a very nice club second only to the good clubs of Calcutta. It had also a race course which ran horse races regularly as in Calcutta. In the olden days, government of Bengal used to move to Dacca for a few weeks so that East Bengal received some importance in the province. Later this practice ceased and the Government House was partly converted into officers residence and partly into a guest house for visiting officials and dignitaries.

I suppose the practice of the Governor moving to Dacca with a small secretariat stopped at the outbreak of the Second World War when this avoidable expenditure was considered improper and the seasonal move was abandoned.

Like all officers of the superior services I joined the Dacca Club which was housed in a nice centrally situated building with many rooms and a large compound. For indoor games, there were billiards, table tennis, cards, darts, etc. There were tennis lawns and squash courts too. There was a couple of good bars where both liquors and soft drinks were served. It was a pleasure to sit in some of the rooms after playing tennis or sitting there after dinner and drinks. On a night of such a party which most of us attended all drinks were served freely by the host. A few young ICS, IP and officers of other services stayed late. About half a dozen of us stayed very late. Except me, all the others were Europeans who had imbibed a lot of alcoholic drinks and were still drinking at their own expense. All of them were inebriate and a couple of them were drunk although they did not go under the table, i.e. they could still sit in their chairs. Being a TT I had non-alcoholic drinks and remained the only sober man in the small group. When it was past eleven at night I saw a stray pariah dog come inside our room and walk freely. All of us kept staring at the dog till it left. The dog came in for the second time and did the same thing and our group also stared at it till it left. I knew that there were some sticklers in the group who had strong feeling about what was proper and improper in the club but they were silent. Being then a newly elected junior member I did not also do anything. The dog came in for the third time when I lost my patience and shouted for the waiter who came and I told him to shoo away the dog and prevent it or any other stray dog or cat from coming in. He chased the dog away. All the others who had become tipsy or drunk heaved a sigh of relief and shouted 'so it is a real dog.' They told me that they had seen the dog everytime and felt annoyed but did not dare to say anything because each thought that liquor had been producing hallucination and making them see a dog while in reality there was none. Each kept quiet so as not to be a laughing stock of others. They thanked me for relieving them of their suspense and shame at being drunk, etc. The party broke up after this incident and we went home.

The Dacca races took place once a week and the horses were smaller than those which ran in Calcutta but certainly larger than those small ponies which ran in Darjeeling races. I decided to put in my horse in the race. I used to ride it frequently in the race course but to make it a race horse it had to be run and put through hard training by a professional jockey. I found a good jockey who was delighted to see my large waler horse and agreed to train it for the races. He used to take out the horse 5 days a week and gave it gradually a hard practice. The result was that the horse started shedding weight and was feeling very much hungry. His daily intake of 2 seer of oats plus grass had to be increased to 8 seers of oats and double the quantity of grass. The training had very good effect in that the horse became slim and fit and could run much faster.

When the trainer-cum-jockey said that it was fit for the race and would be a sure winner I put the horse in the race to run. Most of my friends and many punters put bets on the horse and bought tickets for win. I also put a bet of Rs 10 for a win. The race started and my horse was leading and at the finishing line another horse beat it by a head. I lost my precious ten rupees and was disgusted. I questioned the jockey and he said that he made a mistake and should have kept a sure winning distance from the start to the finish but he had not done so and expected to be able to make the horse take a spurt run at the end but the horse could not do so. He, however, assured me that he would win the next race. I put my horse in the next week's race amongst horses of equal size and most of my friends and outsiders again put their bets on the horse and it did win the race. I had not put any bet and was not sorry. The horse won the third race also. The news that my horse was running a race reached the ears of higher officers and I was told that it was not customary for a high government official to own a race horse or to run it. After the third race I withdrew my horse from the races.

9

Back to Rural Areas and *Shikar*

I joined my new post in Barisal and was lucky to have the old government bungalow. The other Addl. SP was one Sadulla, much junior to me in service who was occupying another house. I was also given the charge of the same south zone as in the past. The curious thing was that one Obaidulla who was the elder brother of Sadulla was the Superintendent of Police in the district. I use to the word 'curious' because it was against government practice to put a very near relative under another relative in the same department.

The local District Club was found to be more lively than during my first stay in the town. Some new faces were seen including European employees of the steamer companies and their womenfolk. One manager and his wife were especially charming and hospitable. I became friendly with this gentleman especially because I wanted to learn more about gardening from him and he had much better floriculture knowledge than I had and had the best private garden in the town. He specialised in canna flowers and had many small plots full of variety of colourful flowers but one plot had plants bearing flowers of one colour only. His garden looked attractive and gorgeous.

I was a bachelor and was invited to tea and dinner by hospitable families including my SP, DM and the District Judge. I forget the name of the District Magistrate but S.K. Halder ICS (Junior) was the District Judge. I had seen him and his fashionable first wife who used to play tennis in Mymansing wearing attractive T shirts and trousers. There were many versions of the manner of her death prematurely in mysterious circumstances. There were gossips which gave many reasons and versions of her death. It was, however, generally held that being a high strung woman and having an expensive style of living the couple often quarrelled. They had a son named Dipak who entered the IPS in later years. The second wife of Halder was a fairly good looking young woman with poor social manners. It was known that she was the daughter of a Bench clerk of a court in Sylhet and she came from a family whose members did not go above rural status. However, I was amazed to see the change in Halder's mode of living and the immense authority his wife wielded on her senior ICS husband. One could easily say that he had become a henpecked husband. Moreover, he had become miserly. On my joining the district I made my first social call one evening and was made to wait in the living room, which was in darkness and the *chaprashi* did not switch on the fan and lights. Halder came in and enquired whether I needed the fan and the lights (it was still twilight) and I replied in the affirmative. He ordered the *chaprashi* to switch on a light and the ceiling fan over me but did not bother that Halder himself was not receiving any breeze from the fan over my head nor that the fan over his had not been switched on. I was offered tea and biscuits. In the mean time the lady of the house burst in and I was introduced to her as the newly arrived Addl. SP who was known to him in the Mymensing days. However, the lady told Halder that the ducks had not come in and asked him to go out and drive them in. I thought it was a strange request to the District Judge husband who however excused himself and went out. I also left saying that I would visit him again.

Coming back to club life, both Mrs Obaidulla and Mrs Sadulla were much club minded. The two ladies were good looking but Mrs Obaidulla was almost a beauty. Both the ladies and their husbands used to drink liquor and their presence livened up the club bar. Many other ladies used to come with their husbands in the evenings and at the noon on Sundays and holidays. They used to come alone also to play cards on other days when their husbands were in office. I was a bachelor and a TT but still I used to go to this club and in all other district clubs because we were told that the club could be a second home and should not be neglected. Being a bachelor and being reasonably handsome I found that I had become a target of attention of a junior colleague's wife. I found her making subtle passes at me when we met each other in the club but I was unresponsive.

One evening when I was sitting on a high stool at the bar and drinking soft drinks, i.e. non-alcoholic, this particular lady came and sat on the empty stool next to me on my left side. There were several others in the bar but they were engaged in conversation. I was sitting on a high stool and sipping my cold drink. One high stool on one side was occupied by a lady. The particular lady sat by me and entered into a conversation and insisted on my taking a glass of whisky. I yielded and ordered two glasses, one for me and one for her. After a while I felt some one touching my feet and later kicking at my feet. As there was another lady on the other side I did not know who was doing this. I did not dare look down which action would draw other peoples' attention on me and on the two ladies on my two sides. I kept quiet in spite of being kicked although I was almost sure the lady on my left had been kicking me. The lady on my right left and I felt a big pinch on my buttock with a full palm and I was now sure that the lady on my left was trying to tease me or wanted me to be more attentive to her. I rebuked her for exposing me and herself to ridicule. She replied that I need not pose to be a goodie goodie innocent man and she knew about my big cocktail and dinner parties in Howrah where gaiety amongst men and women prevailed. I replied that I would speak to her later on and left. One day I could catch her alone and confronted her why she misbehaved and she said, she resented my indifference and unresponsiveness. I told her that I could not commit nuisance at my doorstep and did not flirt with or have an affair with a colleague's wife, sister or daughter staying in the same station and asked her to stop her efforts. The matter ended there.

In the district there were no major problems which were many during my first posting in 1942-43. One thing however I undertook to do this time namely to fulfil a long cherished desire to visit Sunderbans which I had done in my student days when my uncle was the SDO of Bagerhat in Khulna district bordering on the subdivision of Patuakhali and try to do some hunting because the best part of the Sunderbans was in the eastern part of Khulna district which was just across a wide river named Baleswar.

During the jute growing rainy season it was a pleasure to see the jute plants which grew to long heights and produced the best golden jute fibre. After harvesting of jute when the land was soft but waterlogging had disappeared paddy seedlings were sown. With the passage of time, young green paddy plants gradually turned from light yellow to golden brown stretching over vast flat land without trees in sight. This presented an unforgettable sight. The sway of the plant in a windy day brought to mind a wavy golden sea. I used to be reminded that visitors to North Canada had witnessed such scene when the wheat plants ripened especially in the State of Sasket chewan.

My work often took me to Patuakhali subdivision which formed the south-west part of Bakarganj district. In the Khulna district Sunderbans lay across the river. The whole of south Bengal was once covered by the Sunderbans from Noakhali to Midnapore and beyond Bengal along with the forests in Orissa which were all cut down to convert the land good for agriculture, due to increase in population and there being no policy with the then governments to maintain ecological balance. The wild animals were also decimated with the disappearance of their forest habitat. In the olden days wild water buffaloes and rhinoceroses were inhabiting the Sunderbans but became extinct later. I resolved to undertake one or two big game (i.e. tiger) shooting expeditions into the Sunderbans in Khulna. There was a young Muslim gentleman who was a junior officer in the cooperative department of the local government and came to know me and he was very enthusiastic about big game shooting. He pleaded with me to allow him to accompany me if I happened to go to Khulna Sunderbans. He had also a government allotted boat to undertake tours in his jurisdiction which covered the subdivision of Patuakhali. I had told him about my past visits to the Sunderbans when I was a student and my greenhorn efforts to hunt deer, pigs and tiger if I came across and dared to shoot at a Royal Bengal Tiger. These tales had impressed him and he desperately wanted to accompany me during all my hunting expeditions into the Sunderbans. I also liked the idea of having a companion and a second *shikari* to back each other with a gun. I had a gun and also a .423 Mauser rifle. Our Dy. SP at HQ had a .303 single shot rifle which he claimed to be very accurate and I decided to take it when I go. Moreover, I could use .303 ammunition of which I had still a large stock having procured them from an RAF fighter plane which crashlanded in my jurisdiction.

I decided on a date and prepared myself by taking out a license to enter and shoot wild animals and to be accompanied by a companion with a gun. The Divisional Forest Officer (DFO) Khulna issued the license which would hold good for ten days after I enter the forest. I also took 3 days leave and permission to leave the district. My companion did the same. I had a government steam launch at my disposal and chalked out a tour of inspection of police stations and supervision of some important criminal cases in the south-west part of Patuakhali subdivision which were the areas nearest to the forests in Khulna, a wide river named Baleswar separating and demarcating boundaries between the two districts. As my jurisdiction did not extend beyond the district of Bakharganj, I could not take the government launch out of the district and would have to hire a boat to cross the river and enter the district of Khulna and stay in the boat as long as I would be in Khulna district.

My friend accompanied me and agreed to share the expenses of hiring a big boat but each would make his own arrangements for his food. He took dry foodstuff while I had my cook with me. I had told the serang of my launch about my plans and that he would be required to anchor the launch at a suitable point on the bank of or very near the bank of Baleswar river while I and my companion and the cook would hire and travel in a large house boat to be hired by us. I sought help of the officer in charge of the local PS from whose jurisdiction I would proceed to Khulna to find a suitable large boat and he did so after telling the boatmen the purpose of hiring the boat and settling the hire charge. All of us boarded the boat which had its own crew and sailed for going to Khulna district. When we reached the other shore I decided to search out my old *Shikar* guides of 1932 namely one Gani Mia who was then the Union Board President and his neighbour Sobhan Mia both of whom were *shikaris* and had actually shot many tigers, the latter as many as 40 odd in number. It was not difficult to locate them as they stayed in a village next to which the Sunderbans started. I traced both of them and told them of my intention to shoot animals. The two gentlemen were extremely delighted to see me after a lapse of nearly 14-15 years and we recounted some old stories. Both had become nearly old men and Sobhan Mia had developed cataract in his eyes but was still able to see the sights of his gun and shoot accurately. It is Sobhan Mia who agreed to accompany us while Gani Mia had urgent work to attend to. We needed a local *shikari* not only to guide us to the likely spots of finding game but also to act as our guide in the Sunderbans, criss-crossed by hundreds of canals with no land mark where strangers like us would certainly get lost. Without wasting time we left the village of Sobhan Mia and went into the forest areas and sailed our boat as per instructions of Sobhan Mia who took his own boat and his own gun. To travel in the Sunderbans one had to resort to boat trips because one could not walk long inside because of breathing roots of Sundri trees with sprouted roots which kept their tips over the flood water levels. They were like sharp spikes and one had to be careful not only to avoid treading on them but also to avoid tripping up by getting one's foot caught by one of the roots. Moreover, to get down from the boat was a difficult messy affair because the banks had soft knee deep mud and one could only walk across the muddy banks in bare feet. We travelled a lot but had no luck and did not see any animals to shoot but we heard noise of running feet of animals fleeing inside the forest. However, we searched the wooded area on the banks in the evening and early night with 5 celled torch lights. One night I saw a pair of eyes reflecting the beam of torch light and thought I would try to shoot the animal which I took to be a deer or a pig. My friend held the torch light behind my right shoulder so as to illuminate fore and back sights of the firearm. I decided to use the .303 single shot rifle loaded with a solid bullet. I took careful aim because the animal did not move but stared at us. I tried to shoot between the eyes because a successful shot would kill the animal. I fired and we saw the pair of blaring eyes disappear when the animal jumped, turned round and entered the forest. We heard the sound of a larger animal crashing through the forest. Sobhan thought I must have hit the animal. We decided to light the Petromax lamp and three of us namely I, my friend and Sobhan Mia armed with our guns and accompanied by a boatman carrying the lantern got down from the boat barefooted and went to the spot. I thought the animal was a deer and had got hit by the bullet which made it jump up and disappear. After a little search we could locate the place and found that soft earth at two spots had deeply gouged out holes and further examination showed that there were fresh pug marks of a tiger and we realised that it was a tiger I had shot at. We tried to locate the animal in the vicinity but did not find it. As the shot was at the head which was a small target and an actual hit would stun the animal but the animal's hurried flight showed that it was full of life. We could also see some drops of blood and was sure that it was hit at whatever part of the body it might be. We did not feel safe to pursue the animal on foot at night in the light of a lamp only and returned to our boats. We anchored our boat in the mid-stream for the night. Next morning we had early breakfast and three *shikaries* got down with shoes at a less muddy spot where we could walk on the extended root of a tree without stepping into the mud and reached the spot where we saw blood from inside the forest which had dry ground. In day light we saw more drops of blood and the trail led into the forest. Moreover, we picked up a piece of canine tooth which had been chipped off from the animal's jaw by the bullet. We decided to follow the blood trail and came across a spot where there was a small pool of blood indicating that the tiger had rested there for some time while it was bleeding. Further inside we came across small pools of fresh blood and some leaves of small plants also bore marks of blood which had not dried up. We pursued our search and at one spot found a piece of the front part of the lower jaw with pieces of bones embedded in the flesh. There was also evidence that the animal had tried to rub its lower jaw on a low branch of a tree and the piece of jaw with bone must have become detached in the process. From the blood trail it was obvious that the tiger, although wounded had its four feet intact and loss of so little blood could not weaken it much. We pondered over the matter whether we should pursue the trail or not. Sobhan Mia told us that the animal could walk a dozen miles and we would not be able to catch up with it unless it decided to make a stand and attack us. We decided to leave the trail but we were saddened at the fact that we left a wounded tiger in an unsporting way, knowing fully well that it would not be able to eat any animal it killed and would die a slow painful death. There was also the risk of its attacking men and women who might try to catch fish in the canals and search for bee hives but there was one factor which did not make the situation really dangerous because it was not a honey collecting season nor was the canal a fishermen's paradise. We left hoping to get an opportunity to shoot an animal in day light. We were disappointed. On the third day I decided that I would take my friend to 'Katkachar' where one could see graminivorous animals grazing in daylight and hundreds at night time. There was no chance of approaching any animal. Katka Char was a big open sandy field right on the sea (Bay of Bengal) and we had to leave our boat in the canal at a small distance from the sea. We had anchored our boat at the ghat which was built to facilitate use of the boat of the four men who manned a coast guard station. Coast guard stations were quickly built up during the years of apprehended Japanese penetration into Bengal along hundreds of small inlets created by canals in the Sunderbans but such coast guard watchposts still existed in 1946 and later years after creation of East Pakistan. These coast guard posts were huts built on stilts at a height of 12-15 feet. So as to be safe from a jumping tiger. There was a wooden ladder by which the watchers climbed up and down. There were four men all civilians who manned the post and they did duty by turn. One was on duty from morning to early night in two shifts thus using up two men while two watchers kept vigil at night. Those who were not on duty stayed and slept in a boat which was anchored in the adjacent canal and was used as sleeping quarters, kitchen, bath and toilet. Supplies of foodstaff and potable water were made by another boat from the nearest forest beat house. If any information was to be given, the watchers who manned their own boat would go by boat to the nearest forest beat house and inform a forest guard of the beat house office who would inform the Forest Range Officers and it would be the duty of the Range Officer to communicate with higher authorities. Because of anchoring the boat at the site of the coast guard post, we could easily go into the forest without wading through knee deep mud. To reach 'Katka Char', we had to walk a mile or so. Before we left we learnt that man eating tigers (unfortunately majority of the tiger population in the Sundarbans had turned to be maneaters for many many years) the victims were either fishermen and women who landed on the banks to fix long lines of hooks and bait as well as honey collectors who had to go inside the forest in search of bee-hives. I also learnt that some coast guard posts had also lost men who were attacked either in the boat and lifted away or when the unarmed men walked from below the coast guard hut to the boat or vice versa. The only equipment they had was a pair of binoculars and spears. They warned us to be careful and we told our boatmen to anchor in the midstream of the narrow canal when we three *shikaris* left with our guns. After walking in the char area to get an opportunity to shoot a pig or a spotted dear and having failed to get anything within the gun or rifle range, we decided to spend the night on top of two trees in the hope of shooting something or other. We had already brought food for all of us for the night and took our meals early evening. I climbed on top of a tree and so did my young Muslim friend and Sobhan Mia on two other trees nearby. We had torch lights fixed to our guns loaded with Alphamax LG cartridges which would kill any animal found in the Sunderbans except a crocodile.

During the night we heard animals mostly spotted dear passing through the jungles but none seemed to come near the trees we took our perch on. I flashed my torch light occasionally and saw no animals within its range. Dawn broke out and we decided to return to our boat.

We walked in the morning and reached our boats. We were horrified to learn that a tragic incident occurred the previous night when a tiger attacked the coast guard boat and took away one man sleeping in the boat. The other sleeping man did not become aware till the victim gave a short cry when the tiger landed on the bank. The other coast watchers were almost terrorised and decided that all would sleep in the hut though there was not enough space for all. As the camp was short of men, they begged us to take a letter to the beat house which we should hand over on our return journey. We felt very sorry but the watchers joined the coast guard service knowing the risk of being attacked by tigers. The victims' family would get monetary compensation but that was hardly a consolation. The other victims like fishermen and honey collectors who had to take the risk as professional hazard got no compensation from any quarters.

So far as tiger hunting was concerned Government gave a small reward when a hunter killed a tiger and had to produce the tail of the freshly killed tiger when claiming the reward. The tail was to be burnt in presence of the DFO. When we returned to the bank of Baleshwar river it was evening. We returned to our steam launch as per schedule and the launch travelled towards the district headquarters till midnight. We slept in the launch which again travelled from early morning and reached Barisal town by noon which was good enough for me because rules permitted me to reach headquarters by noon of the day of reporting for duty.

In a few months it was known that India would be partitioned. As the date of partition of India had been approaching and as I had opted for India I knew I would not have any opportunity in future to come to Barisal or forest areas of Khulna Sunderbans. It was also known that although the district of Khulna had a Hindu majority it would go to Pakistan in exchange of the district of Murshidabad which had Muslim majority but had been given to India to protect the head water of the Hooghly river which would be the largest river in Bengal. After partition it was imperative that junction place of the Hooghly with the Padma must be protected to ensure flow of enough water into the Hooghly on which stood the important town and port of Calcutta.

As I had failed to do any successful shooting in the Sunderbans, I conceived of the idea of a short almost flying visit to the Sunderbans to start and end in the course of a day when I would take French leave from duty. I did not have the face to ask for leave when hectic preparations were going on in offices to divide documents and material assets between the two countries and most officers were engaged in the work. Actually I myself was not involved but I felt very hesitant to ask for leave for pleasure. Actually I was refused formal leave when I met and enquired from my SP. I, however, told him about my other intention and he had no objection to a day's outing. Hoping to get another chance I had already got a shooting permit from DFO Khulna which held valid for ten days at any time in a particular forest range. There was an important case of murder in the area of a police station in Patuakhali subdivision and I decided to supervise the investigation of the case as there was no subdivisional police officer in Patuakhali to do so during my tenure in Bakharganj district.

I had a discussion with my young companion of the previous expedition and he joyfully agreed. He was in a cadre in which a district transfer was not normal and it was unlikely that he would be transferred and posted in Khulna even if the district became a part of Pakistan. So we set sail to do my official work and to pay a day's visit to the adjoining forest range in Khulna. Actually the forest area in Khulna district bordering on the wide river Baleswar which divided Khulna and Bakharganj districts was the best area so far as wild games were concerned. Hunters from Khulna and Bagerhat did not venture out to the easternmost forest areas on account of non-availability of food and drink like fresh vegetables, milk, meat and even potable water.

After doing my official work I told the O/C about my plans and he agreed to help me. He accompanied me in his boat being towed by the launch and we reached the border village from which we would cross over to Khulna in a hired boat. O/C however, told me that the season was rainy and boat journey to cross over and to return would take longer time than it would take in dry months and we would not have much time to spend inside the forest.

When we reached the village on the river, fortunately there was one big open boat and only small fishing boats were available. The big boat was manned by a crew of 5 men and was slow moving and much less comfortable. There was one long medium sized fishing boat which was available for hire. It was manned by six oarsmen and one at the hull and it had no shelter from sun or rain.Fortunately for us, it was a sunny day and an open boat did not matter.

Before starting on our journey I had studied a map of the forest area in Bagerhat subdivision and located a place which was a small island, triangular in shape in which animals could be driven from the base to the apex and they had not much chance to escape sideways into adjacent forest area's unless they crossed wide water channels on the sides. The *majhis* readily agreed to act as the beaters and were not afraid of doing so in spite of the fact that there might be tigers which might turn back and attack these unarmed men. Before entering the forest we reported to the boat office, showed my license and were told to report again before leaving the forest and going across to the other side.

As planned I and my friend climbed up two trees with our guns and the boatmen went by boat along a canal to the base line as there was a canal at the base. I warned the beaters about probability of tigers being there and in that event to proceed in a manner so as not to disturb the tiger or tigers. It would be a great tragedy if any one got killed and they understood my concern and promised to be careful but would still take the risk because we promised to give them a whole deer if we killed several of them besides paying hire charge for the boat.

The beat started and one or two stags and several does came cautiously towards our line but went past at distances beyond our shooting range. As the beat proceeded we had a number of animals running and coming forward simultaneously and both of us could shoot two after a number of misses. As the beat was nearing our positions many does appeared and ran past. My friend shot one of them and then a stag appeared cautiously and was shot by me. Towards the end a whole herd ran past us and it was a scene of confusion as I could not decide which one to shoot at but I shot one doe. Shooting of does is illegal but unfortunately the does outnumber stags several times over. In a herd there are seldom more than one full grown stag and two or three immature stags. The young stags are driven out of the pack as they grow older and the strongest stag becomes the patriarch and reigns over his *harem* of does. As soon as the beaters reached us we pointed out the places where the dead stags and does might be found and they could pick up all the dead animals and carried them to the boat. We put the two does below the planks of the deck and put one stag and two does on the deck as there was no space to put all four does below the deck in the hold of the boat and prepared to go across. We had no intention of reporting again to the beat office with our illicit kills. But the Beat Officer was more clever and positioned himself with his guard at the mouth of the only canal through which we would emerge. He wanted to see our haul and we pointed out the stag and the two does. Seeing the does the forest officer did not bother to look into the hold of the boat. He demanded our explanation for indulging in an illegal act of killing does. One of the *majhis* said that with one stag shot we could not possibly leave anything for the forest beat office and as such we were compelled to shoot two does and wanted to leave the meat for beat office staff and one for the *majhis.* This satisfied the Forest staff who thought it was compensation enough. They took the larger doe and left the place. We now had to cross the wide river which was at the end of its ebb flow and soon the flow tide would come. Moreover, there would be a strong tidal wave as it was a full moon night. We had to cross the river as we could not possibly stay the night without food and to spend the night outside the district would be highly irregular. It was a full moon night and a strong high tidal bore was expected. We could not cross the river before the bore come and our boatmen did not dare to cross even after the bore passed. The *majhis* of the boat we rented before had refused to cross as they neither had the skill nor was their boat suitable for crossing. They decided to stay back for a few hours till calm water prevailed. So we decided that we would spend another night in the hired boat but there was the problem that I would overstay my leave by a full day and this was not permissible. I should reach my district the same day. As this time we saw a fisherman's long boat manned by six oars men and a man at the helm coming up the river against the ebb tide. They offered to take us across after the bore passed. They assured us that there was not much risk and firmly assured us of taking us across safely an hour after the tidal bore had passed. It was a sight to see a wall of sea water 10-12 feet high rushing from the sea and going up into the interior along the river. As it was a bright full-moon night we could see every thing but could also see the very strong current after the tidal wave had passed which current could take us miles upstream. The Head *majhi* of the 'Chhip' assured us that they had faced such situation before and would be able to row across the strong flow tide with six oarsmen and an expert at the helm. They also told us they could not possibly face the tidal wave which would have sunk the boat and could even sink a steam launch. I knew I was taking great risk and my skill in swimming would not save me. We were, however, helpless and trusted our luck and the boatmen's assurance. I had taken three life belts from the launch when we boarded the boat. I always did so whenever I got into a boat from a launch to travel in shallow or narrow canals. My companion agreed to try our luck. We paid off the boatmen of the other boat which we left behind. We tied the two firearms firmly to one life belt and kept one life belt each for me and my friend. Being equipped like this we set sail and true to their assurances the long boat cut across the strong current although at a somewhat slow speed and we managed to cross the wide river by ten at night taking twice the time ordinarily needed to cross. We paid the boat men the stipulated price and one dead doe as a *bakshis*. This was more than what the men expected. We reached the local PS and told the O/C about our *shikar* and difficulties faced when a tidal wave was expected. He said that he was very anxious as we did not return in the afternoon and thought that we would be compelled to stay the night at the beat house. As we had still one stag and two does we decided to give the O/C and his staff one doe. Still we had the meat of a stag and a doe which I and my friend could take home and distribute meat amongst our local friends. I always used to send deer meat to a Sen family, i.e. the family or parents of A.B. Sen whom I have referred to in the story of Rajshahi period. There were a few other families like the District Engineer with whom and whose wife I was very friendly. I myself did not like venison, i.e. deer meat because fast moving wild animals especially a male developed strong muscles and fibre in their body and the meat did not become soft enough in course of ordinary cooking. There were no pressure cookers in those days.

During my second sojourn in Barisal I used to organise parties to which amateur singers and dancers both male and female were invited. I also invited local friends and some Indian officers to my bungalow on such occasions. The best dancer amongst the girls was one Miss Jayati Sen who later married Rathindra Nath Sengupta, an IAS officer who later became the Chief Secretary. Rathin Sengupta became a favourite of Left Front government in West Bengal especially the major partner CPI (M) and held many important government posts for many years. As a matter of fact he is still employed even though he retired years ago. Sengupta has a pleasant personality and is liked by me and by many officers. He must have such qualities as to make him useful to the Administration.

I remember that while in Barisal I had a proposal given to me to marry the younger daughter of a well-known barrister-at-law late B.C. Chatterjee of the Bhowal Sannyasi suit fame. I consented to visit his house and meet the family during my next visit to Calcutta. During a visit to Calcutta I went to see the family where I met Chatterjee, his wife who was a daughter of late Sir Surendra Nath Banerjee, a well-known patriot, the eldest son Goutam and the youngest daughter Subha. B.C. Chatterjee's became a household name when he was the counsel of the Bhowal Sannyasi suit in the court of trial and won the case for the Sannyasi Raja, who, however, lost his case finally on appeal because of his wife's (Rani's) refusal to identify him as her husband. B.C. Chatterjee received accolades because of his victory in a sensational and unusual case. Later his eldest daughter Boruna got married to a Ry. officer K.K. Mukherjee, son of Sir Lalmohan Mukherjee, Chief Justice of Allahabad High Court. The wedding was given a lot of publicity and coverage in local newspapers and the Chatterjee family acquired a glamourous image in the mind of a large section of Calcutta citizens. I was not an exception.

When I met the family I was extremely well received by Chatterjee and his wife and nearly adopted as a son by the good couple. However, I and Subha, the would-be bride saw each other and had a short conversation. I was not impressed by looks of the girl as I always wanted my bride to be slim, tall and to look soulful which qualities Subha lacked. However, I was thrilled that I had a chance of becoming a son-in-law of a rich well-known family when Chatterjee's informed me the very same day that they would be glad to have me as their son-in-law. I had my elder brothers whom I must consult and broached the subject to my eldest brother, who was an officer in the Bengal Civil Service. He was very much against the marriage as he thought I was from a middle class Bengali family and the Chatterjee's was a high society family. I insisted on marrying into the family and he yielded. The Asirwad or the ceremony of formally blessing the groom and the bride and exchange of gifts was completed and my eldest brother reluctantly performed his part in the ceremony. That night I and my eldest brother were invited to dinner but my brother declined and left but I stayed on for dinner.

After dinner Chatterjee asked me to take Subha out for a ride in the car. I and Subha got into the car driven by a well-uniformed chauffeur. When we were sitting side by side close to each other I could see that Subha was hirsute and had hair or beard on her face which she had shaved off carefully. I politely enquired about this unusual feature and the girl was simple and truthful enough to admit that she had developed rudimentary beard and had to shave before she met anyone outside. There was no cure except a long painful process of removing each hair follicle by electrolysis. Although I was shocked but did not say so. Moreover, I also found that the girl was less intelligent than an average woman of her education and family background. But all this did not shake my resolve to marry the girl because I had given my words and a socio-religious ceremony had been performed.

However, after returning home when I met my elder brother I broke down, burst into tears and said that I had made a blunder and ruined my life by promising to marry the girl who was not only hirsute but was sub-intelligent. My eldest brother wanted to break off the engagement but I would not let him. My other brothers joined and appealed to my sense of honesty in that I had no right to marry a girl whom I did not like and would not love whole heartedly. I said that I would be sued for damages to the tune of lakhs of rupees for breach of promise and my eldest brother wanted to send me away to Australia. I, however, implored them to allow me time to think over the problem. In the mean time my brother told the Chatterjee family about my state of mind and advised them to withdraw the proposal of marriage and to break off the engagement. B.C. Chatterjee started writing to me to help me to realise the social scandal which would occur if I broke off the engagement and gave me a lot of advice to help me to resolve my doubts as to our future happiness. In the meanwhile my brother appealed to my sense of honesty and Brahminaical principles and their arguments finally persuaded me to understand the serious consequences of a marriage which was bound to fail. I also felt that the Chatterjee family was more determined to stick to the promises of both parties because the Chatterjees realised that they would not get a son-in-law of my looks and family and holding an excellent office in government. I also felt that the family should have been honest about the girl's defects especially about her being hirsute if not about her sub-intelligence. I now feel that I was not sued for breach of promise because I could also plead being defrauded by the other party's suppression of a serious defect in a women which was fully known to them. However, both parties became reconciled to the fact that the marriage would not take place. I later learnt from a brother of mine that the eldest son Goutam also suffered from subintelligence. It is a genetic tragedy that two children of intelligent parents and a brilliant maternal grandfather (Surendra Nath Banerjee) should be born subintelligent. B.C. Chatterjee, however, took his complaint to the then Governor of Bengal and requested him to return the diamond earrings I had gifted and these were returned to me through the IG of Police who called me to his office and handed over the earrings. He also asked me to return the five guineas which Chatterjee had given while blessing me. I later returned them direct and informed the IG about it. The girl later got married to an officer of Damodar Valley Corporation. I came to know the gentleman and we became friends. He often joked that what a mess I had landed him in by discarding the girl whom he married in a fit of folly. However, he was more tolerant than I and they were reasonably happy and raised good children. I might as well record here that many years later I made the same mistake by agreeing to marry a girl whom in my position and with my ideas of a wife, I should not have agreed to marry. I broke the very preliminary negotiation and the girl never married. When I actually married I married the girl of my dreams.

News now started spreading that the provisional scheme of forming central government with representatives of the Congress and the Muslim League parties had not succeeded and India would be partitioned into India and Pakistan which latter will be in two parts namely in the north-west and in the east comprising some districts of Bengal and Assam and that all servants and employees of the partitioned states will be given the option of serving either India or Pakistan. Although I felt to opt for Pakistan which would have some of the best districts of Bengal and where I had served most during my serving life except a short spell in Howrah, I finally decided to opt for India hailing as I did from Calcutta and having all relatives in the portion of Bengal which would be in India. I was told to report to the Writers' Building on arrival in Calcutta.

The day of Independence and partition of India soon arrived. I got order of posting as the Deputy Commissioner of Police, Security Control, in the Calcutta Police and was asked to join by 14th August at the latest. I was released from duty a few days earlier and regretfully left East Bengal where I had served for 10 of my 12 years of service. A few Hindu officers decided to opt for Pakistan and stayed on. Unfortunately all of them faced difficulties and had to leave service after democracy ceased to exist in Pakistan under a military dictatorship. Many Muslim officers opted for India but I do not know of any who got into trouble because India managed to believe in a secular democratic government which still exists today. In the Police Abdul Rashid Khan and M.A.H. Maswood both of the IP cadre opted for India and stayed on. It is most unfortunate that A.R. Khan, who was almost a saintly person had to leave service along with his District Magistrate of Midnapore on the charge of corrupt practice during the first West Bengal ministry under Dr Prafulla Chandra Ghosh who was a staunch Gandhian and believed in scrupulous honesty in everything. The corrupt practice only they were charged with and on which they were removed was a triviality, namely, that the D.M. and S.P. of Midnapore were using ARP motor cars allotted to them without paying road tax. In today's West Bengal, nay in the whole of India, such a default when pointed out will be laughed at and the penalty, if any, imposed will be to ask the officer to pay all road taxes for the whole year only. Maswood stayed on till his retirement at the proper age and got all promotions due to him. I know other Muslim officers who stayed on in India and had a successful career. In other states there were hundreds of Muslim officers who stayed on but thousands opted for Pakistan. Most of the Muslim IP officers of Bengal, however, opted for Pakistan and rose to occupy very high posts. There were only three Bengalee Muslim ICS officers of whom one Zaman opted for India, one Murshed resigned before Independence and one ICS officer named Nurannabi Chowdhury joined Pakistan. Most of the Muslim IP officers were efficient, strong minded and tactful with the result that most of those who opted for Pakistan gradually got higher and higher positions in the government like the Chairmanship in Government Undertakings, the Chief Secretary's post in one of the states in Pakistan, as well as ministerial posts in the provincial or central government of Pakistan. In India there was a host of Hindu ICS officers who outnumbered Hindu IP officers and it is they who got promoted and occupied the high posts. In the first three decades Police officers did not get a chance. It was after retirement of all ICS officers who were succeeded by IAS officers that the IPS officers were chosen to be Governors, Ambassadors and members or Chairman of the State and Union Government Public Service Commissions or Chairman of some Public Sector Units mostly after retirement. I suppose the glamour of the Indian Civil Service still stood intact and impressed the rulers, i.e. the Prime Minister at the centre or the Chief Ministers in the states and their colleagues in India and no police officer was known to hold high posts outside the cadre till the breed of ICS officers disappeared.

I got all my household and personal stuff well packed, took valuable things in suit cases and steel trunks with me and despatched other items of furniture, utensils etc. by steamer and goods train. I made over charge, bade good bye to friends and colleagues and left Barisal a few days earlier than 15.8.47. The part of former Bengal which became a part of India and was named West Bengal whereas the rest of Bengal came to be known as East Pakistan.

10

Sequel to Failed War of Independence

Indian National Army

In the year 1942, Subhas Chandra Bose, a great national and patriotic leader of the country who was under house arrest for several months, left his Calcutta residence in disguise for Germany. He arrived there in April and established contacts with leaders of the German government to get political and military support in his endeavour to organise freedom struggle from outside India. Mutual co-operation programme was finalised with German government whereby the latter agreed to help Subhas Chandra in building Indian Army under his leadership, recognising him as 'Netaji' and establishing a powerful radio transmission centre for broadcasting. The formation of an independent army ran into problem as Germany refused to treat such an army as 'Indian National Army'; rather they wanted it to be part of German regular Army and named it 'Indian Legion'. Further the members of this legion were asked to take oath of allegiance in the name of Hitler only. Subhas Chandra did not like this idea but he ultimately succumbed to German pressure.

Members of the Legion were to be drawn from the Indian prisoners belonging to British Army who had surrendered to the Germans in North Africa. These prisoners of war were still loyal to the British and opposed to the idea of severing their allegiance. Subhas Chandra had great difficulty in convincing them and they agreed to join the 'Legion'. But soon he realised that Nazi Germany wanted to use the Legion as Fifth Columnist against the British and not as a part of regular army. Moreover, Hitler was reluctant to declare Indian independence lest this becomes an additional obligation on Germany in future. In fact Hitler never sympathised with the Indian cause as he considered Indians non-Aryans and to be of inferior race. Subhas Chandra naturally got disillusioned with the Nazis and realised that no useful purpose would be served by staying in Germany. Now he turned towards the east where great events had already taken place. Japan had declared war against Britain and other European countries, captured Malaya, Singapore and all colonised countries in South-East Asia including Dutch and French colonies and finally Burma, whereas Germany was engaged in fierce battles on the Russian fronts in Moscow and Stalingrad.

In the east, the preparation of struggle for India's freedom had started much earlier by Indians who were living in far eastern countries for many years. The most important political organisation 'Indian Independence League' was formed in 1924 by Rash Behari Basu who was a great revolutionery by his own right. He was an associate of Aurobinda and Barin Ghosh and was involved in attempts at armed revolution in India. He left India incognito and reached Japan in 1914. He got married to a Japanese lady and became a Japanese national by marriage. This helped him greatly to develop contacts with important influential politicians and military personnel. He formed Indo-Japanese Association and arranged military training of Indian volunteers by the Japanese army.

The Japanese showed great interest in Indian affairs and at the instance of Rash Behari, a conference was arranged by the Japanese government in Tokyo in March 1942. Indians living in East Asian countries participated in the conference. It was agreed that the Indian Independence League should be strengthened and further Japan promised help in Indian struggle for freedom.

Shortly afterwards another conference was held at Bangkok which was attended by delegates from all Far Eastern countries including the Philippines, Malaya, Indo-China, Sumatra, Java, etc. The conference decided on formation of an Indian National Army with 40,000 prisoners of war and 25,000 volunteers, appointment of Capt. Mohan Singh as the Commander-in-Chief of Army simultaneously authorising the League to negotiate with the Japanese Army, procuring all supplies, recruiting more soldiers and volunteers. For exercising absolute control over INA, a four member council was formed with Rash Behari Bose at the head.

Capt. Mohan Singh, a member of the Council and Commander-in-chief was a man of high ambition. He never liked the idea that the army will be under the league and the council will exercise absolute control. The Japanese army wanted INA to serve their purpose and started pressurizing Mohan Singh to toe their line. Initially Mohan Singh collaborated with them but a time came when he was unable to satisfy Japan's ever increasing demands. He was torn between his frustration with the Japanese and his inability to get adequate support from the League. Mohan Singh finally disbanded the Army. Soon after he was arrested by the Japanese and was imprisoned.

For quite some time the League was sending feelers to Subhas Chandra in Germany and immediately after the INA was disbanded Rash Behari invited him to come to Japan and assured Subhas of leadership of the League and INA. Subhas undertook daring and successful undersea journey from Germany to Singapore in a German U–Boat partly and partly in a Japanese Submarine. On his arrival at Singapore he took charge of the League and command of the INA in August 1943. In the presence of a large gathering, the "Provisional Government of Free India" was proclaimed on October 10, 1943 and this proclamation was signed by Subhas Chandra (Head of State-cum-Prime Minister and Minister of War and Foreign Policy), Capt. Mrs Luxmi Swaminathan (Women's Organisation), S.A. Iyer (Publicity), Lt. Col. A.C. Chatterjee (Finance), Capt. Shah Nawaz, Kiyani, Rash Behari Basu (Chief Adviser) and others. Two days later war was declared on Britain and America and this was announced over the radio. This galvanized the entire Indian population of 3 million living in the Far East and they came out with promises of money and other service in the cause of Indian independence. The new Government was recognised by governments of the Axis powers. Japan handed over Andaman and Nicobar Islands to the New Indian Independent government. In the meantime Japan attacked the Pearl Harbour Naval base in Hawaii which was an American colony and thus declared war against the USA.

This was the time when Japan was riding high on its historic victories over the Dutch, the British and the French and one by one the colonial countries were falling under Japanese powers. The British were routed in Burma and in the Andaman and Nicobar Islands by a joint campaign of the Japanese and INA. It was planned to invade India from Burma. At that time Manipur was strategically very important and if the joint army could conquer that area it would be easier to enter Bengal and the existence of the British would be at stake in India. As planned one part of INA assaulted Cox Bazar and other part proceeded towards Kohima and Imphal. Some areas close to Kohima were captured and Indian National Flag was hoisted on the Indian soil. But Kohima could not be held for long. With increasing intensity of American attack in the Pacific region Japan and INA were forced to withdraw from Kohima. More British forces joining in the Burma front enhanced fighting capability of the British. INA was cut off from all vital supplies of arms, ammunition, food, medicines, hospital supplies, etc. The monsoon had also set in and the INA had to continue fighting in very adverse conditions and had to retreat in July, 1944.

The combined army of the British and American forces started its campaign in March 1944 and by early 1945 INA began retreating on all fronts and finally surrendered in May. That year the INA was disbanded and its soldiers were made prisoners of war. Subhas Chandra left Singapore and tried to fly to Japan but the plane he was travelling in crashed into the sea. It is said that preparations of struggle by the INA was considerably late and the most opportune time was the end of the year of 1942 when the British faced freedom movement in India and had been retreating in South East Asia.

The British government shifted the INA prisoners to Delhi for their trial in Red Fort. At the first instance they decided to court martial three top ranking INA officials Capt. Shah Nawaz, Capt. Dhillon and Capt. Sehgal and the trial started in the historic Red Fort, Delhi in the first week of November, 1945. During the war not much was known in India about the heroic struggles of the INA soldiers trying to liberate the country and establish an independent government. But due to heavy influx of Burmese evacuees in Bengal, their bravery and exploits widely circulated and these soldiers were regarded as National heroes. The news of their trial added fuel to fire and people became greatly agitated. Indians of all communities and religions were united against this trial and protest meetings and demonstrations were held all over the country. The city of Calcutta became the focal point of this agitation in Bengal. There were pitched battles with the police and the military. Indiscriminate tear gas shelling, lathi charges and firing made people violent and resulted in burning of tram cars, post offices and police and military vehicles. There was big loss of lives. Assessing the situation the British government released the prisoners.

The next trial commenced in January 1946 and Capt. Rashid Ali and 3 others were court martialled and sentened to 7 years' imprisonment. This was enough to infuriate the citizens of Calcutta again and for 6 days in February, the city witnessed the worst kind of violent demonstrations. Trams, post-offices, army vehicles including American trucks were burnt. Train services were disrupted and 40 people died in police firing. Americans refused to be a party to any military action and withdrew all their vehicles and personnel from the streets and public places.

The struggle spread over to various parts of India particularly in Delhi and Lucknow and all over the state of Bengal. Such a development dealt a serious blow to the British government which realised the futility of repression over the Indians who were eager to win their freedom.

Mutiny of the Royal Indian Navy

Soon after the popular movement for release of the INA soldiers was repressed another heavy blow was inflicted upon the British government. The Cadets of HMS Talwar of the Royal Indian Navy rose in revolt on account of discriminating and inhumane treatment by superior British officers, serving of poor quality food and curtailing other amenities. They marched through the streets of Bombay and people who were already agitated at the unjust imprisonment of INA soldiers joined the mutinous navy. The Naval Cadets in Karachi and Madras also expressed their solidarity with their colleagues in Bombay. Other military and defence personnel in Jabalpur and Indian Signal corps etc. participated in this meeting.

The naval cadets were asked by the Congress leaders including Sardar Vallabhbhai Patel to return to their ship and they were greatly dismayed but had to go back.

Now the British government read the writings on the wall and realized that the British rule in India would sooner or later come to an end.

11

Under a New Flag—In Charge of Foreigners

The Indian Independence Act passed by the British Parliament, conferred the dominion status on the two countries of former India with option of becoming fully independent countries. The British Parliament divested itself of the power of passing any law concerning these two countries and India and Pakistan became commonwealth countries with option of becoming fully Independent countries. This was done by enacting laws in the British Parliament which divested itself of all powers to nullify or modify any further enactment. The same procedure had in the past been adopted in cases of Canada and Australia.

Partition of India was not decided in the beginning when a government formed by representatives of the Congress representing both the Hindus, Muslims and other communities and representatives of the Muslim League representing Indian Muslims who wanted partition of India. Jawaharlal Nehru became the Prime Minister and the Muslim League wanted their representative Liaquat Ali Khan to be given an important portfolio to hold, namely, the Home or the Defence Ministry. Congress would not part with these ministries either and allotted the Finance Ministry to Liaquat Ali, little realising the importance and power of the Finance Minister. I now forget who got what ministries but these details are not of any importance in this narration.

This allotment proved to be an unqualified disaster to the government installed in New Delhi. Congress launched a number of proposals which really benefited the big industrialists and traders in the countries who had supported the Congress morally and financially but the proposed measures were theoretically against the policies and principles which were openly but superficially advocated by the Congress party. Liaquat Ali Khan rejected proposal which benefited the industrialists and traders on the ground that these proposals were against the declared past policies of the Congress and he also agreed with these declared policies which would not make the rich richer and the poor poorer. There were also several other measures which the Congress wanted the Finance Ministry to approve of and these measures involved budget provisions for both income and expenditure but the Finance Minister would not however approve. The result was almost a stalemate in the running of the central government. The Congress Party then realised how important and powerful the Finance Minister was who held the purse strings. Consequently the Congress Party agreed to the partition of India. Looking back upon past events, one is bound to think that the Congress made blunders in not allowing the Muslim League to hold more important positions. Even if the Party allowed the League representative to be the Prime Minister or M.A. Jinnah to be the Governor General in the adinterim government till the election was held under a new government, the Congress or the nationalist minded Hindus and Muslims would not have eventually lost because in future years the nationalists who were in majority could have a government which suited them but the country would not have been partitioned straightway. India was partitioned in spite of the Mahatma declaring that India would be partitioned over his dead body. Nehru and the second most powerful Congress leader Vallabbhai Patel were too eager to be the Prime Minister and Home Minister and became greedy to win Independence at any cost even by paying the price of partitioning India. They entreated and cajoled Bapuji and he yielded. It is a credit to all National Muslims that Maulana Abul Kalam Azad who was the then Congress President during pre-Independence and early Independence years was wholly against partition of India and his feelings and sentiments have found expression in the book *India Wins Freedom* which he authored. He did not allow one chapter dealing with his opposition and short sighted policy of Nehru and his senior Hindu colleagues and capitulation of the Mahatma to be published till after 28 years after his death. Yet he did not castigate the greedy leaders in any harsh language which they certainly deserved.

India was partitioned causing indescribable misery to a large section of people of the Punjab and Sindh which contained a large mixed population. There were widespread revoltingly violent riots involving murder, arson, rape, abduction of women and girls thus ruining thousands of families in the two states of Pakistan and in the East Punjab State of India. There were also riots involving murder, arson, rape, looting and forcible eviction of Hindus in East Pakistan but on a much smaller scale and there were riots of similar types too in West Bengal in India. Thousands of families were ruined in the border states of the two newly formed countries and the erstwhile peaceful law abiding citizens lost members of their families by murder and abduction and all their properties in the riots and departure from their homelands. Lakhs of Hindus and Sikhs fled from Sindh and the Punjab and came to India and so did Muslims of East Punjab and from other provinces in India who fled to Pakistan. There was nearly complete exchange of population between West Pakistan and West India but such events on a large scale did not occur in the provinces of Bengal and Assam. Only large sections of Hindus came to India and few Muslims left the two provinces and flee to East Pakistan. The riots in East Pakistan and West Bengal occurred sporadically whenever new waves of Hindus fled East Pakistan and came to India and such riots continued for many years till East Pakistan became an independent sovereign state of Bangladesh in 1971. When there were severe riots in some parts of Bengal just before Independence Mahatmaji went to Noakhali in order to preach communal harmony and peace and more or less succeeded. While certain parts of the former India were steeped in misery and were becoming victims of Independence on reasons of partition, the leaders, i.e. the statesman of the two countries were joyfully celebrating Independence achieved over one of the great human tragedies in recent world history. The statesmen showed no real anxiety to give relief to the victims in an effective manner but launched half hearted measures. I consider these events to have brought eternal shame to the statesmen of the two countries who did not visualise the tragic events nor did they take steps to meet such contingencies. Simply speaking they lacked foresight, lost touch with realities, failed to learn lessons from past experience and lost ordinary human qualities of the head and the heart.

Moreover in their hurry to grab power the Indian statesmen did not pay adequate attention to the details of the partitioned portions. As, for example, Bengal had a population of roughly 51 per cent Muslims, 47 per cent Hindus and 2 per cent Christians and as such India should have at least got roughly three seventh of Bengal but actually got approximately 1/3 only on the basis of the formulae devised for division of the country, namely wherever there was majority of Hindu community in the district, *thana* and even a village area it would form a part of India and wherever there was a Muslim majority it would form a part of Pakistan. The eastern districts of Bengal across the river Padma had a mixed population of Hindus and Muslims, i.e. all districts except in two coastal districts of Noakhali and Chittagong had a large percentage of Hindus although Muslims had a slight majority. On the other hand, the Western districts in Bengal had overwhelmingly large percentage of Hindus and a small percentage of Muslims. On the basis of the formulae agreed upon nearly 2/3rd of Bengal went to Pakistan and 1/3rd remained in India. Secondly, the district of Murshidabad having a slightly larger Muslim majority was given to India to protect head waters of its main river Ganges or the Hooghly but in exchange the district of Khulna having a Hindu majority was given to Pakistan. This was not necessary as Chittagong Hill Tracts, a large district entirely populated by Buddhist and Christian population was given to Pakistan to protect the head waters of the main rivers in the district of Chittagong. If this was done why was there any need to allot Khulna to Pakistan which got Chittagong Hill Tracts as compensation for loss of Murshidabad. As a matter of fact after disappearance of Subhas Chandra Bose, death of Jatindra Mohan Sengupta and Sarat Chandra Bose's leaving the Congress, Bengal was left with no Hindu leaders or statesmen of eminence who could wield influence in Delhi or over other leaders in the other parts of India.

The other injustice that partition of India inflicted was on North West Frontier Province which had a Muslim majority but the Congress Party had a major following in the province and Khan Abdul Ghaffar Khan was the eminent Congress leader and was called the Frontier Gandhi. His brother Dr Khan Sahib was the Premier or Chief Minister of the province. The ruling party did not want to join Pakistan nor did they think separated from India, they could induce the Muslim population to join India. They could, however, opt to be an independent state but the British government did not allow this option although such option was given to Nepal and Bhutan. This was also an unfair decision because the native states in India and Pakistan were allowed to remain independent without being merged into either India or Pakistan. However, most native states were induced to merge into either India or Pakistan except Kashmir and Hyderabad. Kashmir was contiguous to both Pakistan and India and Maharaja Hari Singh who was the ruler of Jammu and Kashmir hesitated to make a choice as Kashmir had a Muslim majority population but the Maharaja did not want to join Pakistan either. In the beginning he did not join India. When hordes of Pakistani militants started invading the western parts of Kashmir, the Maharaja opted to join India which sent its armed forces to protect the state being run over and taken over by Pakistan which had already grabbed the Gilgit area which was an integral part of Kashmir State. The Indian Forces nearly missed their opportunity to save Kashmir because the Pakistani militants were on the point of taking over the only airport in Srinagar, capital city of Kashmir. The main road link to Kashmir was from Rowalpindi in West Punjab which formed part of Pakistan. There was no vehicular route from India or Jammu to Srinagar. The Indian Airforce and the Civil airlines carried all armed men and materials by air and could somehow stop progress of the Pakistani intruders. India managed to drive the untrained hordes of Pakistanis by using well trained Indian troops but a prolonged war could not be to India's advantage as the Indian Army was greatly handicapped by logistics. Perhaps on the advice of the First Governor General, Lord Mountbatten, Nehru ordered ceasefire and declared a truce thus leaving Pakistan with a strong foothold in West Kashmir besides occupying the whole of Gilgit region. Truce could be ended when India felt strong enough to fight and drive back the Pakistani hordes but Nehru declared that there would be a plebiscite amongst the people of Kashmir to decide whether it would join Pakistan or India. Moreover, unnecessarily Nehru took the Kashmir problems to the forum of the United Nations Organisation. The only saving clause was Nehru's declaration that the plebiscite would be held provided Pakistan vacated the parts of illegally occupied Kashmir and a free plebiscite would be held under the aegis of the United Nations. There was no question of Indian Forces leaving Kashmir which had technically and legally become a part of India as soon as the Maharaja opted for India. Kashmir dispute is raging since 1948 and is the main cause of present hostility between the two countries. Till the 50th year of Independence the dispute is very much alive and it is not known when and how the dispute will end. In course of years, the International community has remembered India's promise of holding a plebiscite and forgotten the important provision that before plebiscite Pakistan must vacate the occupied Kashmir. Pakistan never did so but is insisting on holding the plebiscite. India has poured in thousands of crores of rupees to instal a legitimate government and to improve the state in different aspects and could ill afford to part with the state without jeopardising head waters of many important rivers flowing into India. Even after 50 years of fighting and disputing over Kashmir it cannot be foreseen how and when the dispute would be settled. Pakistan is insisting on the plebiscite being held but India steadfastly refusing to do so on the plea that ground and political realities have vastly changed from those prevailing in 1947–48. It is, however, certain that the result of plebiscite or referendum if held will go in favour of Kashmiris who are mostly Muslims opting for Pakistan unless they are allowed to become an independent state. It is most surprising how Jawaharlal Nehru could even dream that a majority of Muslims of Kashmir would opt to join India instead of Pakistan, if a plebiscite was held, after witnessing the hatred and enmity between the two communities in the days of actual partition.

India made many blunders on the eve of and soon after Independence. First was to agree to partition the country on the basis of two nations theory in the two communities who had lived for 800 years as neighbours for good or evil, to agree to an unequal division of the country, not to agree to peaceful exchange of population and above all to appoint a Britisher as the First Governor General of India who was allowed to offer advice to Nehru on important matters of the State. With continued blundering the Congress politicians have brought untold misery and insoluble problems for Indians of many future generations.

The posting of all personnel to occupy high and middle category posts had been finalised and one Karuna Kumar Hajara, ICS was in charge of posting of all officers in suitable posts. Sukumar Gupta was made the IG of Police in West Bengal. The second most important post in the Police was that of the Commissioner of Police, Calcutta. One Surendra Nath Chatterjee was posted as the CP Calcutta. Both were officers in the IP cadre. As nearly 60 per cent Indian officers in IP cadre in Bengal were Muslims most of whom had opted for Pakistan, there was a large number of vacancies and posts to be filled up by promotion from the rank of Senior Dy. SP's and Inspectors.

I reported to the office of IG of Police and Upananda Mukherjee was the senior Asst. Inspector General who told me to join new post of Dy. Commissioner of Police, Security Central Office in short DC, SCO on 14.8.47 and take charge. I also saw IG of Police Gupta whom I did not know well but had met in the annual dinner parties of the Association of IP officers. I also called on S.N. Chatterjee, the newly appointed Police Commissioner.

Next day was the big day of Independence. Although 15th August was in the height of the rainy season and usually experienced rainfall in these parts of West Bengal, in 1947 the whole day was sunny and all the official functions passed off smoothly without a hitch. I presided over the National Flag hoisting ceremony in full uniform and made a short speech. This was done in the lawn of my residence-cum-office. The important ceremony was held in the Brigade Parade Ground where the three wings of the Armed Forces, Police, Boy Scouts and Girl Guides and contingent of Home Guards would take part in an Independence Day Parade in which the Governor of West Bengal His Excellency Chakravorty Raja Gopalachari would take the salute. All ministers in West Bengal Cabinet, all high officials of the local and central governments had been invited and took part. I did so in uniform and being a cine photography buff took my 8 mm camera to take pictures of the day's proceedings in a colour cine film. The Governor arrived in a well decorated open horse drawn carriage and sat on the dais flanked by the Chief

Minister Dr P.C. Ghosh, who was at that time called the Prime Minister too. There was therefore a confusion between the Prime Minister of India and the Prime Minister of West Bengal or any other state. In consequence, the designation of the Principal Minister in a state was rightly termed the Chief Minister in later months. There was a huge gathering of cheering public who hoped for better days after Independence. It had also been announced that the local Government House, i.e. Raj Bhavan in Calcutta would be thrown open to the public and this decision spelt disaster. Thousands of people thronged and entered the government house except a few bed rooms and dining room and moved all over the place. They considered the Government House as belonging to the nation and indirectly to the public. Some unscrupulous people took away silver articles and valuable objects de-art and pictures too. The Commissioner of Police had to send words to the DC South and also asked DC HQ to take a contingent of policemen and clear the Government House of all members of the public and that was done with great difficulty. Thousands who had been waiting outside had to be asked to leave the place to their great disappointment. There was also a garden party at the Government House in the afternoon and I attended. The Governor Rajaji was attentive to most of his guests and sat at many tables to have a talk with his guests.

From the next day I had to attend office and bring normalcy to departmental work which was greatly interrupted during the few weeks before actual partition when most British and Irish officers left the service. Most Muslim officers left for Pakistan and all Hindu officers who opted had not yet joined or had not yet been apprised of their posting.

I had taken charge of SCO from one British officer on 14.8.47 and he was James Jameson of my batch. Besides there were one Addl. DC named Richardson and a special officer named EOC, both Englishmen who did not leave and were experts in their job. Security control office was a part of the Calcutta Police Department but was also partly controlled by the Intelligence Bureau of the Government of India in New Delhi. The office was in charge of receiving passport applications. Verifying character and antecedents of the applicants and making a report recommending issue of a passport or otherwise. Passports were being issued by the West Bengal government as in the British Rule days but later the central government opened passport issuing offices in each state and the SCO received applications of only residents in Calcutta Police area and the District Magistrate dealt with applicants in the districts. This office was also the centre of direct registration of all foreigners in Calcutta and also received periodical reports of all registered foreigners in the districts in West Bengal and an annual report had to be sent to the Intelligence Bureau in New Delhi. Besides this office undertook intelligence work on some foreign countries especially Soviet Russia and China as well as kept watch and information about important personages. The work of monitoring outgoing and incoming foreign mail was undertaken by this office. There was some common work between Special Branch office of Calcutta Police and SCODC. SCO wielded some special powers described hereinafter. D.C. could permit stay of three days to foreigners who had no visas or gave permission of three days of extra stay beyond the date of expiry of a visa.

Besides looking after trading and commercial interests of their own countries consulates of foreign countries and the UK. Dy. High Commissioner's office in Calcutta were in charge of welfare of their own citizens staying in or passing through Calcutta. My office was in close touch with all the consulates and all senior and junior officers were well acquainted with members of the Consular corps. DC was much sought after as he was the first officer charged with the duty of permitting a foreigner to stay without a visa for three days. It was the local authorities of the Foreign Airlines which touched Calcutta who needed help of this office mostly to allow foreign passengers who did not have a transit visa but wanted to visit the city for shopping or sight seeing to land and stay in a local hotel. In some cases, the Aircraft needed some minor repairs and had to stay for a day. In rare cases, an aircraft was found not to be airworthy and another aeroplane had to come to carry passengers of the defective plane. In both events the passengers had to move into the city to stay in a hotel and had to be given permission by the DC. DC was invited to attend all parties given by the consulates on the National day of each country. So were the two Add. DCs. Big cocktail parties were thrown in which foreign liquors and soft drinks were served along with nice tasty snacks. Caviare was served in some parties of rich countries. The important consulates were of the USA, Italy, Belgium, France, Holland, Spain, Germany, Thailand, China and British Dy. High Commission. Although I was a middle rank officer equivalent to a Dy. Secretary's post, the hosts used to be very attentive to me because I played a critical and useful part in their affairs. The Consul General of China during Marshal Chiang Kai Shek's regime, one Dr Tsai, was a very nice and friendly man and we came close to each other. He invited me to other parties held by him and I attended some dinner parties too at his residence.

France was waging a war in French Indo China and there was a French Airforce Liaison office in Ballygunge Park and I became friendly with the two Principal officers of that office. One was Marcel Bouyat who was a bachelor and the other was his senior and a married man.

SCO was housed in an old building on Pretoria Street and my residence was on the same street opposite to my office across the road. It was a nice two storeyed house with a large lawn. I occupied the first floor and the ground floor housed the Special Officer Cowen's office and some electronic and photographic gadgets. We had a Kodak copying machine which took photographs of documents and pictures on a 16 mm cine film frame and could develop and print enlargements. The hire charge was Rs 6,000 per annum. There was also an automatic telephone tapping wire recorder which was operated with government permission accorded during the World War years and we were authorised to link our line with any telephone line we wanted to tap and the telephone department carried out our direction. This machine was a recording unit with a large spool of magnetic recording wire before magnetic tapes came into vogue. This machine would start functioning as soon as any call originated from or was made to the particular number the machine was connected to. In the latter case the machine would start functioning as soon as the receiver was lifted. It recorded all conversation from or to the particular telephone number. We used to rewind the wire and listen to the previous day's or a few previous days' conversation and the stenographer would take down if the conversation was of any importance. When I took over, the machine was connected to tap the phone of one of the most important persons in Bengal before Independence and could record all his conversation with others. The telephone of this person was being tapped in the hope of getting important information about his present political activities and future plans. Unfortunately we were disappointed. Most of his calls were personal and social and were of no importance to us. We were, however, surprised to discover that this bachelor politician had managed to cultivate intimate acquaintance with wives of some high officials and other society ladies. It was apparent that he was a lover of some of them. It was a shameful revelation as these ladies had placed themselves in this position in order to promote service interests of their husbands or to get small advantage for themselves in pre-Independence days.

During my tenure of 9 months, several incidents occurred which are worth recording. I had to put two foreigners to be held as prisoners because they had been unwanted visitors who landed without visas and they were to be kept in SCO prisoners' cell till they got visas or a foreign Airline agreed to take them out of the country at the intervention of the country's Diplomatic Representative in Calcutta or New Delhi.

One day the local Manager of PANAM Airlines came to see me and invited me to travel by their Airline wherever I wanted to go. Simultaneously he offered me two airline tickets good for a round the world trip. I enquired about the normal price of each ticket and he said that the question of price of tickets did not arise. On my insistence, however, he said that each ticket would normally cost Rs 6,000 but these were being offered to me and my wife as complimentary gifts. I told him that I was a bachelor and there was no need for a second ticket. Later I explained to him that under the extant government officers' conduct rules I could take a gift valued upto Rs 20 and told him that I would be guilty of gross violation of conduct rules if I accepted any such ticket. I told him that I would retire on 30.6.68 and would be very glad to accept such tickets if offered to me on or after that date. He was disappointed but understood my objection. I thanked him profusely before he left.

Another notable incident occurred during my tenure. While selecting foreign mail letters for opening and scrutinising the contents, my officers got one addressed to Sarat Chandra Bose, elder brother of Netaji Subhas Chandra Bose. The contents were simple. The letter (which was dated a year or so after Subhas Chandra Bose disappeared from his house in Calcutta and left India) informed his elder brother that he was keeping good health and that he had married an Austrian lady and asked for his elder brother's blessings and also sent his compliments, i.e. *pranam*s to him and other elders. The letter ended by the simple word 'Subhas'. This letter was opened and closed very carefully so that no suspicion was aroused. This letter was photographed and a copy was sent to the Intelligence Bureau, New Delhi. As a matter of routine we had to send a monthly resume incorporating important contents of all letters intercepted by us. After all a Congress party government was in power in the state and Sarat Chandra Bose was a renowned leader, although he had quit Congress. I knew one son of Sarat Chandra Bose named Amiya who was a year junior to me in the same school. He became a Barrister-at-law but did not seriously take to practice of law. He always boasted of his uncle Subhas and also his family and accused us of being minions of a useless government and used other pejorative epithets. I met him many times but could not tell him about his uncle's marriage to a foreigner. Amiya became a Forward Block Party leader and organised meetings against the Congress government in the state. The opposition parties consisted of the Forward Block, the Communist Party of India, RSP, RCPI and other parties.

This myth of avowed bachelorhood not to marry till India became free continued. In my opinion there was nothing wrong in a staunch patriot and nationalist marrying and participating simultaneously in a freedom struggle. For a terrorist it is wrong to marry because he may lose his or her life in a shoot out or after a trial and leave his or her partner a widow or a widower and in grief. While I read this letter I could not help conjuring up the vision of Lila Roy neé Lila Nag of Dacca whose inamorato was rumoured to be Subhas Bose whom she knew from before her marriage and loved and most people expected that her love would not be in vain. I saw Lila Nag when she used to come to the Police Control Room in Dacca to complain against police failures. What a marvellous handsome and dignified couple the two would have made. Lila Nag later married another reputed Congressman Anil Roy after she came to know of Subhas's disappearance. Soon rumours floated that Subhas Chandra had got married and this rumour must have originated from the high official circle of New Delhi where the Prime Minister, Home Minister and several high officials came to know from the contents of the intercepted letter. Alternatively the news might have originated from a foreign country after the war was over. At this rumour Amiya became mad with rage and practically abused all official circles for maligning his uncle in order to demolish Subhas's image with his country men. Amiya and members of Bose family must have known the true facts from the hand written letter Sarat Bose received which bore a postal seal of several years back. But Amiya and his brothers and other Forward Block workers preferred to carry on with a palpable lie. Many people in India did not believe even when it became public knowledge of Subhas Bose's marriage to an Austrian lady till the lady herself came to India many years later accompanied by her daughter by Subhas.

Agitation of the opposition parties mainly took the form of daily demonstration near the two wings of the Legislature, i.e. Legislative Assembly (Lower House) and Legislative Council (Upper House). They shouted slogans like "E AZADI JHUTA HAI", "E SARKAR BADALNA CHAHIYE", "SAB GADDI CHHODO", etc., i.e. this Independence is a mockery, this government must change, government must quit, etc. and the demonstration was against the Congress Party of which Pandit Jawaharlal Nehru, the then Prime Minister was the president. This went on daily and the DC's had to perform duty alternatively to be in charge of police arrangements. Sometimes the demonstrators became rowdy and unruly and the police had to use tear gas to disperse the unruly crowd, especially the stone throwing mob. So far as I remember, this agitation went on as long as I stayed in the Calcutta Police.

During my tenure I had to recommend deportation of a few undesirable foreigners and the government of India seldom rejected my recommendations which were supported by facts, figures and an overall appreciation why the foreigners' stay in India was undesirable. Amongst those recommended for deportation there was a Greek merchant of Calcutta. He had been a trader, importing and exporting goods but had a shady side to his business. I got several reports and also came to know that he was deported from India a few years back during the British regime but had managed to get a visa again and stayed to do business. However, this Greek merchant apprehended his deportation and engaged a famous top Barrister lawyer named Amiya Kumar Bose who was also the President of the Calcutta Club and was well known to me. Barrister Bose sought an interview with me and I promptly agreed to see him in my office and gave him a date and time. Bose came and saw me. After a few minutes of pleasant small talk, Bose broached the purpose of his coming to see me, namely, to find out some means to withdraw my recommendation to the Government of India about deportation of the Greek merchant but I declined. He tried his best to convince me about the hollowness of reports about the Greek's undesirable activities and that my officers had fabricated the reports. I told him that deportation was a serious matter and we had to cross check each information and to get the materials verified from different sources. I told him unambiguously that there was no chance of withdrawing or modifying my recommendation for deportation. The interview was over in 20 minutes but Bose begged of me to allow him to sit in my office for another 30 minutes so that his client, the Greek, who was waiting in a car on the road outside would think that he was pleading his case vigorously for an hour. As Bose did not show any signs of leaving I had to ask him to leave because I had to see other visitors. He said that he had taken the assignment for two days on a fee of Rs 20,000 per day and requested me to permit him to come next day when be would only sit in my office room and smoke cigars without disturbing me. I firmly refused to do so because such an act would make me a party to cheating his client. He left with a saddened heart saying that I had robbed him of an easy earning of Rs 20,000.

While serving in the Calcutta Police we had to deal with minor communal troubles which continued even after the partition and Independence. The awkward thing that happened was illegal occupation of Muslim residential properties especially Muslim houses by Hindu neighbours when the Muslim residents had left for shelter in safer places for fear of life and abduction and found that their houses had been occupied by the Hindus who refused to leave on the plea that such events were occurring much more frequently all over the East Pakistan. The local police would help in forcing the intruders out. It was left to the higher officers of the rank of AC's and DC's to manage. Often they succeeded by giving good advice, by haranguing and cajoling the intruders but sometimes they failed. There were occasions of stiff determined resistance by the illegal intruders who were supported by their neighbours.

Such an instance not only required use of force but such force may extend to use of guns to fire at the men taking part in rioting. I and Prasad K. Bose Dy. Commissioner of the Special Branch who were perhaps more conscientious than many others, decided to seek advice from the Commissioner of Police who directed to see the DC HQ who was a senior I.P. officer named Hari Sadhan Ghosh Chaudhuri. We two DC's saw him but he could not give us any firm advice or direction and we three decided to see the then Premier or Chief Minister Dr Bidhan Chandra Roy who had replaced the first incumbent Dr Prafulla Ch. Ghosh, who was a staunch Gandhiste and had strict moral principles which did not suit the legislators who wanted him to be replaced. Dr B.C. Roy had been selected to be the Governor of the United Provinces but he opted out of this post of a titular head and kept himself free to take up an assignment suited to his abilities and genius. He was asked by the Congress High Command to become the Chief Minister of West Bengal and he took up the reins of government of the problem ridden impoverished and truncated state of West Bengal. He, however, governed the state very successfully from 1948 till his death in 1962. Dr Roy launched many important projects for economic and industrial development of the state. To mention a few there are Kalyani satellite town and industrial estate, Bandel thermal project, Durgapur township and industrial area, Haldia port, creation of Salt Lake City by bringing up sand from the bed of the river Hooghly, Farakka barrage, Chittaranjan Locomotive Works being sited in West Bengal and many others. He has been rightly called as 'Paschim Banglar Rupakar', i.e. 'The Creator of West Bengal'.

However, reverting to my story of seeing Dr Roy we did go and see Dr Roy, posed our problem and sought his orders. It was an awkward problem to ask him to solve namely to do justice to Muslim victims without taking violent measures against the Hindus. He was very nice to us during the interview and said that we were in service long enough to find an acceptable solution and must have faced such problems during the British regime and solved them satisfactorily, etc. Finally, he advised us to use our good sense, and experience and tactfully manage such situations. Such advice I had received later many times in my service.

As we did not feel satisfied at whatever advise we received from different quarters we decided that we should see Mahatma Gandhi who was camping in a house in Beliaghata Road in order to bring communal harmony in West Bengal soon after Independence. We went to Gandhiji without making an appointment, gave out our identity to the Police on duty and saw him. We bowed to him and posed our problem and sought his advice. He was straightforward and told us to believe in truth and justice and act according to our conscience and in the instances we quoted we had no alternative to evicting the intruding Hindus by use of minimum force or adopting non-violent means and thus allowing original Muslim owners/occupants to return and occupy their residence. By this time I had met three great sons of India, namely Rabindra Nath Tagore, Jawaharlal Nehru and Mahatma Gandhi and had long discussions with all of them. I was most impressed with Gandhiji's simplicity of thought and clearcut advice as how to solve our problem. We had to wait for a few weeks before we could induce the Hindu intruders to leave and to enable the former Muslim residents to occupy the houses.

As the three senior officers in the SCO were receiving regular invitations from the offices of the local Consulates and Dy. High Commissioner of the United Kingdom we thought that it would be a good idea if we ourselves threw a cocktail party inviting our regular hosts and their senior officers. IG and CP, the Chief Secretary, the Home Secretary as well as a few of our personal friends would also be invited. We printed cards for invitation fixing a date which was not a National

Holiday of any country. We made out a careful list of invitees and the minimum number came to be 120 gentlemen and ladies. It was decided to serve foreign liquor, local soft drinks and snacks of different kinds. I knew that some guests would stay beyond the scheduled hours and it was proper they were served with a simple dinner. Food for dinner of a dozen or more people was also prepared. Most of the invitees responded and the guests who attended numbered 106. I still remember the number as it was the largest party I hosted except at my own wedding reception a few months later. The party went off extremely well and the foreigner guests said that they had not been invited to such a party by the police in the past. As expected by me a few guests stayed on after 9 pm the hour set for the end of the party and we decided to have some dancing with the help of a radiogram and parlophone dance records (discs) serving as the dance band. Some time later, a simple dinner was served but most people who had eaten plenty of snacks took little food. After dinner all guests left and I retired for the night. Next day was a Sunday and there would be rest for all the hosts. I may record here that the reciprocal cocktail party became a tradition for the next few years when my successors were working as the Head of the Security Control.

During the cocktail party some guests whom I knew to be the committee members of a fashionable social club named '300 Club' enquired which club I was a member of. On learning that I was a member of the Calcutta Club, they insisted that I must become a member of the '300 Club' too and they would see to it that I did become a member. A couple of weeks later, I got intimation that I had been elected to be a permanent member of '300 Club'. I had not signed any application form nor did I know who proposed and seconded my name. Such was the magic of the post I held as the Dy. Commissioner of Police and Asstt. Director of the Intelligence Bureau, Government of India. I got congratulations from a senior ICS friend A.D. Khan who at my request had tried earlier to induct me as a member of the '300 Club' before Independence and was compelled to withdraw my name because one senior Englishman colleague in the police considered me as a difficult person and had objected to my membership.

I and my two colleagues were doing our work smoothly. Richardson and Cowen were well trained in intelligence work and knew about foreign intelligence, how to recruit agents and how to analyse newspaper reports and published commercial and industrial statistics. Before the end of the war, foreign intelligence concentrated on Germany and her allies in Europe and Japan in Asia. After the end of the war intelligence offensive was directed against Soviet Russia in Europe and China in Asia where President Chiang Kai Shek was fighting a losing battle with the Chinese Communist Party under Mao Ze Dong who eventually took over the whole of China. Richardson used to do very clever intelligence work not only about Soviet Russia but also some Soviet satellite countries in Europe and Cowen did the same good work in respect of China under General Chiang Kai Shek and communist activities in that country.

Richardson soon decided to leave and government appointed one officer from the local Intelligence Branch to act in his place. He was a very much inferior substitute for Richardson. After some time, Cowen also decided to leave as he had been offered a very attractive post in the South East Asian Council (SEAC) to be posted in Singapore. As the incumbent of this post need to know Chinese language and characters both to read and speak, we were in real difficulty to find a suitable person. I conceived the idea of visiting China to find a suitable successor to cowen as well as to fulfil a promise to the Chinese Consul General in Calcutta that I would pay a visit to his country to fulfil a long standing invitation by Dr Tsai, the Chinese Consul General in Calcutta, to visit his country.

12

Sojourn in the East

Some months earlier in 1947 I had received my first passport which was British and bore the emblem of the Lion and Unicorn as India was still a commonwealth country with a Viceroy and Governor General as the Head of the State and as the representative of the crown of the United Kingdom. The first use I made of my passport was to obtain a visa for Burma from the Burmese Consul's office in Calcutta and undertook a journey to Rangoon where I stayed in a hotel for 3 days and did all the sight seeing. It was certainly thrilling for me to be able to visit a foreign country. Burmese were great eaters and the wayside hotel did brisk business throughout the night till early hours of the dawn. Another thing was peculiar. The barbers' shops (saloons) remained practically open throughout the day and night except 3–4 hours in early dawn. Shwey Dagon pagoda was the most famous and popular Buddhist temple in Burma and had its pagoda covered in gold sheets. There were many Buddhist monks inside as well as visiting from elsewhere. Besides there were hundreds of pilgrims. I visited some shops where valuable jewels like rubies, sapphires and other precious stones mined in Burma were sold. As I was a bachelor I had no idea about their price nor any desire to buy them. I just wanted to see the precious stones mined in Burma. I also learnt that a senior ICS officer named B.N. Chakravorty ICS, was the Minister in the Indian Embassy in Nanking which was the capital of Kuoming Tang government in China under General Chiang. A large part of China was occupied by the communists who were totally against Chiang's rule. I wrote to B.N. Chakravorty whom I knew well and the purpose of my visit. He agreed to help me and to allow me to be his guest during my stay in Nanking.

I had to get foreign exchange and I got two thousand dollars sanctioned by the Reserve Bank of India on the recommendation of the then Chief Secretary whom I told the purpose of my visit. The cardinal mistake I made was not to inform my boss, the Commissioner of Police, causing him great annoyance as subsequent events proved. I took Chinese visa and also a US visa because there was also a remote chance of my visiting the USA which was served by a Chinese Airline from China to the West Coast of the USA and back.

As I could not afford to pay a regular Airlines fare to China and back nor could I take a free complimentary ticket, I decided to travel by a Chinese military plane which carried cargoes only like in the Second World War days and could not take fare paying passengers. The Chinese Consul General made all the arrangements and I travelled by a Chinese military plane which flew from Calcutta to Chittagong and then take a long circuitous route via Rangoon, Chungking, Hangchow and finally to Shanghai. In flying to Chungking the plane had to fly over the 'Hump' which the Burmese Himalayas in the Chinese air-route used to be termed in those days. During the actual days of the war, the allied military and civil planes had to take this route to go to China because the littoral areas and other East Asian countries were under Japanese occupation. While crossing the 'Hump' I remember that I felt faint and had to lie down at one point of the flight. I could not sit up or enquire about the reasons but this condition disappeared after an hour or so. To my query, the co-pilot who could speak English told me that to fly over the hump the plane had to rise upto 17000 or 18000 feet above the sea level and in that altitude oxygen was much less than normal. This happened because our plane was not pressurised and breathing air with less oxygen caused my feeling of faintness. As the crew had become accustomed, they did not feel faint or suffer from any other difficulty. In Shanghai I went into a hotel which the representative of the plane service arranged. It was a nice, small and fashionable hotel where lots of Europeans stayed. I used to eat at the hotel restaurant and seldom went out to eat. I contacted the Indian Consul General who was one Captain Sathe, formerly of the Royal (India) Airforce. He was delighted that I had come and would go on to the capital Nanking. He invited me for a meal next day and sent his car to fetch me. Captain Sathe who was in the Foreign Service was a polished handsome young man and later married a daughter of the then Indian Ambassador in China, named K.P.S. Menon, a very senior ICS officer. Sathe also lent me his car to do sight seeing in Shanghai which was the most important city and a sea port in China. In the old days Shanghai was full of foreigners mostly residents of European and North American countries and was the scene of a lot of activities in business, fashion and espionage. This was so also in pre-war days. In my student days I had seen a cine picture titled 'Shanghai Express'. Both European and Chinese food was served in the hotel. There was one Indian whom I came to be acquainted with. He was a businessman and had married a Polish girl who was an exceptional beauty with green eyes and seemed to be devoted to him.

After staying a few days in Shanghai I took a night train to Nanking. I travelled in a sleeper coach in which dinner was served and clean comfortable bed was provided. They served warm tea water for cleaning one's mouth before retiring. I found that green tea leaves were plentiful and was supplied hot or tepid to most passengers on the train or at the railway station. At the Nanking Rail Station I was received by an officer of the Indian Embassy who took me in the Embassy car to B.N. Chakraborty's residence. Chakraborty lived with his wife, a schoolgoing daughter named Gouri and an infant son. Mrs Chakraborty was busy with her son but both the children received great care and attention. The daughter who was the first and only child for many years was perhaps a little spoilt by over indulgent parents. I could see this from her way of talking with and behaviour towards her father. My impression was confirmed when the daughter was one day heard telling her father "Don't be silly" who did not rebuke her nor cautioned her against using such language in an educated highly placed Indian family. There were several places of sightseeing including the Great Chinese Wall which is 2400 kms long, 7.5 metres average height, 7 metres at base and 3.5 metres at the top. I called on the Ambassador and his wife next day. K.P.S. Menon and his wife were excellent people and treated me not as a junior officer but as an honoured guest. I had accompanied Chakraborty and his wife and we were all invited to come to tea a few days later. He had perhaps two sons staying with him and they were studying in English medium schools in Nanking. Incidentally Menon's eldest son joined the Indian Foreign Service and rose to become the Principal Secretary in the Ministry of External Affairs in India. Earlier his son-in-law Captain Sathe had also held the post before his retirement. In the mean time both Sathe and young Menon held several Ambassadorial posts in different countries. I had visited New Delhi when Sathe and later Menon were acting as the Chief Bureaucrats in the Ministry but resisted my desire, if not temptation, to congratulate them and renew old memories. I, however, desisted because there was no point in my seeing them in their elevated positions unless my work demanded that I should do so.

I told Chakraborty about the need to find suitable Chinese knowing Indians one of whom could be induced to join my office. The Embassy could find 3 persons but only one in my opinion might suit the post in my office. He was one Sumal Sinha and was considered by me to be the most suitable man but he refused to leave China where he was getting a handsome salary in the teaching profession. I was disappointed in my search and returned empty handed so far as my main mission was concerned. In later years Sumal Sinha joined the Ministry of External Affairs in the Chinese section.

I was taken to see the Great Wall and climbed on to its top. I also visited two interior towns to see rural life. The average citizen in post-war China lived a life like an average Indian. The Chinese were, however, more hard working. I saw a bamboo and wooden residential structure start and be completed during my eleven days' stay in Nanking. I was at first aghast to see Chinese peasants taking basketloads of human excreta in bamboo basket slung on a bamboo pole on the shoulder to be used as fertilisers of the farm lands. I did not see many heads of cattle but saw horses used in ploughing. There were water buffaloes in some places and were used to draw the plough. One small town in the interior named Hangchow, was recommended for my visit, Hangchow now renamed, had a beautiful lake. I travelled by train to the town and spent a day in the town. I had a boat ride in the lake and found women paddling the boat with both hands and feet. I had taken an 8 mm cine camera and used it extensively. The most important event was my attendance as a member of the Indian Ambassador's group at the meeting held in memory of Mahatma Gandhi who was assassinated a few weeks back in New Delhi. General Chiang Kai Shaik, President of China and Head of the Kuomingtang government presided at the memorial meeting and addressed the gathering. I tried my best to film the event but there was not sufficient light except that flashlights of still photographers lighted up the scene and my film showed the presence of General Chiang.

Return journey was by civilian plane which started from Shanghai, stopped at HongKong, Rangoon and Calcutta. As there was need to change the plane I had to spend a night and half a day in Hong Kong and was put up in the very best hotel in Hong Kong named Peninsular. Next morning the British Flying Boats airline, in which the aeroplanes took off from and landed in water made their last flight from Hong Kong harbour and was watched by many people including me.

When I returned from my China tour, I got an order posting me as the Superintendent of Police in the district of Hooghly. This post fell vacant due to the then SP H.N. Gupta being promoted to the rank of DIG of Police. I was to be succeeded by one Sudhir Kr. Sinha, an IP officer 4 years my senior. I was very upset because I was to get married in 8 weeks' time and all my plans already made had to be altered. I approached the Commissioner of Police but he was not helpful. I could feel that he was very displeased with me because of my failure to inform him of my intended visit to China and search for an Indian who would be a China expert. He came to know of my tour to China and its purpose from a small newspaper report. I should have told him the details of my tour as well as my impending wedding. I regretted my folly and left SCO with a heavy heart.

The most notable event which occurred during my tenure in this office was the assassination of Mahatma Gandhi, Father of the Nation. I heard the news over the radio and also heard what the Prime Minister Nehru had to say. He was weeping and one could just understand his speech between loud sobs. All public and private engagements were cancelled for the whole period of mourning. There was no television and we could only hear news and views on the radio and read in the newspapers. The whole country was in deep shock and mourning that the apostle of '*Ahingsa*' (non-violence) and of Truth died by the bullets of a rabid fanatic, named Nathuram Godse, who was later tried and hanged.

13

Marriage, Prison Revolt, Influx of East Pakistan Refugees, Terrorist Outrages, Telengana Type Movement

I joined Hooghly as the Superintendent of Police and had my headquarters in the town of Chinsurah. I was housed in a spacious residential quarters which formed a part of barracks of British officers in the East India Company's days. It was situated on the bank of the river Hooghly.

Chinsurah was the headquarters of the district as well as the seat of the Divisional Commissioner of Burdwan Division and the Range D.I.G. The Commissioner had an independent large house which was built in the Dutch period and was more than 200 years old. The DIG of Police lived next door to me occupying a portion of the barrack which housed three officers, namely, DIG, SP and the Civil Surgeon on the first floor and one Addl. SP, one Addl. District Magistrate on the ground floor in which was also situated the Circuit house. There was also the Superintending Engineer living in a rented house in the town. The Range DIG was my old boss in Rajshahi namely H.N. Gupta and the Superintending Engineer was the former P.W.D. executive engineer of Rajshahi both of whom I came to know closely in Rajshahi. Therefore, I had two friendly families in which I was always welcome. I joined sometime in March 1948 and soon I had to apply for a month's leave for getting married and later to spend some time on honeymoon. I went to see Gupta, IG of Police and had to see Upananda Mukherjee who was then the Senior of the two Asstt. Inspectors General of Police posted in IG's office. Upananda did not favour my seeking a month's leave and asked me to reduce the period to a fortnight, if not a week and he also added that IG would not sanction a month's leave. I got irritated and told him to his face that he was acting the IG's role but I would not change my application. This caustic remark of mine did not certainly please him. He was merely two years my senior and I did not look upon him or his post with fear or reverence. He got up and went in to see IG and asked me to go in. I do not know what he told IG. My application was in IG's hand and he only wanted to know if I could do with a lesser period but I replied that one got married only once in one's lifetime and I had not taken any leave since 1945 and needed the leave. He promptly sanctioned the leave and wished me good luck.

I got married to one Miss Gouri Bhattacharyya, the youngest daughter of one Nagendra Kr. Bhattacharyya, an eminent Advocate in Berhampore District Courts. Miss Bhattacharyya was a student in B.A. course but had to suspend her studies because she contacted plurisy and was under treatment. Her doctors had forbidden much movement and as such she desisted from attending the college. She was a student in Berhampore Women's College which had recently been founded and my maternal uncle, Bishnupada Bhattacharyya, IAS, the then District Magistrate in Murshidabad, was the President of the Governing Council and also an honorary professor teaching Sanskrit in the same college. It was my maternal uncle who first suggested that I get married to Miss Gouri who was a tall girl of rare beauty and of excellent manners. After meeting her and her senior relatives I and my family approved of the alliance but I was asked to wait for one year to allow her to get completely cured of her ailment. As such I used to meet her occasionally when I was stationed in Barisal and later more often when I got posted as a Dy. Commissioner in Calcutta Police.

As my wife's family were residents of Berhampore, Murshidabad, they wanted the wedding to take place in Berhampore but I would not agree. The family therefore thrust on me the responsibility of finding a suitable house for the wedding and I had to find a suitable house for my wedding reception *(Boubhat)* also. I was lucky to have the garden house in Alipore of late Hanuman Poddar, a thorough gentleman and a friend whom I knew closely as a member of the Calcutta Club and also the ground floor of the palace in Calcutta of Raja Kamala Ranjan Roy of Cossimbazar whom I came to know closely while serving as a probationer in Berhampore several years back. The wedding was held in the garden house on May 1, 1948 and the *Boubhat* and reception were held a couple of days later. I invited the Inspector General and the Commissioner of Police, several high officials in the ICS, IP and other services and also all my former colleagues in the Calcutta Police and colleagues in the West Bengal Police. The ceremonies passed off smoothly. The Calcutta Police officers presented a heavy sterling silver plate made by the reputed silversmith Cooke & Kelvey bearing signatures of all the Deputy Commissioners of Police of Calcutta and a silver cigar box was presented by three I.P. officers serving in West Bengal. Senior officers like the Chief Secretary, IG and CP gave separate presents of their choice. I greatly cherish the silver plate which bears not only signatures but also my and my wife's names and the date of wedding. The reception had perforce to be a very simple affair as Dr P.C. Ghosh, the former Chief Minister had imposed a spartan fare in all ceremonies which permitted serving of nuts, fruits and sweets only as eats and the practice continued while I got married. Soft drinks, coffee and tea were also served. I did not dare violate the guest control orders in the least because the guests were mostly officials some of whom themselves might have been enthusiastic about strict imposition of the order and might report to the Chief Minister or initiate departmental proceedings against me. I had, however, another small function with close relatives of my wife and mine in the Bengali style with *pilau,* fish, meat etc. After a couple of days I and my newly wed wife accompanied by my cook left for Darjeeling to spend 3 weeks on honeymoon. An old industrialist friend lent his superb bungalow in Darjeeling and allowed his own suite of rooms to be occupied by me and my wife. I had become a member of the Darjeeling Gymkhana Club during my stay in Darjeeling in 1946 and we often visited the Club. I do not remember who were the Dy. Commissioner (District Magistrate) and the Superintendent of Police in Darjeeling at that time but we paid them courtesy visits. In the Mall we met many friends and acquaintances and time did not hang on our hands. I returned to Chinsurah to join my post as SP. There my wife was cordially received by the DIG of Police and the Superintending Engineer and their families who were my old friends of Rajshahi days. Touring in Hooghly was difficult as the police stations were not directly connected by road with the district headquarters in Chinsurah. There was a childrens' theatrical show in which several children of the DIG H.N. Gupta were to participate. My wife took charge of training the troupe and the show was a reasonable success. At that time I came to know that my wife had musical talents, especially a fine ear for music. SP's office had a notorious Head Clerk whose passion was to send anonymous petitions against SP and other officers. Unknown to me he did so against me also. I was once informed by the IG's office that allegations of corrupt practice had been made against me in that I had been drawing horse maintenance allowance and that I had drawn travelling allowance for my wife's journey from Calcutta to Chinsurah although I was not married at the time of joining as SP Hooghly. It was also stated that a secret enquiry was made and the allegations were found to be true. I was asked to offer my explanation. I was very annoyed as well as amused and thought the higher authorities might have enquired of me directly instead of getting enquiries made by officers of the Anti Corruption Department behind my back because these events could not be altered or suppressed even if I tried to do so. I also knew that the person making the allegation was not aware of the actual facts. I replied that my horse had developed some troubles and was kept in the Government Veterinary College and was therefore not being used by me in Chinsurah. Government rules permitted drawing of horse maintenance allowance for four months when a horse is ill and without actually using it. As regards my wife's travelling allowance, the T.A. rules did not say that the officer need be married at the time of joining a new post but only that the wife and family to follow in six months' time. I am ashmed to record here that the government was mean enough to introduce a modification that T.A. can be drawn provided the officer had a wife at the time of transfer, although government admitted that I was right and did not commit any irregularity.

In August I received a transfer order to join as SP 24 Paraganas which was the most important district in West Bengal. Sachindra Mohan Ghosh, an IP officer, a year senior to me, was serving as SP since the Independence Day and the vacancy occurred as he was transferred to IG's office as the Senior AIG after Mukherjee the incumbent got a promotion as DIG of Police.

24 Paraganas was one of the two districts which stretched from the Bay of Bengal inland and the district was 4000 square miles in area and had a population of 4 million in 1948. It was the only district which has a bit of the Sundarbans, the greater part of which is in Khulna district which was then in East Pakistan, now Bangladesh. SP had a nice two storeyed house in Alipore with a large compound in front on the south side and there was a larger plot of land in the rear which could be used as a kitchen garden. Besides the household staff namely the cook, bearer, the syce and the driver had their living quarters. The bathrooms were all fitted with English bath tubs and gas geysers and there was a gas cooking range in the kitchen. There were dining and living rooms and an office room on the ground floor and three bed rooms on the first floor. My wife was very happy to live in this house which was the best house in possession of the West Bengal Police in Calcutta at that time. My wife learnt riding on my horse with the help of the syce in the rear plot of land before venturing out on to the Calcutta Race Course where both of us did some riding for a few days.

During my tenure I had four ICS District Magistrate as my senior colleagues. They were Rabindra Kumar Mitra, Hiranmoy Banerjee, two senior ICS officers and later Bijoy Krishna Acharya and Sankar Nath Maitra ICS officers of my seniority. As it was customary for the Superintendent of Police to pay an official call on the District Magistrate as well as the DIG of Police and the Divisional Commissioner, I called on R.K. Mitra, who was already serving as the DM of the district. R.K. Mitra asked me to report to him every week and apprise him of crime and law and order situations in the district. I considered this as a tall order and did not intend to carry out his order or advice. I called on him after a fortnight and gradually lengthened the gap so that it was seldom more than once in two months. Mitra got transferred and Hiranmoy Banerjee was his successor. I called on him too but he did not ask me to report to him personally or otherwise. However, I used to telephone to inform him about the District

Police Administration. He was soon transferred and was succeeded by Bijoy Acharya on whom also I called. As was proper, he also called at my office once or twice to have a discussion. This pleased me immensely. He was also transferred and was succeeded by Sankar Nath Maitra, an ICS officer, originally of Assam cadre who opted to come to West Bengal. He was the most friendly amongst the four DM's I have had. We became very friendly and he often dropped into my office. My wife also became a friend of his wife with whose parents we also came to have close friendly relationship.

In 24 Parganas I spent two years and a half as SP. Some important and tragic events occurred in the district during my tenure details of which are given herein after.

Hindu refugees were constantly coming from the then East Pakistan and they came in waves if there were communal riots which were mainly one sided, Muslims oppressing Hindus by murder, loot, arson, rape and abduction. Hindus in West Bengal sometimes retaliated on innocent Muslims in the state. I had to take measures to control such communal riots as far as my resources permitted. Things came to such a pass that Prime Minister Nehru and Chief Minister Bidhan Chandra Roy decided to go to the border and see things for themselves. The District Magistrate and I accompanied. Nehru was physically very fit and walked at a brisk pace after leaving the motorcade. Bidhan Roy took his own time and followed him at a distance and gradually fell behind. I heard Nehru call the CM as 'Bidhan' and the latter called the PM as 'Jawahar' and they appeared to be fully on equal terms. This was possible only with Bidhan Chandra Roy. Bidhan Chandra Roy was several years older in age than Nehru. Nehru visited some transit camps and questioned some men and women about the reasons for running away from the East Pakistan and heard the usual tales of atrocities. After 1946-47, killing was not so frequent but looting and forcible occupation of houses and threats of abduction of Hindu women and girls continued thus forcing the Hindus to leave their valuables and immovable properties and flee to India. Soon after I learnt that General Cariappa, the first Indian Chief of the Army, had decided to visit the border and I was directed by the government to accompany him. I saw the local army authorities who were busy polishing their brass and getting two jeep cars thoroughly checked and adjusted for the General to travel in. They told me that Cariappa drove his own vehicle and unfortunately in the past such vehicles broke down en route to the General's great annoyance. They showed me the two cars and expressed satisfaction at the purring noise of the engines. On the particular day, we went to Dum Dum Airport and received the General. He boarded the fully and especially checked and tested jeep car accompanied by his ADC. I was travelling in my new Chevrolet car but the General asked me to get into his car and sit by his side so as to guide him to our destination. The General was found to be a nice polite gentleman but appeared to be spartan in outlook. He drove very fast and I was afraid that we might get involved in an accident. Such an accident could certainly result in death or grievous injuries. It was difficult for the cars behind to keep pace. As a matter of fact he drove ahead of the pilot car and became the first car in the cavalcade. After some time, the car stopped and would not start. The other army officers including the Transport officer came up, apologised and offered the reserve Jeep car. The General and I got into the car and he drove fast as before. It may sound strange but the second car also broke down and the General cursed for the first time and called his officers useless and incompetent. He became red in his face with anger and annoyance. The army officers came up, apologised profusely and explained how much care they had taken to prepare and check the two cars but ill luck dogged them to put them in such an embarassing situation. The Transport officer offered his own vehicle, a jeep car and we again changed car and the General drove to our destination without any hitch or breakdown. The General met the border officers and questioned some refugees as did the Prime Minister earlier. He had also come to study if there would be any defence problem in case border skirmishes started. We returned to Calcutta without any mishap. The General thanked me and left for rest and luncheon at the Fort William. Frankly speaking I did not see what good would come out of short visits of an hour or two by the PM, CM and the Army Chief. In PM and CM's visit there might have been some political mileage gained but in any event both the visits had been morale booster to some victims and the border officers.

There were also industrial as well as communal riots in the industrial areas. Some areas in Jagatdal P.S. were perennial trouble spots for communal troubles and I had to rush many times to ensure effective police action. I had five Addl. Superintendents of Police to help me but they were all promoted officers. They were all very good and conscientious officers but were older than me and did not have the requisite boldness to take firm action. I also knew that I would have to go in the end and it was better that I took charge of the situation as soon as practicable. In 1950 there was a large exodus of Hindu refugees from the East Pakistan into my district and there were widespread repercussions. There were communal riots in many areas, especially in the form of Hindu crowds setting fire to Muslim houses at night. Moreover, hundreds or thousands of refugees took shelter in vacant lands and large houses all over in my district were occupied by the Hindu refugees. There were not many vacant plots in the Calcutta Police areas and, moreover, the Calcutta Police could be more vigilant to prevent squatters and illegal occupation of others properties in the town area manned by the police officers and men of many police stations in the city equipped with cars and radios. In contrast many police stations in my district had as large an area in one police station jurisdiction as the whole of the Calcutta Police area having as many as 20–25 police stations in the jurisdiction.

In Barrackpore subdivision many cases of rioting occurred in the month of January 1950. I remember I went out on 27 nights out of 31 to help local officers to quell disturbances. Towards the end I was feeling fatigued and wished that I could have a few more nights of good sleep. Although Barrackpore subdivision had two active and effective officers, namely, Raghunath Banerjee as SDO and B.C. Chakravorty as SDPO but still I was called out to help these officers. I remember about one night when Banerjee, SDO telephoned to me and requested me to take charge of a situation which he and the SDPO could not control. I replied that with two able officers in the subdivision, it should not be difficult to manage but he would not yield and besought me to come and clinched his argument by saying that he had seen many riots in his life including riots in London, Birmingham and Liverpool but the rioters there were not so violent or ferocious. I knew Banerjee to be a braggart and bluffer but not a liar. He had been to the U.K. for a year or less in the past to appear in the examination for recruitment to the Indian Civil Service after having tried and failed twice in India. Age limit was a year more for recruitment into the ICS in the U.K. and many Indians had been known to avail of the test in U.K. as a desperate step to get into the I.C.S. Banerjee utilised his visit to the U.K. to refer to his experience of witnessing or handling riots in some Industrial towns in the U.K. I did not understand how a visitor and an would-be examinee could have anything to do with riots in the U.K. Reluctantly I left my bed and went out with two armed guards and reached the place of rioting. There were some rioters and many huts were burning. I found both the SDO and SDPO standing at a safe distance with a large posse of policemen armed with *lathi*s, teargas and rifles. O/C was there waiting to be led by either SDO or SDPO. I took charge and obtained orders of the SDO to open fire if I need to. I shouted to the apparent rioters to disperse and asked policemen with *lathis* and guns to advance and to make a determined *lathi* charge first. Rioters on one side dispersed but a few on the side of houses on fire did not. With a few armed men I advanced and found a few men trying to save household goods from the burning huts. As they did not disperse on seeing me and the armed policemen, I approached cautiously when a few men and women came to me weeping and saying that they were Muslims and had been attacked by the Hindus. Police came and opened fire on them who were the actual victims instead of on the Hindu rioters. I pacified them and told them that I would take steps to protect them from further assault. I ordered O/C to take two severely injured men to be taken to the hospital and could not do anything about two men shot dead. SDO and SDPO did not accompany me. I questioned them and learnt that SDPO Chakravorty who owned an automatic US .30 carbine had opened 4 rounds of fire at the rioters who were not rioters but victims of rioting, thus killing two men and injuring two others. I questioned Chakravorty who said that he was puzzled and made the bonafide mistake of shooting at the victims. I now understood that after SDO and SDPO realised their blunder, they did not dare to take any further action and wanted me to pull them out of a difficult and awkward situation. We had to report all cases of police firing to the IG and government. I did so and mentioned about the bonafide mistake made by the SDPO in presence of the SDO.

On another night I had to go out to deal with a riot at night in spite of there being a very competent officer incharge named Durgadas Ghosh, a sub-inspector of police. When I reached I saw actual rioting and had to ask two constables to open fire in two different directions. Opening fire immediately dispersed the rioters. When we scoured the place we could not trace the dead or injured persons nor could we make any arrests. Arrests were almost impractical at night because of darkness and confusion reigning on all sides. I returned to the police station and found the O/C with a superficial bullet injury on his belly. A doctor was called to attend to the wound the officer received. On enquiry I learnt that one of the constables fired in a clumsy manner and the bullet grazed O/C's body at the lower abdomen (belly) region. He did not cry out nor did he give up his efforts to help me in order to get medical aid. Actually he helped me for half an hour or more in completing the police operation. I was full of praise for his physical courage and endurance and considered that my high opinion of him already formed was fully justified. There were many other occasions in the past when S.I. Durga Ghosh showed efficiency and courage in discharge of his duties. I remember I recommended him for award of the Police Medal for meritorious service and he did get the medal. I had also made up my mind to ensure that he got promoted to the Inspector's rank which he did not attain because of his failure in departmental examination for promotion. A few years later when Durga Ghosh had not yet got his promotion, I made out a strong case to the government to exempt him from the promotion examination by citing a series of instances of valiant deeds by him in the interest of the police administration. My efforts convinced both the IG of Police and the government, the latter granting Durga Ghosh exemption and ordering promotion as an Inspector without passing the prescribed examination. So far as I remember this was the only occasion till my retirement when a sub-inspector of the investigation cadre was promoted to be an Inspector without passing the qualifying examination.

During my tenure important law and order problems of new types occurred in the district. First was a terrorist raid in the beginning of 1949. It was a Sunday when the District Police was due to have its annual sports meet. I was in my chamber in the police office allocating prizes for each event when I got a message that armed raiders had tried to attack the District police armed guards at the Dum Dum Airport Gold Vault but left on being unsuccessful to loot the vault. I also got news of an attack carried out on the staff in a section of the big sprawling Jessop factory in DumDum and that the raiders had been heading towards Barasat. At once I alerted the armed police and the control room in IG's office and added that I was leaving with a small armed force in pursuit of the raiders. There used to be a small standing force with one NCO and 10 constables with a truck to leave the police lines in order to tackle any emergent situation in 5 to 10 minutes and another force of such men to leave in 20-30 minutes to act as reinforcements. I ordered both the contingents to leave but left with the first contingent and took my Armed Inspector of Police, one Kailaspati Dubey with me. I was in mufti but always carried my revolver and so did my orderly. I had a new Chevrolet car and travelled in that. I cancelled the sports meet and informed my wife over the telephone that I would not go home for lunch and was leaving to tackle an emergent situation. We travelled along Jessore Road and went to Jessop factory where I learnt that the raiders burst in and opened random fire. They got hold of two Anglo-Indian foremen and threw them into the furnace of a big boiler to die a painful death. I also learnt that the raiders had opened fire on the sentry at Gauripore Police outpost while driving past the place. At the airport I learnt that the armed guard spotted the raiders from a distance and opened fire thus scaring them away and they left without any loot. Nearing Barasat I stopped at a police wireless station situated at Champadali at the point of bifurcation of Jessore Road in two directions, namely one to Bongaon and the other to Basirhat both bordering on East Pakistan. I learnt that the raiders had headed towards Basirhat. I asked Inspector Dubey to go ahead while I stopped to send a wireless message to

Basirhat PS and the Inspector of Police warning them of the approaching armed raiders and to be prepared to intercept them. My message read 'Armed terrorists heading towards Basirhat. Be ready to intercept them'. I was pleased that I could send a message of warning and followed the first party. I reached Basirhat in late afternoon and found the P.S. building and a special tent to accommodate extra posse armed policemen were all deserted and the remnant of the first police party were found huddled in the PS. I learnt that Inspector Dubey and one constable got killed in the encounter when they got out of the police vehicle and exposed themselves to terrorist fire in the open. The raiders had already set fire to the PS office building but none were killed or injured. I was shocked by the tragic events which could easily be prevented if Inspector Dubey and his men had taken simple security precautions which must be taken by any police party facing enemies armed with firearms or any other missiles like bombs, bows and arrows, etc. By this time the second batch of stand-by force arrived from headquarters and morale was restored. I visited the local subtreasury and learnt that they saw raiders who came near the barbed wire fencing when a constable opened fire and the raiders did not dare to attack and fled in their motor cars towards the Pakistan border. I sent words to the O/C and police station staff who were in hiding and they returned. Unfortunately the guns in the PS were all looted from the *malkhana* where a few muskets were kept in reserve. On enquiry O/C told me that they had received no wireless message which actually arrived the same evening after a delay of 3–4 hours. With a few armed constables left at the P.S. I sent O/C and rest of the armed police in cars to hunt for and arrest the raiders I ordered shooting and killing them if there was any resistance by the raiders. They were ordered to keep up the pursuit and hunt till they were satisfied that no more raiders were there to search for. I sent message to my residence expressing my inability to return the same night adding that I was safe and well and prepared to spend the night at the P.S. I remember buying some food locally and eating in the evening. I slept on a bench the whole night. I also asked for more vehicles to be sent to carry the dead bodies and prisoners if any could be caught. I also arranged to search all buses and trains from Basirhat or near about and look for raiders and arrest all suspicious persons. The fiasco of the wireless message arriving late was due to my failure to mark my message as 'most immediate' with the result that the operator treated it as an ordinary message and sent my message after other ordinary messages received earlier for transmission. The operator had not the intelligence to understand the great importance and urgency of my message and contributed to the good luck of the raiders and misfortune of the Basirhat Police personnel.

Police parties sent out in pursuit of the raiders returned to the P.S. next morning with 14 raiders in custody and all the firearms looted from the P.S. recovered. I learnt that there were more raiders but they had managed to get across the border into East Pakistan now Bangladesh. To my great disappointment I learnt that the raiders had all thrown down their weapons and surrendered meekly so that there was no occasion to use force against them, not to speak of shooting and killing any one. I sent wireless messages to the IG's office and to my own control room intimating developments. As passport system had not yet been introduced between West Bengal and East Pakistan, the raiders did not have much difficulty in bluffing their way through the Indian and Pakistan border checkposts. They did not carry any arms. An elaborate FIR was written down and a criminal case was started in Basirhat. There were several other criminal cases started in Dum Dum P.S. over the incident in Jessop factory and at the airport.

I returned the next afternoon after leaving the Circle Inspector and O/C to manage. One Addl. SP who was called from headquarters also had arrived and he was left in overall charge. En route I found policemen checking all buses and trains at several places but on questioning what they were searching for I learnt that they were searching for refugees from Burma and Burmese currency notes. I had issued orders to send men to search trains and buses to detect raiders trying to return to Calcutta. I was therefore greatly disappointed at the poor briefing of men put on duty and I did my best to instruct them correctly and ordered them to carry on till next morning. This search did not yield any result. I had earlier sent the dead bodies and the arrested culprits to Calcutta and the culprits were produced before a Magistrate who ordered their lodging in the local jail till it was decided whether they would be in police or in judicial custody. Actually the District Police had no arrangement to hold so many people in police custody. The bodies of the dead policemen were laid out in the parade ground and I made a short speech paying high tributes to them and they were later cremated with many senior officers and their colleagues attending the cremation. It was learnt that the raid was carried out by Revolutionary Communist Party of India (RCPI) under the planning and leadership of one Pannalal Dasgupta. It was also learnt that they had planned the raid a day earlier but had postponed it by a day. This postponement saved my own life in the sense that on the two previous days I had gone to and returned from Basirhat after inspection of the P.S. I would certainly have met the raiders en route and they would have been too glad to kill the Superintendent of the District Police. This incident made me take out an accident insurance policy of a lakh of rupees at my own expense because I foresaw the danger of leaving a penniless young widow. At the time I am reminiscing about, widow of an officer killed in action got the maximum pension which would have been due to the officer himself if he was invalided out. Besides my life insurance policy had a clause if the insured person died in any accident the nominee would get double the amount. An accident meant death by unnatural means and included murder and culpable homicide. This clause would have given my wife a little more money. For the next few weeks I was busy in forming a team of investigators called from the District Branch of the Detective Department. The Investigation was, however, taken over by the Intelligence Branch functioning under the then DIG of Police, IB and CID, Hirendra Nath Sircar. More people involved in the planning and conspiracy were gradually arrested. I do not know how many were sent up in chargesheet to stand trial in the court of Sessions. What I remember is poor result of investigation and prosecution. The first trial took place in the Court of one B.K. Basu, a senior ICS officer posted as the District and Sessions Judge in 24 Parganas. The colleagues of the accused persons habitually threatened the Judge by writing letters that he would forfeit his life and leave a widow if he passed a stiff sentence. Borderless white *saris* were also periodically sent to the Judge's wife at her residence to cause fear in her and her husband's mind. We arranged armed escort for him to come to and go back from the court and posted armed guards at the Judge's residence. As a matter of fact we had to post armed guards also at my own residence and that of the District Magistrate. The trial proceeded and it was funny that I was not cited as a witness in the trial although I played an important role. I suppose that happened because I myself did not arrest any one nor did I witness the atrocities of the terrorists. On the day announced for passing judgement there was pindrop silence in the Court room and some of the culprits in the deck looked pale and frightened. They were certain that some of them would get death sentence and no dead man comes back to live another day. As soon as the judgement which did not order capital sentence on any one but transportation for life which meant imprisonment for fourteen years for a few and lesser prison sentences on others was passed there was continuous shouts of 'RCPI Jindabad', 'Vande Mataram' and other slogans and the under trial prisoners at the dock showed visible relief and joy that none would go to the gallows. It may be said that the prisoners at the dock remained subdued throughout the first trial. The sentenced accused went up in appeal to the Calcutta High Court which ordered a retrial. I still do not know on what grounds the retrial was ordered. The second trial took place but the prisoners at the dock were boisterous throughout knowing that none would be sentenced to death. The second trial ended with sentences of varying terms of imprisonment. A few were also acquitted. Again the sentenced persons went up in appeal to the High Court which again ordered retrial. By this time 5 or more years had elapsed and I had left the district. In the third trial, the accused were given much lighter sentences of imprisonment, the maximum being 7 years or so. The judge took the period of imprisonment as under trial prisoners into account while passing the sentences. Appeal to the High Court against the conviction and the sentences was dismissed. Thus ended the trial of notorious murderers and political criminals with a whimper.

During this time RCPI activists showed a great deal of militancy by attacking policemen and police stations and outposts in my district. We had to post double sentries and again instruct all policemen about first principles of security. As a matter of fact I wrote out a small brochure about security in the police and asked officers to instruct and train their men. It is a sad omission in the Police Regulations of Bengal that there is no chapter on security nor is the subject taught in the Training College/school for officers and constables to benefit the police officers of any rank. I wrote to IG's office about incorporating a chapter on security in the Police Regulations noting the principles of security and giving adequate practical training in the training college and school on the basis of my brochure or in any other effective way. But all these suggestions fell on deaf ears of officers in the higher echelons. Police continued to pay heavy price for this omission and consequent absence of a sense of need to learn basic principles of security.

I remember that solitary police camps were attacked with explosive and acid bombs by RCPI militants. Some policemen were injured and two were so grievously hurt that one died and the other had been blinded for life and had to be invalided out. Gradually RCPI militancy subsided.

There was another very important and sinister development during my stay in the district. Important and dangerous political prisoners used to be lodged in the Dum Dum Central Jail. One day there was a jail riot and the prisoners chased out the prison guards inside but could not manage to escape as there was a high wall and the guards had managed to lock the gate from outside the compound in which lay the prison barracks and prisoners cells. The prisoners could not, however, be driven inside the barracks or cells nor could food be served. The jail authorities sought police assistance and I was ordered to tackle the situation. I took half a platoon of armed policemen and requested the District Magistrate Hironmoy Banerjee to accompany me. We arrived in early evening and saw a large number of undertrial and convicted prisoners in the open ground between barracks and cells. They were throwing brickbats and broken bottles if any one approached the locked gate which they were wanting to break open. The jail guards had, however, managed to drive them away from the locked gate by firing into the air and threatening to fire at them if they actually tried to break open the big gate.

On reaching the jail I discussed details with the Superintendent of the Jail and his senior officers to know the history of the riot and of efforts by the local jail authorities to tackle the situation. Later I spoke on a portable loud speaker and requested them of behaving in a disciplined way and bring back normalcy. I assured them of redress once jail discipline was restored. My appeal was answered with more brickbats thrown at us. I formed a hollow square with the armed policemen although there was no need to use policemen at the two sides and in the rear. In spite of flying missiles I appealed again to the prisoners to go back into their cells and not to force a situation which might necessitate opening fire with guns. I told them with the help of the portable loud speaker that I would wait for 15 minutes and then force them inside by opening gun fire. In response they shouted in defiance. After 12 minutes had expired I again issued a warning that I would open fire within three minutes if they did not go back into their cells. There was no movement of the prisoners who continued to show defiance and throw missiles at us. I told the DM (H. Banerjee) the need to open fire. Banerjee who accompanied me and was present throughout was a witness to what was happening and our efforts to persuade the rioters and heard formal warnings given repeatedly, permitted me to open fire. Although the policemen under my control did not face any real danger but I could see that they had become frightened and jittery. I told them that they should not feel frightened as there was little chance of the prisoners breaking out and attacking them. I did not see much perceptible change in my men's sense of fear. In the circumstances, I felt that tear gas would not be effective and ruled out its use. I touched the shoulders of two policemen and asked them to open one round fire each. They did so but two policemen from the rear rank also opened fire without orders and the bullets whizzed past my head as I had taken my position inside the square. I ducked my head and got out of the square as I considered the jittery policemen to be undependable. The first four rounds did not have any effect except that a few went inside. I reprimanded the policemen in the rear for opening fire without order and asked all the men on the sides and in the rear to cease to be in the firing position and they lowered their rifles. I asked all the men in the front rank to open one round of fire and they did so. I could see some men fall on the ground and the rest of the rioters scampered inside the compound adjoining the cells. They kept on shouting abuses and slogans. This place was not visible from where we stood nor could the prisoners throw brickbats and other missiles at us. There were no means to enter without unlocking the main gate but this could not be done as it might prove to be a tactical disaster. The prisoners might make a determined rush at us, overwhelm us and the jail guards unless we were prepared to kill many of them. The only solution was to put the policemen in a position from where we could see the area which the prisoners occupied and open fire to make the prisoners go inside the cells. The only probable site was the roof of a prison barrack which was a two storeyed building. As there was no staircase I enquired of some officers and men if they could climb upto the roof but they pleaded their inability. I decided to undertake the task myself and after putting a rifle across my shoulder I clambered up an iron ladder fixed wholly upright with single rods as rungs but managed to reach the roof. From there I could see some prisoners still outside and fired a couple of shots at intervals and all went into their cells. The cells could not, however, be locked by entering the compound at night and it was decided to leave a batch of policemen and the senior Jailor was asked to put policemen in front when opening the gate next morning and entering the cells. The front and rear compounds should be manned by armed jail guards. Accompanied by the District Magistrate I left and communicated details to IG, Police. The DM informed the Home Secretary of the happenings.

Next morning I learnt that the jail authorities found 4 men dead and they removed the dead men for post mortem examination. I do not remember how many were injured. A criminal case was also started against the prisoners in Dum Dum PS. I learnt that the prisoners did not create any more trouble and allowed the jail staff to serve food and drinks. After news of the shooting in the jail broke out and became common knowledge, there were meetings of the political parties opposing the Congress government and they condemned police firing at imprisoned men. There were also some small processions demonstrating against the district police and the government.

Guards were doubled at the residence and office of both the DM and SP who reasonably feared an attack on them or their families. Both travelled in cars in which there was one rifleman besides an orderly armed with a revolver. As the SP and DM were involved in firing, the Divisional Commissioner, J.N. Talukdar, ICS had to hold an enquiry into the police firing. In his report he praised my action especially my hazardous climb up to the roof of a building at night with a rifle in order to drive the rioters back into their cells.

The third important incident was a prolonged long drawn affair. The Communist Party of India (CPI) which had not yet split into CPI and CPI (M) increased their militant activities a good deal in the southern parts of the district especially in Kakdwip PS area. The PS area stretched from the Bay of Bengal inland and was between two large rivers, the Hooghly on the west and the Ichhamati on the east. A large area bordering the sea had scrub jungles in the eastern side with no human habitation and on the west side was the Sundarbans in West Bengal. For a few months reports were coming that *zamindars*' kuchhery houses and rich jotdars farm houses were being burnt down and the owners were being threatened with bodily violence unless they left. A criminal case started in each instance and police investigation was undertaken. No culprits could be detected and consequently no arrests were made. I sent out officers of the District Intelligence Branch to the area but they could not find any clue. We, however, knew the identity of local communist leaders but they could not be tied up with the cases of arson. The district leaders were Kangsari Halder and Somnath Lahiri, genuine communist activists. Activities increased and residential houses were being set on fire at night and threats of looting and violence continued. Several Jotdars left the area with their families. Policemen and some other government employees feared to go into the area to do their normal duties. Communist newspapers gave out that a part of Kakdwip had become a 'Muktanchal'. i.e. an area liberated from control and administration on the lines of Telengana area in Andhra Pradesh. This was a menacing declaration. I set up a number of armed police camps men from which would undertake patrol at night and prevent incidents of arson and arrest suspicious persons moving about during day or night. Although incidents did not occur in the vicinity of the police camps but they continued to occur in other areas as frequently as before. No arrests were made. I had doubts if the camp police were doing their duty as ordered. This was proved by an occurrence of several arson cases occurring in the vicinity of one camp from which flames could be seen. I decided to look into the several incidents which took a minimum time of 30 minutes to accomplish, which took place very near an armed police camp. I learnt from the persons affected that no policemen went to any place of occurrence during the actual heppening. On a visit to a particular armed camp I found that there were four out of six policemen present and they deployed themselves to guard their own cooking pots and pans and their bedding, ration and a spare uniform instead of going to the villagers' help and trying to arrest the culprits who had operated for about half an hour. The policemen had no explanation for their negligence or foolish behaviour and all were placed under suspension and sent back to the headquarters. This suspension had a salutary effect and other camps managed to arrest a few suspects and send them to Kakdwip police station. But incidents of arson and sneaky night attacks still continued affecting innocent victims. Actually things were gradually getting worse and no intelligence reports were forthcoming about the real culprits or their leaders. The higher authorities became worried and urged on me and the District Magistrate to take more vigorous steps which must be planned in a way to be effective. We got some names of leaders and suspected culprits and special contingents of policeforce under a *Subedar* or Inspector were posted to carry out raids for their arrest but the culprits took shelter in the scrub jungles and could neither be located nor arrested. I was getting a bad name for failing to be effective. The District Magistrate had deputed his Addl. D.M. to liaise with me and give all help. The officer was one A.B. Chatterjee, who retired from the rank of a Lt. Col. in the Army. Chatterjee was a very pleasant and helpful officer. I devised a plan to undertake a combing operation starting from the sea shore through the scrub jungles into the open area which was free from trouble. I decided to lead the operation and asked Chatterjee to accompany me. I arranged to raise two platoons of armed policemen, one from the headquarters and another by winding up some of the local ineffective police camps. We took three steam launches to take the contingent from Alipore and we sailed from Diamond Harbour for Kakdwip. Local O/C's and inspectors were also ordered to join. On the evening before the actual operation we had assembled about half a dozen junior officers, 60 armed policemen and they were kept ready for launching the operation at dawn next day. We set sail in three launches with all the men who were to be commanded by the officers who were fully briefed. Chatterjee, ADM and I were to be with two columns or rather eagle sprèad contingents. We reached the sea beach when it was just dawn. I put the men on the shore and ordered them to spread out to cover the entire width of the area from one river on the west to the other on the east. South Kakdwip was an island.

The operation started and we could hear noises of some animals going forward but backtracking through the police line. There was, however, noise of a different kind as made by human beings running away. We got evidence of men hiding in the scrubs where we found remnants of cooking utensils and ovens but none were found in the jungle area. After we reached the first village we searched each house and its outhouses and rounded up all adult males found therein. We could catch some of the wanted men also. When the operation was over, the men were kept in a big kuchhery house of a *Zamindar* with police guards all around. We interrogated all the men about the identity of the culprits who committed the atrocities and got a good number of names but a few people were found to be common culprits in several cases of crime. Some of those men who were known to be leaders or to have committed actual crime were already caught in the police net and held in our custody. We interrogated them and got admissions. Excepting these we released others to go home. As we had recorded statements and admissions of all, we asked O/C Kakdwip P.S. to name the culprits as accused in several criminal cases already started and to send them up to the Magistrate in Diamond Harbour praying for being kept in police custody. The court officers were instructed to oppose bail severely.

After the leaders and the persons involved in actual crime had been removed from the locality and it was known that they were accused in specific cases and had become undertrial prisoners without being granted bail, the militant movement for creating a 'Muktanchal' or an area free from the state control gradually subsided. Trials were held and many got convicted and this led to complete cessation of the local communist movement on the lines of Telengana in Andhra Pradesh.

In 1950 communal riots in East Pakistan and oppression on the Hindus created panic and hordes of Hindu refugees came to India and a host of them into my district. Most of them told the horrors of Muslim oppressions and some tales were perhaps exaggerated. Some of them even urged Hindus whom they met to avenge the atrocities they suffered from by committing the same atrocities on the Muslims living in West Bengal. The result was that there were widespread riots in the north and east side of my district. As the refugees mostly settled in vacant plots of land and houses or became tenants or guests of families in or near Calcutta, riots in the police stations in the suburbs of Calcutta were intensive and widespread. We were sorely tried to control the riots. I sought help of extra policemen and several platoons of the Eastern Frontier Rifles were sent to assist me. This crack force in the police were sent to me to reinforce my own arrangements. I tried my best to control the riots and to give protection to Muslims who did not leave India but sought shelter in Muslim majority areas. I had to protect the vacant houses from illegal occupation by the Hindus. Almost all police stations in the suburbs of Calcutta, namely, Dum Dum, Baranagar, Khardah, Noapara, Naihati, Barrackpur, Titagarh, Jagatdal and Bizpur (Kanchrapara) in the north and Tollygunge, Behala and Mahestola in the south were affected.

There were a few instances of Muslim families converting into Hinduism so as to escape oppression and not be forced to leave their ancestral hearth and home. Conversion was rightly frowned upon and condemned by the authorities and I and my police officers saw all the families reportedly having been converted and offered them all protection to be reconverted to Islam but they refused saying that they had taken the decision after a good deal of thinking and in their firm belief that ultimately all religions believed in the same Supreme Being who was common to all mankind. I had renewed my efforts several times but in vain.

We got an information of rioting in Baranagar area and I accompanied DIG Ghosh Choudhury and a section of EFR and went there. The actual rioters fled on seeing the police. We had already asked our men to open fire on rioters in action without warning them. There was a boy standing at his own doorstep and one EFR rifleman shot him dead before DIG and I could stop him. We reconstrated with the man for shooting a boy who was not seen taking part in any rioting. We reached a house where about 2 dozen Muslims had taken shelter but Hindus had surrounded them, locked the doors from outside and set the rooms on fire thus killing all the Muslims by burning them alive. No culprits could be arrested on the spot. We imposed curfew for several days and searched for the culprits. On another occasion D.M. Sankarnath Maitra and I rushed out with a force to quell disturbances in Barrackpore PS area and found some Hindu young men rioting and setting fire to Muslim houses. On our approach some fled but other bolder men shouted that we were Hindu officers and would do not harm them and so their comrades need not run away. I asked the policemen to round up as many as we could capture and put them in a small open place surrounded by policemen with *lathi*s and rifles. Then DM and I proceeded to disabuse the rioters of their notion that Hindu officers would not take action against Hindu rioters but would be willing spectators to oppression of innocent Muslims. That evening we beat the men very severely with *lathi*s and I still remember that at least half a dozen skulls were split with forceful *lathi* blows. They shouted for mercy and we stopped. As we had inflicted enough physical punishment which was more severe than a jail sentence we did not arrest any one and left them to fend for themselves and run back to their own homes.

On another night I had to go to an area in Jagatdal PS where I saw young Hindu boys setting fire to vacant Muslim houses. As I had a stengun in my hand and so had the officer next to me, both of us could open rapid fire and kill a dozen of the boys. As no inhabitant came out of the burning hut nor was there any cry for help, I took pity on the young boys setting fire to vacant huts abandoned by their erstwhile Muslim occupants. I chased them away and they fled. This was perhaps the only occasion when I did not open fire at rioters caught in the act of communal rioting. Riots gradually subsided but the government appointed a one man Commission of Enquiry and report on the extent and cause of rioting in the districts of West Bengal and failure of the police, if any, and to suggest remedial measures. Justice P.B. Mukherjee of Calcutta High Court formed the one-man Commission and he embarked on his job seriously. I was one of the few important witnesses who could provide more or less full details and accounts of the riots to help the Commission to conduct its enquiry officially and rather smoothly. I found Justice P.B. to be a very intelligent and sociable man and a bond of friendship gradually developed between us. Later he asked me to go to his house and I and my wife became very friendly with the Judge's family consisting of his wife Mrs Gita Mukherjee, an active social worker and their young son named Partha who was a pert well-read young student. As Justice Mukherjee was a keen cine photographer and so was I, we had a common subject to discuss and compare notes, I took my films to show and so did he show his own films to us. This friendship lasted till his death. I was sorry when I learnt that Justice Mukherjee was denied his promotion of becoming the Chief Justice in Calcutta High Court on the charge of a nearly corrupt practice in buying the house he lived in at a throw away price. This happened when another brother Judge set aside the sale and passed very adverse comments on Justice Mukherjee's conduct. The matter went up to the Government of India and it is rumoured that the then Prime Minister, Jawaharlal Nehru himself wrote a note stating that Justice Mukherjee must never be given promotion. However the ban was removed through the efforts of a prominent barrister-at-law, one Snehangshu Kumar Acharya, who was a personal friend of Jyoti Basu, the powerful Chief Minister of West Bengal and a henchman of the Communist Party of India (Marxist). Justice Mukherjee became the Chief Justice of Calcutta High Court during Jyoti Basu's regime and retired from that post. As Justice Mukherjee was appointed a Judge at a very young age, namely 42, he would perhaps have gone up to the Supreme Court and become the Chief Justice of India. His youngest brother Sabyasachi Mukherjee, however, became the Chief Justice of India many years later. Sabyasachi was also well known to me.

He died of a heart attack in the UK when I was there. I did not know whom to call upon and where to go to express my condolences.

During my tenure as SP 24 Parganas the first Indian IG in Bengal named Sukumar Gupta died of a heart attack while having a siesta after lunch. I was asked to make all arrangements for his funeral and provide a contingent of policemen at the cremation ground to pay him last respects in a nearly military fashion. With a very heavy heart at the IG's death who liked me and whom I too liked, I worked feverishly to complete the arrangements in course of the day. IG's office informed all officers to be present at his cremation which took place in Keoratala. The buglers sounded the last post and the Armed Police contingent reversed their rifles to pay their last respects to the departed Chief while the officers also gave their last salute in the prescribed manner.

14

In the Mainstream of Administration

Although the seniormost efficient officer available was Surendra Nath Chatterjee who was serving as the Police Commissioner he was not selected to be the next IG of Police. The next efficient seniormost officer was Hirendra Nath Sarkar, DIG of Police, IB & CID, who was selected thus superseding several other I.P. officers senior to him. Suren Chatterjee was not considered as he had earned an unsavoury reputation by having a too friendly personal relationship with a Jewish lady and the government, especially the Chief Secretary Satyen Roy, frowned upon the relationship and had advised the CM not to appoint Chatterjee as the IG. We did not know at the time that government had other plans about Chatterjee. Sarkar took charge immediately and Hari Sadhan Ghose Choudhury was posted as Sarkar's successor. In the meantime Sachindra Mohan Ghosh who was working as the senior AIG was also promoted leaving a vacancy in the IG's office. Soon I was called to attend an informal meeting in the IG's office by Ghose Choudhury. I went to attend the meeting in AIG's office where I saw Ghose Choudhury, Upendra Mukherjee and Sachin Ghosh to be present. They told me that they wanted me to be the next senior AIG to succeed Sachin Ghosh. I was not prepared for such a proposal. The reasons were that I was happy in 24 Parganas and had the best house in Calcutta belonging to the West Bengal Police. Secondly, Hirendra Nath Sarkar was an unknown quantity amongst his colleagues to many of whom Sarkar was a persona-non-grata. I was reluctant to be Sarkar's right hand man and be so close to him. Even Sarkar's looks were not attractive. However, I was very reluctant to join the new post but my senior colleagues argued that the other officers must have a reliable efficient officer in IG's office who wanted to look after the interest of the officers and also would give good and correct advice to the IG H.N. Sarkar who was a person of virtues and vices unknown to most other officers, consequently they became apprehensive. I reluctantly agreed to join and the other officers, expressed their happiness over my consent. Later working with Sarkar I found out that he was the most knowledgeable and technically efficient policeman we had amongst us and it was a pleasure to work with him except when he expressed his likes for a few officers of subordinate ranks who were close to him in the past and his suspicion of his colleagues in the IP cadre many of whom he did not know well. However, in my tenure of two years and a half I fully justified the confidence of my fellow seniors who urged upon and induced me to accept the post.

I joined IG's office as the senior A.I.G. and one Gopal Chandra Dutta, an IPS officer promoted from the rank of Dy. SP joined as my successor in 24 Parganas. Dutta was a bachelor and I asked him to allow me to stay in SP's house till I got some accommodation. A few days later I invited Gopal Dutta to stay with us (i.e. me and my wife) as a guest so as to make it easier for him to attend office and receive visitors. The arrangement lasted for a month or two during which Dutta started telling my wife that he would like his mother, brother and sister to stay with him and it would be better if we left. I had no alternative but to leave the house. I was, however, accommodated in a spacious flat on Burdwan Road owned by a friend of mine one Gangjee. But my stay there was only for a few weeks because I was asked to vacate the flat in favour of Suren Chatterjee who had earlier gone on leave and on return was not posted as the Commissioner of Police. Hari Sadhan Choudhury was appointed C.P. and continued to hold the post till he became IG of Police on Sarkar's retirement after about ten years. As accommodation was not available anywhere else, I was in difficulty and approached Sankarnath Maitra, my last DM in 24 Parganas to help me out. I knew he had a huge house on Ronaldsay Road next to which was the Presidency Jail. The ground floor rooms of this house remained mostly vacant. I suggested that I might be given two ground floor rooms with adjoining kitchen and toilet and he was kind enough to agree. I and my wife stayed there for 2 months or more and friendship between the two families further grew into a kinship. Maitra had two good looking very young daughters: one was Munnie aged about 6-7 years and the other a toddler nick named Nannu a short for Narayani aged about 2-3 years, both of whom became very fond of my wife. She also reciprocated their love fully because we had no children and my wife loved children. Fortunately for me a flat in a newly built house at 9/1 Hungerford Street was available and I moved in there. It had four rooms and a central hall and accommodation was adequate for two of us. I had Saibal Kumar Gupta, a very senior ICS officer, who occupied the top 3rd floor flat as my neighbour. I do not remember who occupied the first floor flat but the ground floor rooms were used as the Enforcement Branch office of the Calcutta Police.

I worked for two years and a half as the senior AIG (D) and had quite a busy time. Before Independence Sarkar was sent to the Scotland Yard for training when he was working as the Dy. Commissioner of Police in the British days. He fully utilised his deputation and took copious notes. As IG West Bengal he got an opportunity to put many useful ideas into practice and procedure which were all meant for better performance and gave clearer guidelines and helpful suggestions to improve the police administration in the state. In me he found a very willing and useful assistant to carry out the reforms by issuing police orders, circular letters and memoranda. In the course of my 13 years service I had also accumulated many ideas and kept written notes for better functioning of the police and most of them were circulated with the IG's approval. Both of us were happy as we both believed in efficiency and improvement. Knowing that he was not close to his colleagues Sarkar used to throw cocktail parties and small dinner parties which were a way of the Chief's eagerness to be hospitable and popular. He also arranged musical soirees and it was in his residence that I heard the famous musical Maestro Bade Gulam Ali singing classical songs.

Recommendations for award of the Police Medal and the President's Police and Fire Services Medal used to come to IG's office from DIG's and DM's. During this period a recommendation came from Sankar Maitra, my last DM in 24 Parganas recommending award of the Police Medal to me. Upananda Mukherjee DIG, HQ, was still sitting in IG's office and thought that I deserved to be awarded the President's Police and Fire Services Medal which was a higher award than the Police Medal in appreciation of my past good and effective police work. He went up to the IG and requested him to consider me for the award but the IG disagreed saying that some awards might be left for me to win in future. I got the Police Medal and was decorated by the Governor in a Police Parade. Chief Secretary S.N. Roy himself wrote the citation.

I was a poor concealer of my thoughts and Sarkar knew that I did not like him personally as much as I should have. He, however, appreciated my whole hearted efforts to help him to carry out IG's duties successfully. There were awards of the Medals first once a year, on the eve of the Independence Day on August 15 and later twice a year, i.e. on the eve of the Independence Day on August 15 as well as the Republic Day on January 26. Recommendations were channelled through me and I had to comment on the suitability or otherwise. I also originated some recommendations sent to the state government which on its part forwarded them to the central government. Although Sarkar was not popular with his colleagues because they did not know him well and had heard critical and disparaging tales about him when he was working as SP Rangpur in Bengal with one Abdul Majid, a promoted officer as the District Magistrate. Sarkar, however, knew a large number of Dy. SP's and inspectors of police whom he liked and who were devoted to him. Recommendations frequently came for award of a Medal to some of them, perhaps on the suggestion of the IG conveyed informally but most cases did not deserve to be forwarded to the state government. I often pointed this out but IG used to insist on my forwarding them. As expected several cases came back from the state Govt. and I showed the Governments decision. I was, however, mischievous and rubbed it in by noting 'I told you so' before sending the file on to IG. Such a note did not certainly please IG Sarkar.

During my tenure as AIG, West Bengal, a Miniature Rifle Shooting Championship was held in the shooting range of the South Calcutta Rifle Club. This club was formed under Sarkar's patronage and his active advice and help. The range was the same as used by 24 Parganas police in Tollygunge Police Lines for their regular firing practice and test. I and my wife had become members of the South Calcutta Rifle Club when I was SP 24 Parganas and my wife was taught and trained to shoot by the Club Trainer. During the all State meet IG directed me to help the organisers in organising the meet successfully. IG and I had both put in our names as competitors in the revolver and heavy bore rifle shooting. I still remember the day the heavy bore rifle contest was held. IG was somewhat boastful in small matters and he took a rifle, perhaps a .303 of the police which was tested for accuracy. During the contest his turn came and he fired the customary ten shots and asked me to scrutinise the target carefully so that he did not miss any point due to carelessness on part of the official score board scrutiniser. I went up and saw the target blank, IG having not a single shot hitting the big target even at the periphery. The target was not removed and replaced but was used for the next shooter. When I came back I.G. enquired what was his score and I replied that they did not replace the target meaning that he had drawn blank. I should have expressed my sorrow at his performance but I rubbed in salt to his wounded pride. I had developed a bad habit of rubbing in salt into a wound. I used to boast that I was recruited to a superior service by the Secretary of State for India in London and I would never behave in a way which did not become an officer of a superior service. This motto did not pay me dividends and I dearly paid for this vanity throughout my service career. I was always proud, correct and unbending but this attitude cannot be kept up in service. From my experience I advised my colleagues and juniors not to fight or criticise a boss unless they were favourites of the 'Boss's Boss who would openly support them in the face of the boss's opposition.

During our working days IG often said that there was not enough work for the two AIG's and one should suffice Once when he said this in my presence I replied that I agreed but requested him to transfer me out. Actually I.G. was teasing us the AIG's. Sometimes I had to get up at 2 a.m. in early hours of the morning to dispose of files I was compelled to take home. Taking files home was a regular feature with me that I could not avoid in spite of my wife resenting this practice. There was an All India Police meet in Bangalore and IG decided to attend and leave me in charge of the office. I was not at all nervous at this prospect including seeing the CM Bidhan Chandra Roy and answering his queries. I had to attend two such calls and I handled the situation with confidence. Once CM called me and I went in. After entering CM's room I was confronted with the query what I wanted of him. I reminded him that he had called me and I did not know the purpose. Then he would remember and discuss the subject he had in mind. After IG returned and found his office in order and correct actions had been taken, he was full of praise for me and said that he did not know what he would have done without me. This happened on another occasion when he went on casual leave.

My promotion to the next higher post was being delayed and there was no early prospect of getting promotion. At this time Bhola Nath Mallik, I.P. who was the Director of the Intelligence Bureau in the Union Government paid a visit to IG's office and enquired if West Bengal could spare a good officer to act as a Dy. Director which was a post equivalent to a DIG's. IG thought of me and presented me before Mallik who put a few questions and the interview ended. Later my name was sent recommending my deputation to the Central Government to work as a Dy. Director. To my great sorrow, a reply came that Dr K.N. Katju, the then Home Minister, scrutinised my records and considered me as unacceptable because I was somewhat proud and thought highly of myself. These remarks which were incorporated in my confidential reports were not untrue but I did not consider them as defects in any one's character. Some time later I was recommended for training in the U.K. under the Colombo Plan and there also I failed to be selected. I was so depressed at all these happenings that I thought of going on leave outside India especially to attend the coronation of Queen Elizabeth, the Second.

I asked for 8 months leave outside India and was sure to get the leave applied for but IG called me and tried to persuade me not to go on leave at all leaving him in some difficulty. Even if I did so, it could be limited to a month or six weeks. His argument was that he could not find a suitable replacement for me and he and his office cannot be looked after as well as I did by anyone else he knew. I countered his argument by saying that he thought that there was not enough work for two AIG's and one should be released. He smiled broadly and recommended my leave for four months only. Before I proceeded on leave I could know that he made adverse comments in my annual confidential report on the ground of my insistance to go on leave and consequently to leave his office. However, Bisweswar Chatterjee, an IP officer of 1940 batch, was posted as my successor. He was a competent, pleasant and tactful officer and no better choice could be made for this post.

15

In Distant Shores

As I could not pay the large fare to London charged by a regular Airline I managed to find a Chartered service specially arranged to take visitors to the UK to attend the ceremony of coronation of the queen of Great Britain. I paid Rs 1,100 only for me and my wife each to travel one way for the outward journey. On the plane we met a few known persons and my wife was delighted to meet the Head Mistress of a school in Mymensing where she studied for a few years. The teacher was also immensely pleased to see her old pupil and renew old bonds of affection. At that time an Indian travelling outside India was granted permission to buy £ 600 per head in foreign exchange and the two of us got £ 1,200. Besides I applied for drawing my salary in the UK and this permission was also granted with the result that I could draw my salary in pound sterling from the office of the Indian High Commission in London. In those days a pound was equivalent to Rs 13 and 10 annas and a dollar to Rs 3 and 12 annas only. All this meant that we could buy £ 1,200 easily with Indian money and would have enough funds to spend during the holidays and to make some purchases. At the time of writing these reminiscences a British pound is equivalent to Rs 70.00 and a dollar to Rs 48.00.

My wife had a younger brother in London who was a student of Engineering in the London Polytechnic. During our stay he was of great help to us, especially because he received us at the airport and took us by bus to a room he rented for our stay in London. The rent was low, i.e. less than a pound a day with facilities for bath and toilet but we had to arrange for our food. Our room rented in London was very centrally situated and was furnished for comfortable living and had a gas room-heater. My brother-in-law also stayed at a place not far away but he had to use the underground Metro (tube) Railway or a bus to come to our place. Our house was within walking distance of such well known places like Dorchester Hotel, Hyde Park, Windsor Park and two Metro stations, namely, Regent Park and Knights Bridge.

We had taken a few letters of introduction but the most valuable were three letters, one from Mr Bartos, Managing Director of Bata India (P) Ltd. to the Chief Officer of Bata's in London, a second one from the General Manager of Hindustan Motors to their Agent in London who acted as the liaison officer with the Morris Car Manufacturing Company and the third one was from the Managing Director of Boseck and Co. Ltd. a famous retail shopping complex dealing in imported clocks, watches and silverwares. In the first letter was a request to give all help to me and my wife in providing a car for sight seeing visits to places in the neighbourhood of London and to arrange for our stay in a Bata guest house in Paris.

I telephoned to see the Bata Officer and handed over Mr. Bartos's letter to him. He promised to provide a car and advised us to see the Oxford University and the Windsor Castle by car. As coronation was a few days away, we arranged to visit the two places as advised by the Bata Officer. After breakfast we travelled in the car and first visited the Oxford campus which was a sprawling place and could only see the buildings of the University and of some well known colleges because the University was closed for summer holidays. Later we went to Windsor castle which was a eleventh century building and was entirely built of stone blocks at least on the outside of all walls and some domes. There were other visitors and we accompanied them to see all the places inside and outside to which access was permitted to visitors. There were Grenadier Guards at the Castle wearing tall black bearskin hats and immaculately clean and well pressed red coats and black trousers. They were famous for their disdain at jokes or to be provoked by visitors' remarks or their antiques and were never seen to laugh or even to smile while on actual duty as guards. We returned in the evening and thanked the driver for being helpful during our tour of the day. One new thing I noticed during the journey was that the roads were all numbered so that even after crossing a circus from where several roads radiated one could continue on the road one had chosen. This was an excellent idea and was indispensable to motorists driving in a new place. Inside the city areas the roads were not so marked but if the same road again emerged after crossing the city area, it would bear the same number on the emerging side.

As we had decided to visit as many countries in Europe as practicable, we had taken out multi-journey visas from the foreign consulates in Calcutta for France, Germany, Belgium, Holland, Denmark, Sweden, Norway, Switzerland and Italy. Because of my past contacts with the Consular offices, we were given visas gratis and were spared a good deal of expenses in India. Visas were not, however, expensive in the old days as they were in subsequent years or are at present. I also thought that driving by car would give us freedom of movement and would be a cheaper means of travel than by tourist bus or railway trains. I approached the Agent of Hindustan Motors who helped me to get a Morris 8 Sedan car from the special quota of Hindustan Motors who were importing Morris cars and selling as Hindustan cars in India. In India there were Morris cars of 8, 10, and 14 horse power. As there were two of us, I preferred to buy the smallest car which also cost me the smallest sum of money, namely less than £ 400. I say special quota because in Great Britain there were long waiting lists of intending buyers and one had to wait two to three years before one got a car in the lower price ranges sold to him. The Agent was a middle aged Jewish gentleman who treated us with courtesy and even promised to take us out for lunch in the posh Dorchester Hotel. This lunch in Dorchester did not materialise but he took us out for tea there one day and later for lunch at a good cheaper restaurant.

My brother-in-law bought two visitors tickets to occupy reserved seats in the gallery to watch the coronation procession. We were warned that we would have to leave at early dawn if we wanted to reach the gallery and occupy the seats as there would be unending streams of cars and people in our route on the day. It was a cloudy day when I and my wife started before day light broke out. We had been given full directions in a leaflet attached to each ticket how to travel from the nearest Metro station, bus stop and car parking place. We travelled by Metro and reached the specific station. Streams of people emerged from trains on different lines and we could walk very slowly perhaps at a pace of two miles per hour and one did not have an opportunity to overtake any one in front. However, we reached the gallery and with the help of guides could find our reserved seats. Both of us had raincoats and only one umbrella to share. We reached about a couple of hours before the vanguard of the procession appeared and went past us. I was a cine photo enthusiast and had my Bell and Howell 8 mm Camera which was extensively used to film all worthwhile places and events during our sojourn in Europe. While we were waiting it started to rain and I felt sorry that filming would be difficult and colour would not be vivid without sunshine. The procession went by and we saw the British Prime Minister Winston Churchill and the Indian Prime Minister Jawaharlal Nehru driving past. The former was lustily cheered by the British public and the latter by the Indians present as well as citizens of commonwealth countries. They waved their hands at the spectators. As a matter of fact, all were cheered by the spectators. The Queen drove in a gilded horse-drawn carriage and was cheered wildly by all present. In spite of rain I managed to film the event extensively keeping the cine camera under the umbrella. Finally, we went back to our room exhausted but happy.

My brother-in-law saw the event on the television screen. All the cinema halls showed the events by filming with television cameras and showing them live. As a matter of fact from a position on the gallery we could not possibly see the actual coronation inside the Westminster Abbey, nor the beginning and end of the procession. All these were, however, shown on the television screen. In order to see all the events of the ceremony we decided to go to a cinema hall later and saw the entire ceremony which was filmed in colour and shown on the cinema hall screens. We could see the entire ceremony from crowning to the point of entry back into the Buckingham Palace.

We made full use of our stay in London by undertaking sight seeing all important places including London Tower, Tower Bridge, Hampton Court Palace, Madam Tussaud's Wax Museum, British Library, Parliament Houses, etc. Simultaneously we attended concerts conducted by three famous conductors namely Sri Thomas Beecham, the then oldest and most famous English conductor and a worthy successor of Sir Henry Wood of yester years, Sir Adrian Boult and Sir Malcolm Sargeant. We saw some British stage plays and skits. We went to art galleries and the Whipsnade open zoo.

These events, functions and sights cannot be attended to and enjoyed unless you be in the countries where these were being performed. Consequently we tried to take full advantage of our visit to and stay in the UK. We saw several shows in the Wembley stadium including one wonderful ice-skating show by Sonja Henie, a former World figure skating champion in winter Olympic Games and her troupe. There was enough light to enable me to film the show in colour but due to folly of my bankers the film got lost. We went to the Epson Race Course and watched the race on the Derby day. The Queen also attended and gave away the winner's cup. We attended the tennis grounds of the All England Tennis Club in Wimbledon and watched some games played by top players like Donald Budge, Lew Hoad, Ken Rosewell, Maureen O'Conolly nicknamed Mighty Moe. Budge and Miss Conolly went on to be that year's champions in men's and women's finals. Only amateurs could take part but very good players had still been keeping themselves in the amateur circuit but in years to come all good players became professionals to earn money and the amateur title matches had to be abandoned in favour of all players of the game and huge sums of money were later distributed not only amongst winners but runners up as well as those who lost in the semi and quarter finals.

Besides the letter received from Bartos, I had three important letters of introduction, namely, a letter from Rodda and Co. Ltd. Gunmakers & Sellers of Calcutta to their principals in the UK namely Greener Gun Co. in Birmingham, from Boseck & Co. Ltd. to their principals in Sheffield who supplied sterling silver and good quality cutlery to Boseck and Co. in Calcutta and another letter from Boseck to the General Manager of Rolex Watch Company in Geneva, Switzerland of which Boseck & Co. was the importers and salesmen. These letters helped me to get a gun made to order and sold to me at the dealer's price. I also got very good quality silver plated cutlery at the importer's price, i.e. sold to the shop keepers in Calcutta. I had already placed order for a DBBL Greener shot gun for duck shooting and a full set of cutlery for 12 persons which I paid for and collected to take back to India.

I did another important thing. I learnt that Bhabesh Chandra Roy and Gopal Chandra Dutt two IPS officers promoted from the rank of Dy. SP, the former holding the post of D.C., D.D. Calcutta and the latter holding the post of the Principal, Police Training College, Barrackpore, had been sent to undergo training in the New Scotland yard and to receive training in other police institutions. It was obvious that I.G. Sarkar had deliberately left me out and did not even mention to me about these nominations. I learnt that Dr Bidhan Chandra Roy, the then Chief Minister, West Bengal, was in London. I saw him and sought his help in getting training in the Scotland Yard and in Paris Interpole as well as with the French Police. He was kind enough to write two letters, one to B.G. Kher, the then Indian High Commissioner, UK in London and to H.S. Malik, ICS, Indian Ambassador to France in Paris. I went again to the High Commission and showed the letter. The High Commission arranged for 15 days of training in the New Scotland Yard. I joined Bhabes Roy for the 15 days. Besides I was shown a training institute of promotees in the Police. I was highly interested in the crime map room, the method of maintaining card index which was in the form of the old but now discarded Hollerith system with wires and punch holes. A visit was arranged also to the London Forensic Laboratory. When I saw the Director, he enquired if I had visited the Forensic Laboratory attached to the FBI in the USA. On receiving my reply in the negative he said that FBI had an elaborate extremely well furnished laboratory and his laboratory was a poor unit compared with that in Washington. He, however, chose to tell me a part of his conversation with the Director of the FBI Laboratory. He said that he wanted to know the most valuable work done in the Laboratory, the FBI Director recounted how examination and tests carried out in his laboratory on the exhibits seized in several cases of robbery, some with murder, had established the prosecution case beyond doubt and clinched guilt on the suspects who were all convicted after trial. The UK Director said he enquired how the exhibits were located and names of the suspects were found and the FBI expert replied that the very first clue came from 'squealing', i.e. betrayal of inside information by an accomplice. He laughed with me and said that a laboratory does not detect a crime but tries to prove whether evidence collected is beyond all reasonable doubt. Incidentally the Laboratory was not controlled by the Police but came under direct control of the Home office. This created confidence in the minds of the trial Judge, the public and the legal profession. I was also given an opportunity to study the working of a Police Station at Ascot. At Ascot the Police also arranged for me to see the races which was attended by fashionable well dressed ladies and gentlemen. I also saw the opening of a superior criminal circuit court. I was very much impressed by the solemnity of the proceedings. First, there was a ceremony in the local church. The Judge in full regalia entered the church followed by other well dressed court officials and took a special seat. The clergyman in charge conducted a religious ceremony after which the Judge appeared at the pulpit and prayed to God for giving him wisdom and power to do justice and pass correct judgements so that no innocent men suffered in cases he tried. Thereafter we entered the court room. There were 32 cases on the cause list, all being sessions triable cases and there was the jury also. During the course of two sittings in the forenoon and afternoon, 27 cases were disposed of as most of the accused persons pleaded guilty. Moreover, there was the system of 'taken into consideration' in respect of cases not detected by the police mostly burglary and theft but committed and admitted by the accused persons in Court so that the guilt of the past undetected cases could not be fastened on the culprit at any future date. This also helped the police in showing many more cases as detected and convicted in the police statistics. I was amazed that respectable male citizens were found guilty of homosexual acts and confessed. Such acts were then serious criminal offences in the UK but this is no longer so in that country.

We attended the ceremony of 'Trooping of colours' attended by the Queen as well as lighting of fire works on the bank of the Thames. The most impressive ceremony was inspection of the fleet off Portsmouth or Southhampton to attend which I managed to get admission cards from the High Commission. We travelled by train and were allowed to board the flagship of the Indian fleet, aircraft carrier, Vikrant. Rear Admiral Adhar Chatterjee, who was a brother-in-law of the Police officer Upananda Mukherjee and a college student of my years of study, was the Principal Officer on the ship. Pandit Jawaharlal Nehru, V.K. Krishna Menon, B.G. Kher and many Indian dignitaries came on board the ship and we had a grand stand view of the fleet of the UK and the commonwealth countries including India which was inspected by the Queen who received the salute. I did a good deal of filming on the day which was sunlit throughout. We also spent a day on the beach at Brighton one day where many people got drunk and slept on the beach or shouted obscenities and irrelevances.

While in England I met a group of young Belgians who were members of the Belgian Royal family and we became very friendly. They were planning a *shikar* trip to the Belgian Congo in Africa. On learning that I was a keen *shikari* they invited me and my wife to join the group. I did not have my own weapon but they promised to give me the best weapon available to them and promised to pay for me and my wife's fare to and back from Belgian Congo. I wondered whether there might or might not be ladies in the group but was hesitant to enquire. I did not want to be alone with my young handsome wife in a group of unknown young men. Secondly, I had already made my plan of travel by car in the countries in Europe and did not like the idea of abandoning the plan. Lastly, I thought that I myself might be able to go to Africa and undertake some big games shooting in Kenya or Uganda during lifetime but such shooting became a dream in later years because of the disastrous fall in the exchange rate of Indian rupee vis-a-vis the dollar, the sterling pound and all other hard currencies and also due to the unconscionably high rate of license fee to shoot big games in the countries of Africa.

Another curious episode occurred when I met an Iranian Prince in London and became friendly. He narrated how he had travelled all over the world and asked me why I was not doing the same. I pleaded that I had limited foreign currency and could not afford to go to North and South America. He readily offered me a loan of 30,000 pound sterling and said that I might gradually repay when I could do so. Those were the good old days when people trusted in others; otherwise this gentleman could not offer a huge sum of money to a complete stranger whom he had come to know a few days ago. However, I did not accept this offer because I could not afford to pay back nor was it permissible under government servants' conduct rules.

At this time I got delivery of my car and made out a tentative date of departure for the continent. It was a mistake not to use the car in London for a few days before setting out for the continent. Both I and my wife had international driving licenses. I became a member of AAE and got a carnet for my car and a key for using telephones en route in the UK. The carnet was necessary so that I did not have to pay custom duty or to give a promissory bond to take the motor car out of the countries I visited in Europe. We vacated our residential room in London, our possessions being left with my brother-in-law.

Two days later we started in the early morning so as to catch the first ferry across the English Channel from Dover to Ostend, a port in Belgium. En route to Dover, the car stopped several times due to over flooding of the carburettor and I sought help of AAE men on patrol as well as mechanics of the workshop of the agents of Morris cars. Just wanting to seek help we were greatly delayed and managed to catch the last ferry just in time and reached Ostend and later Ghent in the evening. We drove to the town and lodged in a hotel for the night. There was a club across the road and many couples were seen dancing on the dance floor. We went to the verandah to watch the dancing and listen to music. Seeing my wife in *sari*, still a new and bizarre dress for many people in Europe, many women came out on the verandah and started beckoning to us to join them in the dance. Although the crowd appeared to consist of decent people but I did not want to take a chance in a foreign country at night with a young handsome wife accompanying me and shouted 'tomorrow we shall join' and went back into our rooms. Next morning we drove out and reached Brussels, the Belgian capital. We stayed in a hotel, moved round in the city, saw the museums and art galleries and statuettes of the boy for two days and left for Rotterdam in Netherlands. In Rotterdam we stayed with a Dutch family whom we came to know in Calcutta while attending meetings of a movement known as the World Disarmament

Movement with its headquarters in Caux, Switzerland. This family had invited us and we stayed two days with them. The family members tried to make us as comfortable as practicable and took us out for sight seeing in the big port city. We were taken to the harbour area and saw many war and merchant ships. From Rotterdam we moved on to Amsterdam which was the largest and most important city of the Netherlands. Amsterdam was the cutting and polishing centre of world trade in diamonds. My friends offered to help me in buying some diamonds for my wife but we had to decline because we had not enough money but more importantly we were also afraid of being cheated. We loved the city with its man-made waterways or canals in which were plying motor boats, tugs and other vessels. Food was cheap and we lunched on open sandwiches which were a Dutch speciality. There was a big amusement park named Tivoli Gardens. We visited the zoological gardens and the Art Galleries. Visits to these two places were number 1 and 2 items in all places in our itinerary. From Amsterdam we went to the Hague which was the seat of the Dutch government and my old senior friend B.N. Chakravorty was the Ambassador. We telephoned and saw him and his wife and expressed a desire to stay for two days. He, however, regretted his inability to keep us as guests because he had one guest already. His reply and the grounds advanced somewhat surprised us because the Ambassador's house was a Palace with many rooms and many attendants. Chakravorty, however, offered us luncheon and advised us to visit Scavening on the sea nearby. After lunch we went to the sea beach which was full of people, men, women and children most of whom were basking in the sunshine and some were playing games or swimming in the sea. We returned to Amsterdam and after a couple of days left northwards. We went through North Germany. While crossing into Germany we were suddenly faced with huge concrete blocks which, we learnt later, were the remains of the German Sigfried Line. It is an irony of fate that neither Maginot lines built by France nor Sigfried line built by Germany stood in the way of German army sweeping into and overrunning the Netherlands, Belgium and later into northern France. We went to Copenhagen, the capital city of Denmark. We drove through hundreds of acres of fields growing poppy flower of various colours, shapes and sizes. Denmark was then a country which grew and traded in cut flowers which were sold to the rest of the world. The Danish women were not handsome looking but were fair and sturdy. Most of them gave an impression of coming from farmers' families. There were thousands of pedal cycles which were the most popular mode of transport in post-war years in Denmark. That the country was a big producer of cow's milk was evident from the stack of varieties of cheese and milk products. We were taken to see a cheese factory and wondered at the quantities and varieties of the factory products. In Copenhagen we met a young Indian with a Danish wife whom we used to meet on all the days we stayed in Copenhagen. As we had a car there was no difficulty in movement of all four of us. We were taken to see the Sea Mermaid statue and later to dine with them. The husband enquired of his wife where to go to and his wife suggested a restaurant on the seaside on the outskirts of the town. As we entered the restaurant I had a premonition that we had gone to an expensive place where we were served by liveried waiters. The hostess asked us to see the menu card and order food. We wanted to take soup and fish only. Large bowls of delicious soup were served followed by fish cooked in wine. We noticed with apprehension entry of fashionable ladies and gentlemen wearing smart dress and ornaments and were sure that the host and hostess had landed themselves in trouble. When the bill came my host fished out his wallet and counted all the money inside. There was not enough. He asked his wife who poured out the contents of her purse and still there was not enough. They were in a very embarrassing position. I went to their rescue and paid the balance falling short. Later the husband told me sotto voce that although his wife knew their financial condition she had expensive taste and habits and often landed him in similar embarrassing situations after a meal or a purchase. In case of a purchase he could return the goods but meals once eaten could not be returned. I asked him not to bother because I had paid much less than what it would have cost two persons to have dinner even in a cheap eating place. We promised to see them on our return journey from Sweden and Norway when we would have to pass through Copenhagen after crossing the straight known as 'the sound' separating Denmark from Sweden. We put our car on a combined rail-cum-car ferry and landed in Sweden in

Helsingborg from where we drove north by a highway. I had bought a guide book titled 'Europa' which served as a good guide for motorists and all visitors by including maps with route numbers, places of interest and their history and a long list of hotels, expensive as well inexpensive. It was a bright day and we passed big beautiful lakes in South Sweden with blue water reflecting the sunshine. We carried pack lunch which we ate by sitting on a lake side. Before dusk we reached Stockholm. Actually it was 9 pm but there was bright sunlight. We stayed in an inexpensive hotel but were impressed with the cleanliness maintained there. The waitresses were good looking young women who were attentive and helpful. We went round the city and saw places of interest. As Sweden was a monarchy, we went to see the palace from outside and watched the change of guards as in Windsor Castle. The guards wore blue dress which was not so gorgeous looking as those of the Grenadier Guards in the UK. The first night we spent by sleeping practically during day light because darkness fell for only an hour at that time of the year. We learnt that if we drove further north beyond the Arctic circle we would have daylight throughout 24 hours and could also see the famous Aurora Borealis, a phenomenon not fully understood nor explained by the scientists.

There is another phenomenon in nature which is not fully understood nor can be explained by the scientists. It is the clouds which become charged with millions of volts of static electricity and produce long and repeated thunders and lightnings which would burn any tree or break any man made structure if a strong lighting struck.

As we gradually moved north there was a marked fall in temperature and we had to use heavy winter clothes. Studying the maps and estimating distances we found that we would have still to cover a thousand miles to go beyond the Arctic Circle or into Norway to drive along the west coast with scenic beauty of the Fjords. I felt tired of driving and we abandoned the idea of going further north or into Norway and decided to relax. Moreover, we had yet to see Germany, Switzerland, Italy and France which offered many more popular and famous sight seeing places. We returned by crossing the strait of skagerak from Goteborg to Frederikshaven in Denmark and thus bypassed Copenhagen.

On the return journey from the north, we entered Germany and our first place of visit was Hamburg which was perhaps the largest city in West Germany under occupation of three Allied powers, namely, USA, Great Britain and France. The fourth segment having Berlin in its jurisdiction was under Russian control and known as East Germany. All the four countries were in control of a segment in the city of Berlin which was the old Capital city of Germany. West Germany had its capital in the city of Bonn but East Germany had still Berlin as its capital. Russian segment of Berlin was separated from the rest by building a dividing wall, very high and well protected against any one going or coming from one side to the other. There are sentry posts too. There was a narrow corridor from Western Germany to Berlin through the Russian Segment surrounding the city and this weak link was very vulnerable. There was a formal gate to go through known as 'Check Point Charter'. At one time the Russians closed the corridor and the people of Berlin in the segments under control of the allied powers were given supplies of food, medicine, clothes and other necessities by airlifting them. This was the largest air lifting operation known in history. The blockade was later lifted.

Hamburg was a nice city and we stayed a few days in the city which had a number of large inland lakes in and around. Some had floating restaurants and all were suitably lighted up at night. Hamburg had an excellent zoological park which we visited. We also went to see Kiel canal where our car was taken down by a large elevator which enabled us to drive through the under-water tunnel to the other side. In West Germany we visited the factory manufacturing engines of Marcedes de Benz motor cars. In the factory we saw a huge high powered Mercedes car which was used by Adolf Hitlar. As I wanted to buy Contax cameras we went to the headquarters of the manufacturers in the city of Stuttgart. The other three good German cameras namely Leica, Zeissicon and Exact were produced in other cities, the last in East Germany. Stuttgart is a picturesque city with half the city built on a hillside. I bought a Contax and a Contafles both of 35 mm frame with high powered lenses. The factory authorities were highly pleased at the fact that an Indian couple had gone to Stuttgart to see a camera body and lens manufacturing factory. They agreed to sell the cameras at the concessional rate allowed to dealers which meant a reduction of nearly forty per cent of the scheduled price. From Stuttgart we went into Switzerland where we spent many days.

Switzerland is a small country and can be criscrossed easily by car in course of a day or two. We went to Zurich which had a good zoo. We went to Berne, the capital city which was known for its bear pits. Geneva situated on the beautiful Geneva Lake with its famous jet fountain shooting water into hundreds of feet high into the air. Geneva was famous for making the best and most expensive watches. We went to the Rolex watch company and bought two gold watches for my wife and a gold and a stainless steel watch for me. As we had the letter of introduction from their Calcutta agent Boseck & Co., we got the watches by paying 40 per cent of the catalogue price. We had boat rides in the lake and left Geneva to go to Caux, the headquarters of Moral Rearmament Movement. Geneva has one great drawback. There are big clock towers all over the city and big clocks sounded every 15 minutes all over the city for 24 hours of the day and night. An important incident occurred when we left the hotel in Geneva. I had encashed traveller's cheques for four thousand or more Swiss Francs which I thought I would need to buy the watches but the watches did not cost much and I had a lot of cash left with me. On the night before our departure, I kept the money under my pillow instead of in the suitcase as usual. In the morning we had breakfast in the hotel and left. After driving a few miles I remembered that I had forgotten to collect the money more than 2000 Swiss francs kept below the pillow and panicked. I cursed myself for being so forgetful and drove back to the hotel with little hope of getting my money back. I got the key of the room, went in and found the money intact. This happened because the chamber maid had not yet entered the room to change the linen.

We reached Caux which was on the top of a plateau above the plains and stayed in the MRM guest house at a cheap price but no guest was allowed this concession of stay of more than 3 days. The highest mountain peak Matterhorn was nearby and we went to the foothills and took pictures from positions of vantage. A well trained mountaineer can climb up to the peak and come down in course of a day. I had no such ambition although local guides offered to take me up.

In Caux, we all had food together and paid for food at a subsidised price. I met Lady Sinha, wife of the second Lord Sinha of Raipur, India. She had stayed for a couple of weeks and was pleading for being allowed to pay for her stay and meals at concessional rate although a guest was not permitted to enjoy this rate for more than three days. I felt ashamed when Lady Sinha pleaded her poor financial condition and insisted on getting undue advantage of the hospitable institution.

From Switzerland we drove south to north Italy. I took an apparently short route to Italy but going along I encountered a mountain road and was continuously climbing. I was at a loss to know why it happened. I wondered if I had taken a wrong route but road signs indicated that the road led to Italy. At the summit of the road I read the sign FURKA PASS at 7975 feet above the sea level i.e., I had driven along many miles of circuitous mountain road before reaching the pass.

We reached Milan where we spent some time. North Italy was and still is the industrial area of the country which stretches down upto Rome. Milan had good art galleries which housed many of the works of famous artists and sculptors. It had also the famous La Scala opera house (Treatro alla Scala). There was no question of watching any performance as La Scala remained closed during the summer months when most people would be interested in outdoor activities, like motoring, trekking, mountaineering, fishing, sailing and playing outdoor sports. We went to the Scala premises just to see the building. Milan is the centre of a big industrial zone and it had the highest per capita income in the country.

We halted at the next place of great interest namely the town of Florence. Florence is the town which contains some of the best art galleries and museums of picture, sculptures and objects d'art. It used to be called the jewel of Italian renaissance. We visited all the museums and art galleries. The famous art galleries were Palazzo Veccio, the Uffizi Museum, the Pitti Palace and many others. These museums and art galleries contained works of Michael Angelo, Leonardo da Vinci, Raphael, Donatello. The art galleries contained works of hundreds of other artists and sculptors, like Botti Celli, Titian, Ammanati. It was in this city that Michael Angelo, Leonardo da Vinci, Raphael and Donatello who headed the long list of artists and sculptors had spent their working life. Seeing the works of art one wondered to what height of artistic excellence the Italian Masters had reached. It has some of the most famous Italian palaces and was the seat of the Medicis. The cemetry in Florence is also famous for its artistic head stones and monuments which are a feast to the eyes.

Our next halt was in Rome which houses an old big Roman amphitheatre and many other ancient Roman buildings of lesser importance. Rome's plazzas and roads were mostly built in recent years and were of no less importance. We went round the ancient as well modern Rome. We visited its museums, art galleries and zoological garden. The most important was the visit to the Vatican and we could see the mural paintings of Raphael and Leonardo da Vinci on the ceiling and walls.

We drove on to south to reach Naples, an important town in south Italy. There was a marked change in the atmosphere and living standards of the people which reminded us of Asia and the East. People seemed to be poorer and wore simple inexpensive clothes compared to people in northern parts of the Italy especially Rome and further north. Food was cheaper and one felt the heat. Food in the form of long thick threads, tubes and ribbons made from wheat flour paste, some with eggs and some without, were available. These bore different names like ravioli noodles, macaroni, vermicelli, spaghetti etc. People were seen eating these as their principal items of food. Pizzas were also made and sold but they were mostly vegetarian dishes.

Our main interest was to see the most notable volcano Vesuvias which is still active. We read in history how the towns of Pompeii and Herculian were completely destroyed and buried by the volcano's eruption in A.D. 79. The volcanic ashes fell and *lava* flowed the towns so suddenly that all living creatures and organic matters were completely burnt up but were not fully destroyed. They were all sealed and made aseptic with the result that many people, cattle and household articles have been kept in the same posture and position as they were when engulfed by the volcanic eruption. The archaeologists have been able to uncover portions of Pompei and have kept the identifiable objects in a specially built museum. Some people and cattle and houses have been left in their original sites in the same position and posture as when they died in the inferno. We saw the preserves of the burnt people, cattle and goods in aseptic condition. We visited the specially built archaeological museum to have glimpse of age-old relics.

We then decided to see the volcano itself. Many men offered to act as guides and we took one who agreed to take a small fee. We were made to walk long distances up a slope which was formed by molten *lava* which solidified on cooling. At some places we saw smoke coming out from some underground source. The guide tried to pass these small holes or craters as the volcano. When he said that we had several miles to walk, we decided to turn back. When we reached the flat ground we enquired of some shopkeepers who said that the guide had bluffed us and wanted to cheat us by charging a fee. On hearing this, the guide decamped.We learnt that there was a definite route to reach the crater of the volcano which we should take. There was also a funicular railway to take us upto the crater. We availed of the transport facility and went up to see the crater which was full of smoke and hot gases were coming out slowly. The crater was a few hundred yards in diameter. As it was very warm and uncomfortable, we decided not to go further south and left for the north. We had yet to see Venice which we could not afford to miss.

We drove northwards passing through Bologna and many central Italian towns. We crossed the Apennine Ranges and reached Venice. The city was completely divided into segments of Islands by canals which joined the Adriatic sea. There were gondolas and bridges. There were probably 177 canals spanned by about 400 bridges. The palaces were great works of architecture which were not seen anywhere else in Italy. We went to Lido, a small townlet on the sea and stayed there. It was a great gambling centre with a casino and many gambling tables with different types of games. We were there for some time but I did not do any betting because I did not understand the games except roulette. In our hotel there was a band and we danced after dinner and a photographer who was intrigued to see a lady in a gorgeous *sari* took a number of pictures. Unfortunately I did not collect the prints next day.

From Venice we took a westward route and reached the town of Verona where we had to halt. We tried many hotels and guest houses which all were full. A steward of a good hotel told us that we had no chance of finding any accommodation as the town was to have an open air performance of the opera 'Aida' by Verdi in the local amphitheatre. He said that nearly 30,000 people had come from outside to watch the performance and many who had come in the morning to book accommodation were also disappointed. He suggested that we buy two tickets and watch the opera after dinner and the opera would end in the wee hours of the morning. He would, however, let us sleep on the sofas in the lounge room especially because we had come from as far as India. We bought two tickets from him, had dinner in the hotel and left for the amphitheatre. It was difficult to find a place to sit and we had to go up many flights of stairs to find places to sit down. The opera started and we could hear each word of the actors and actresses but did not understand any, as it was all in Italian. The opera was about opening of the Suez Canal and there were efforts to create an impression of digging the canal and linking the Red Sea with the Mediterranean through the peninsula of Sinai. We returned to the hotel after 2 a.m. and the concierge who had already been instructed by the steward allowed us to park the car inside the hotel compound and to sleep on the sofa without changing dress. Next morning the steward allowed us to use the toilet and bath and we left after breakfast in the hotel. The steward enquired of our destination and I said we would be heading for the west coast say for the port town of Genoa. He advised us not to miss a drive along the nearby lake Garda which has a good road on all sides of the lake which we should take. After circumscribing the lake, we may emerge on the west side and head westward. We did so and enjoyed the beautiful sight of the lake and hills and later headed towards west. Italy is not long in its width and by evening we reached Genoa and halted at a small seaside resort hotel near the border with France.

Next day we crossed into France and halted at Monte Carlo, capital city of Monaco, a semi-independent area with a hereditary person in charge of the government who had the official title of Prince. At that time Rainier was the Prince who later married the well-known American film actress Grace Kelly who came to be known as Princess Grace. She later died in a motor car accident when driving along the Riviera road. I spoke to the local Police Chief giving my identity and he promised to send a guide to show us round. The guide who was a police officer, took us round the town and the harbour. He also came in the evening to take us to the famous Monte Carlo casino. There was an entrance fee which was not demanded from us, accompanied as we were by the Police Guide. We went to several gaming tables and every table was surrounded by fashionable ladies and gentlemen in expensive clothes who were also gambling. We watched and heard cursing by most people betting. In the nature of things only the bettors who put their money in one box won and sometimes even that did not happen. The croupier was merrily collecting the lost bets. We did not gamble and moved into the dining room where we had dinner after thanking and bidding goodbye to the police officer. There was a band in attendance and we danced for a while. We stayed for two days in Monte Carlo and then left taking the road along the sea, east of the mediterranean riviera. We passed through well known towns in the French riviera. The scenery was beautiful both during the day and at night. Although winter was the riviera season, the beach had lots of people bathing in the sea and basking in the sun. It was a season of grapes which were sweet and luscious. We bought and ate a lot of grapes as long as we were in that area. We came across such well-known places as Nice, Cannes and Toulon. Cannes was famous for holding an international film festival and was the fashionable riviera town in France. We stayed for a day in Cannes but there was hardly anything for us to do. From Provence we took the road northwards by-passing the big port city of Marseilles. We, however, wanted to visit the Black Forest area in West Germany and as such decided to enter Paris from the east. It was two days before we reached Freiburg, the main town in the Black Forest area. The main road through the Black Forest was very smooth and was an avenue through forest trees with no break or disharmony with the result that one was apt to fall asleep while driving for long. There was a ski resort nearby and we went there and halted. Next morning we had a cable car ride upto the spot from where skiers start their downward journey. There was no snow nor skiers but only tourists like us. In Freiburg we stayed in a hotel mostly patronised by skiers. The hotel served good food and we enjoyed our stay in peaceful sylvan surroundings. From Freiburg we crossed into eastern France and drove along an almost straight road westwards. This road passed through farmlands which did not seem to be fertile and did not pass through any important towns either. People seemed to be farmers and of farming families. Many of them had rustic manners. We found dozens of women defecating themselves in the fields by exposing their buttocks but facing away from the road. After two days of driving we reached Paris and went to Bata's guest house. From the guest House I telephoned to a senior officer of Bata organisation in France who called the cook and the maid and gave them instructions saying that we would stay for two or three weeks. Actually we stayed 17 days at a stretch on this occasion and two more days on our return journey when we boarded a Calcutta bound French Military plane from Paris to Calcutta.

Seventeen days of stay in the heart of Paris with a cook and maid in constant attendance and a motor car of our own as conveyance would be a great luxury for any one. We had to spend money only to buy raw foodstuff for the cook to prepare meals, simple but wholesome. The cook or the maid took money and went to the market. We ourselves only bought and ate fruits everyday. I called on the Indian Ambassador who was one H.S. Malik of the Indian Civil Service. He received me cordially and invited me and my wife to have tea with him the next day. Before leaving I handed over our Chief Minister Dr B.C. Roy's letter secured earlier in London and requested him to ask a chancery official to arrange my attachment in the French Police. He asked his first secretary to do the needful. The Secretary telephoned to an officer in the Home Ministry under which the Police worked and he arranged for my attachment to Paris Police as well in the office of the Chief of the police force in the countryside. He also arranged for my visit to the office of the Interpol which has headquarters in Paris. French Police were organised more or less on the lines in India. The Head of the Civil Administration was the Prefect both in the Metropolis and also in the districts. The Prefect was a civil servant under whom all officers of other departments including the police worked. This system prevailed in India except in the Metropolitan cities. Paris prefecture was most important and Paris police was the largest compact unit. I reported to the designated officer who received me with a lot of courtesy and arranged for my visits to and study of working in all the departments in the Paris police. He also ordered two officers to be attached to me to act as guides whenever I needed them. I remained attached for a week or so and worked only in the forenoon. I got a map of Paris from the Tourist office and went to all places of interest in Paris. Louvre Museum, the church of Notre Dame, the Eiffel Tower, the Arche de Triomph, Monmartre area where we saw artists working, the local United Nations building etc. Paris had very wide roads with broad sidewalks on which stood restaurants, taverns and patisseries. These were always crowded with people both in daytime and in the evenings. The police officer guide who came in the evening offered to take us to night club shows and assured that we would not have to pay any entrance fees on the strength of being guests of the Paris Police. He took us to see shows in the four most famous night clubs, namely Mouliu Rogue, Folies Bergere, Lido and Nouvelle Eve. Cancan dancing in different forms was the main theme of all shows in Mouliu Rogue. Lido and Nouvelle Eve had dancers who did not wear any upper garments but the shows were presented in such artistic manner that one would not see the nudity of the female dancers but would watch the dancing and remain absorbed in seeing the theme of each dance sequence. We were taken to many other night clubs where the nude shows were hardly artistic and could not hide the nakedness of female dancers. There were far too many night clubs and we took three evenings to visit most of the good and tolerably good night clubs. The smaller and less well-known clubs did not charge any entrance fees to visitors but made large profits by selling alcoholic drinks. French cognac and wines were everywhere and Scotch whiskey was hardly demanded or served nor was beer a popular drink as it was in the UK and Germany. Although roads were wide in Paris driving was a nightmarish experience. The drivers in Paris were most indisciplined, if not reckless and did not follow traffic rules. They would pass a car coming from a road crossing both in front and behind. A driver may find one car crossing his path in front and another crossing in the rear. The state of automobile traffic in Paris reminded me of the story I heard from the Traffic Training Instructor of the London Police. He said that his predecessor had been given charge of training ten Paris traffic policemen who were given the usual course of training as given to the traffic constabulary in London, namely, how they should stay in the middle of the road or at a road junction where there were no traffic lights to regulate traffic. After a few years, he paid a private visit to Paris and looked for some of his erstwhile trainees on traffic control duty. He did not find any one of his former pupils but he went on trying till one day he found one of his trainees regulating traffic by standing on the sidewalk. He approached him and introduced himself. Both were delighted to see each other after a few years. The Instructor enquired how it was that he had not been following the instructions given during his training in London but was regulating traffic by standing on the side walk. He also enquired where were the other trainees. The particular traffic constable told his former instructor that his nine colleagues had tried to follow the instructions given to them in London and had all been run over by cars and got killed or so severely injured as to be compelled to retire from the force on an invalid pension. As he had decided not to follow the mode of regulating traffic in the way he was taught he was still alive and was determined not to follow the London instructions so long as he was employed as a traffic policeman. The story may be a little exaggerated but vividly described the chaotic conditions of automobile traffic in Paris at that time. Personally I do not know how I avoided collision although I took out the car quite frequently. Paris had an underground Metro Railway which we used frequently for longish journeys. The Paris Metro cars used to run on steel wheels and rails and made a lot of noise, more than that what we found in London tube trains. All this had changed when I visited Paris in 1990 and 1992 when I found trains on the Paris Metropolitan Transport and Rapid Transit Systems had wide pneumatic rubber wheels and had become practically smooth and noiseless. Besides all the mad driving had changed and Paris drivers were found to be as rule abiding as in London. So there were important changes in noisy Paris underground system as well as on the Paris roads.

At the Interpol office also I was received with courtesy and offer of helping me to understand working of the office. I also visited the printing section which published the Interpole magazine. I learnt how they were trying to economise the expense of this publication by doing everything on a special type writer and doing printing from a specially prepared raised type script on a thin metal sheet which was later strengthened with a layer of resin. The same attempt at economy was made in the statistics section which used manual methods by using punched cards and stainless steel rods to pull out the type of information from cards which had both punched holes and cut out channels, the latter to escape being pulled out wrongly. The police system in the countryside was slightly different from that in the metropolis. The armed police force were under a central command although utilised by the District Police who controlled them for operational purpose.

We spent a weekend to go round the Versaille Palace and Gardens as well as the Museum housed therein. We learnt there was to be a performance of an event like a water-ballet with dance and music with water fountains in the background the same evening. We were foolish not to buy entrance tickets during the morning visit and decided to buy them when we actually went to the show. After dinner we managed to go but failed to get entry because we could not buy any tickets which had all been sold out. We came back to Paris feeling foolish and frustrated. As we did not stay in Paris till the next weekend we missed the popular spectacular show.

We did not make any purchases in Paris except French perfume. The First Secretary of the Indian Embassy helped me to buy petrol at concessional rate by giving me his coupons. Similarly, he helped me to buy perfumes at the rate allowed to members of the Diplomatic Corps. My wife bought a lot of perfumes of the best known brands. These were actual perfumes not eau-de-toilette or colongne bottles which are frequently bought these days because of high price of actual perfumes due to very adverse exchange rate of the rupees vis-a-vis any other hard currency.

I had not yet chalked out my plans of return to India. There was no chartered return flight in the months after the coronation. The charter flight system was over a couple of months ago before we decided to return. I then remembered my friend Marcel Bouyat in the French Air Force Liaison Office in Calcutta who had told me that French airforce planes made regular weekly flights from Paris to Saigon via Calcutta. I also knew that he was posted in the Airforce Department in the French Ministry of Defence. I telephoned to the Defence Ministry and they managed to locate the officer and intimated me his telephone number. I telephoned to Marcel Bouyat who was delighted that I and my wife were in Paris and invited me to go to his office which we did. He took us out for lunch during which I broached the problem of returning to India without spending a large sum of money on tickets for travel by regular Airlines. He said that it was possible to accommodate me and my wife as passengers but he had to take permission of higher authorities. There was no question of charging any fare but travelling would not be as comfortable as in regular passenger airlines. He promised to contact me after a decision was reached and the decision would be communicated to me before I left Paris or in London. After a couple of days he telephoned and told me that the Ministry had agreed to give us permission to travel as civilian passengers and gave me the date and the name of the Airforce officer at the aerodrome I should report to. He promised to be at the aerodrome on the day of departure. We returned to London and got a room rented at a much higher rent. As there were still a couple of weeks left before our return we decided to go to Edinburgh by car and my brother-in-law agreed to join. He could not drive a small car nor did my wife dare to do so. I had to prepare myself to drive a small car all the way to Edinburgh and back. We left one day early morning and travelled the whole day and reached Edinburgh in the early afternoon. The same day we did whatever sight seeing we could, tried to find accommodation in hotels which were all found to be too expensive and we decided to return to London. We started late evening and travelled the whole night eating fish and chips en route. There was rain and fog almost throughout our journey back and we reached London next morning. I still wonder how I managed to cover a long distance on unknown roads and in bad weather and poor visibility without getting involved in an accident. In London we made last minute purchase and faced the problem of disposing of the car which would otherwise create a problem in garaging the vehicle and in maintenance. As a result of an advertisement I could sell my car two days before the day of my departure. The buyer paid me the same price I paid in buying the new car. He wanted a car in a hurry to give unexpected surprise to his wife who was in a hospital to deliver a baby and would come out in a week's time. This last minute deal settled all my affairs satisfactorily.

We left London 3 days earlier and travelled on a special train running from London to Paris and vice versa which was known as the 'Golden Arrow' in England and 'Fleche d'Or' in France. One boarded the train, crossed the ferry by sitting or sleeping in the car and reached Paris late next morning. It was a most comfortable journey and food served in the car restaurant was good and delicious. In Paris I got a cab and again took shelter in Bata Guest House. As we had no independent transport of our own we walked some distances and visited La Fayette gallery a shopping complex and ate at a good Paris restaurant. On the whole we were delighted at our pleasant and successful stay for five months in Europe, having travelled to most Western European countries except Spain and Austria and the entire holiday did not cost us much. After 2 days we went to the aerodrome in the company of my French friend who came in his car to give us a lift to the airport and boarded an airforce plane which landed us at Dum Dum airport the next day. We had bought so many clothes and other goods that the old clothes had to be sent from London by sea. I took the newly bought things, the gun and the cutlery as my personal baggages and got custom clearance without paying any duty. The gun and cutlery were delivered on board the plane to avoid paying local sales tax. In those days an Indian citizen could bring foreign goods of much greater value. Later government reduced the quota because some people used to bring foreign goods and sell them in India to earn a large profit.

16

First Police Revolt—Penalty for Intransigence

While I was still in the UK I got a message through the High Commission to return as quickly as practicable as I had got promotion as DIG of Police and had to join a vacant post in Jalpaiguri. It was in the year 1953. I decided to return before my leave period actually expired. Before departure on leave I had well packed all my personal belongings in Calcutta and left them in the Harrington Street Palace of the Maharajah of Chanchi with whose son-in-law we were on very friendly terms. I reported my arrival at the IG's office and left for Jalpaiguri. Most people feel sorry to leave Calcutta for a muffasil town but I was not feeling sorry because I knew I would have an opportunity to try to do big game hunting in the forests of Jalpaiguri and Darjeeling and fishing in the hill streams. Actually my posting in Jalpaiguri was in a leave vacancy which should have continued for about 2 years on account of other DIG's taking their turn to go on leave to create a vacant post for me. That was the usual practice which the Head of the Department encouraged. Because of the reason that I annoyed IG Sarkar who was displeased with me, he did not encourage DIG's to go on leave so that I might face a reversion to act in SP's rank for want of a vacancy.

In Jalpaiguri I had a two-storeyed brick built house which had 3 bed rooms, with spacious attached dressing rooms and toilets on the first floor. The ground floor had an office room, a living room, a bed room with attached bath, a dining room and a kitchen. The house had a large compound surrounding it and was designed for very comfortable living. The house had eight staff quarters in a part of the compound. My office was separated by a narrow canal named 'Karla' over which a wooden bridge existed and was used to walk over to my office. There was, however, a wider well built bridge further up in the congested town area for use of motor cars, buses, cyclists and large groups of people.

I took up my duties as a DIG seriously and tried to improve the administration of my office. I started going to office at the scheduled time and found that almost everyone was coming late to attend office. I tried to enforce punctuality and reprimanded those who were late in attendance in spite of being warned. This made me somewhat impatient and occasionally rude. This attitude of mine was both foolish and tactless and easily raised the hackles of some office staff who sent an anonymous letter to the IG of Police complaining against my rude behaviour and that I did not fully respect the ceremony of the Republic Day Parade preferring to go out on tour instead of attending the ceremony. The latter was true because the District Magistrate used to preside over the function and hoist the National Flag, I used to feel small and tried to avoid. This attitude was not correct because the DM would be the presiding officer even if IG or the Home Secretary was present. The Divisional Commissioner or a Minister and finally the State Governor would only take precedence over the DM who was known as the Dy. Commissioner in Jalpaiguri as a relic of the olden days when in some districts like Jalpaiguri and Darjeeling the DM wielded more power and was designated as a Dy. Commissioner. As, for example, in the old days the DC could award imprisonment upto seven years in a criminal case which provide such long sentences or imprisonment. Ordinarily the power is now limited to 2 years imprisonment by all First Class Magistrates and an accused is tried by the Sessions Judge or one of his Additional or Assistant Judges if an accused is to be tried for an offence in which the punishment prescribed exceeded 2 years. I got the letter of complaint sent by the IG asking me to give my comments. As regards my strictness I explained that the office staff had got into bad habits of unpunctuality and slip shod work and had to be pulled up. As regards not being present at the ceremony of the previous Republic Day on the 26th January, I went out to inspect border outposts on that day because I did not play any part in the ceremony and there was no office work to do. I, however, assured him that I would be present on the future occasions.

There were five districts in my Range. One Himangshu Roy was SP Jalpaiguri and one B.C. Bagchi, IPS, was SP Darjeeling. A.K. Banerjee was SP CoochBihar, my brother-in-law, S.N. Bhattacharyya was SP Malda and S.K. Guha Majumdar was SP West Dinajpore. One Raghunath Banerjee who had a mouth for big talks was the DM in Jalpaiguri and Saradindu Dutta Majumdar was DC Darjeeling. The largest river in North Bengal, namely, the Tista flows by Jalpaiguri town and there are other somewhat smaller rivers namely the Jaldhaka, the Rydak and the Torsha further east. The first three rivers divide the district into four segments. The easternmost river Sankosh forms the boundary with Assam. There were motorable roads all over but no bridges existed over the Tista or Rydak in the district. One could cross the Tista over a bridge at Sevok in Darjeeling district. But this route was long and circuitous and officers in the district mainly crossed the rivers by putting their vehicles on a large ferry platform formed with two boats. This ferry could take cars and buses aboard. In the district there were small forest areas all over upto the bank of the Sankosh river which formed the boundary between West Bengal and Assam. All forest areas were under the Forest Department of the State Government and each district had a Divisional Forest Officer in charge. The Raja of Jalpaiguri owned a small forest area beginning from a line a few miles north of the Jalpaiguri town. All the police stations on the east of the Tista had forest areas dotted by numerous tea gardens. Prosperity of Jalpaiguri depended on tea which made many Bengalee families rich and prosperous. One had to take the Raja's or his family's permission to hunt wild animals in the Raja's forest. After I joined the old Raja died and his only child Rajkumari Prativa Devi inherited his property. Rajkumari married one Dr Sudhangshu Kiran Bose, who was the elder brother of Jyoti Basu who was a staunch communist in early years and later became the communist Chief Minister of West Bengal continuously for 5 terms which started in 1977 and should last till 2001. Dr Bose was a Dentist trained in the USA but did not practise his profession. He was always busy to save the Raja's properties for his wife and their children.

The tribal Raja used to have other women as mistresses who were given almost the status of official wives. Their children laid claims of inheritance on Raja's properties as his legal heirs and Dr Bose spent all his life after the Raja's death to fight suits filed by a number of the so-called heirs, children of the Raja's mistresses claiming a share in the properties. He managed to win or compromise all the cases and the family got compensation from the government when it took over the Raja's lands and forest areas. Dr Bose, one Sri Rahut, members of some prominent Bengalee tea planters' families and many other prominent citizens called on me and we became friends for the rest of my life. I and my wife were often invited to have meals with them and we also had to reciprocate their hospitality. Well known tea gardens owning Bengalee families were Ghosh's, Roy's, Rahut's, Bhowmik's to name a few. The Bengalee owners tried to earn as much profit as practicable by not growing new plantations, ploughing back an adequate percentage of profit to improve and maintain the tea bushes. The result was all Bengalee owned gardens became less productive both in quality and quantity and had to be sold out to non-Bengalee Indian businessmen. There were many gardens owned by big British commercial and manufacturing houses like Jardine and Henderson, Mcneil and Barry, Finlays, Goodrickes who maintained their gardens well and had professional managers both of the British and Indian stock. But continuous labour trouble and other administrative difficulties created by new government policies induced these foreign owners and Trading Houses to sell out their gardens and pull out of tea plantation business. Moreover, many of the foreign Trading Houses became Indianised by sale to Marwari and Gujarati businessmen and they kept the gardens in better condition than Bengalee owners. However, India's international trade, i.e. export of tea was not as profitable as in the past as Ceylon (Sri Lanka) and Kenya in Africa became keen competitors. I suppose China gradually became a big and important factor in international trade in tea. I visited all the sub-divisions of the five districts in my range and many police stations. This was an arduous task because I had to travel a lot, sometimes to distant places, by road, rail and boat. I also tried to travel by car to Balurghat District Headquarters of

West Dinajpur but could not do so, as the road to Balurghat was not completed.

For some years discontent was brewing amongst lower ranks of the police mainly the constabulary on account of low pay, bad service conditions and bad treatment they often received at the hands of superior officers namely of the Superintendent or Dy. Superintendent rank. This discontent erupted in 1954 in a statewide pay strikes in the whole state in that they would not take their pay or salary but would not stop performing duty. There was strike in districts in my range except in Darjeeling. SP's managed to pacify the force in Cooch Behar and West Dinajpur. In Jalpaiguri I had to intervene as the Superintendent of Police failed to induce the policemen in not continuing with the strike. I had to assist SP Jalpaiguri to break the strike. The strike in Jalpaiguri ended when I assured the policemen that their grievances would be looked into and redressed. But in Malda men were more adament and the Superintendent of Police failed and sought my help. I went there and held two meetings in the morning and afternoon on the same day. The strikers grievances were receipt of low pay and policemen were often made to work as household servants by some Superintendents, Dy. Superintendents and Inspectors of Police. I told them that strike by a disciplined force was most undesirable and unacceptable to the authorities. I would certainly recommend removal of their grievances, especially their utilisation in non-police duties. I exhorted and appealed to them. Fortunately they responded favourably and gave up the strike and joined their duty. Actually it was in Northern range that the strike ended ahead of districts in other ranges. IG Sarkar called all the Range DIGs and DIG, IB and CID to attend a meeting. I went down to Calcutta. On my arrival I learnt that Sarkar had gone to meet the striking policemen in Howrah district. I went to see him there. In my presence the force were insulting the IG and he could not convince them to return to duty. He failed in his efforts and came back frustrated. SP, however, managed the strikers and made them agree to end the strike. The statewide strike gradually petered out when the force learnt that policemen in most districts had ceased to be on strike and thought it unwise to continue and be singled out to be recalcitrant and indisciplined policemen.

Before we joined the meeting with IG Sarkar in his room there was a conference in the AIG's room with DIGs, SPs including the seniormost DIG, Upananda Mukherjee who was DIG, IB-CID and Ghosh Choudhury, Commissioner of Police. Most of the officers thought that lowering of the dignity and authority of the Superintendent of Police was the main reason that the Superintendent could not control their men. IG Sarkar was himself responsible for lowering the dignity of the post of the Superintendent of Police by writing nasty letters and/or rebuking them in presence of subordinate staff. A little later we were called to IG's room and there was a conference and the reasons of the strike were discussed threadbare as far as were known to the officers in the meeting. The main reason that was discussed in the preliminary discussion in the AIG's room which was attended by the Commissioner of Police, DIG, IB and other DIGs that it was IG Sarkar's treatment of SPs which reduced their authority was not mentioned at all. Nobody spoke about it but I could not help in not referring to the subject. After seeking IG's permission and apologising beforehand I spoke about the points not mentioned. IG was stunned and denied that he was even responsible and enquired of all other officers present but most kept quiet, i.e. indirectly supporting me. IG Sarkar became red and blue in the face with annoyance and apparent humiliation. He became completely antagonistic to me. My colleague Masood told me that I was very unwise and tactless and should never have raised the very sensitive point while I was officiating in the post of a DIG. I told him that there was no proper time in an officers' service life to speak unpleasant truth. While the officer was officiating he has to be cautious and timid lest he is not confirmed. When he works in a post after confirmation he has also to be timid and cautious to avoid annoyance to his boss lest he misses a chance of promotion. So an officer has to be bold to speak the truth. This attitude of mine was right but was deprecated by other officers who thought I had done a good deal of harm to myself and this proved to be tragically true.

17

Outdoor Life

My security officer who belonged to MP cadre and knew the state well invited me to visit Kanha game sanctuary which was one of the best in the country. After leaving the nearest rail station we travelled by a car over a dirt road to reach the sanctuary which had not yet been developed as a tourist spot. The forest guards manning the entrance gate stopped and informed us that we had to take permission of the local Divisional Forest Officer, who was fortunately for us staying in the Forest Bungalow inside. We went in and introduced ourselves and were cordially received and got permission to stay in the bungalow and enter the sanctuary. The DFO was one Deep Singh who was staying with his wife. My wife made friends with her and we had meals together. Deep Singh had a chevrolet car and he promised to take us round in his car. He was only apprehensive that the battery of the car was in a low state of charge and he could not take us out at night.

Next day after breakfast, we four, i.e., Deep, his wife, my wife and myself went out. We saw herds of chital, deer and black buck which I filmed with cine camera. We saw a tiger. Again in the afternoon we went out and saw the same animals as well as a tiger. Besides we saw a pack of wild dogs who were powerful killers of all games except tigers, leopards and large graminivoroes. There were no elephants, rhinos or baffaloes in the sanctuary.

After dinner, I decided to go out by myself for a short distance in spite of warning by the DFO that I shall not be able to put the head lights on because the car might stop. Accompanied by my wife, I drove and went along a wide forest road and crossed the dry sandy bed of a small stream. I flashed my torch light on but saw nothing. I decided to return but during my return journey I put the head lights on for a while and the car engine stopped while crossing the riverbed. The motor car was thus stalled in a depression and it was not practicable for two of us to push the car and take it to a portion of road on plain ground. I sensed the awkward situation I had put my wife and myself due to my foolhardiness. The self starter would not work fully nor would the engine start. We were faced with the prospect of walking at night about a mile without a firearm in a defenceless condition. With a lot of embarrassment I asked my wife to push the car while I kept pressing the self starter switch. To our great relief the engine started and my wife clambered in. I drove the car for a mile in complete darkness with the torchlight to help and reached the bungalow. I cursed my folly and obstinancy in not listening to the DFO's warnings. We left Kanha but promised the DFO that we would keep in touch and requested him to do so.

Next day a beat was organised in another part of the jungle. Deep and I took our perch on two small *machans* on two trees. During the beat two tigers were seen to come up one after the other. The first ran fast and I did not try to shoot it. A second tiger came out and stopped for a while and I took a broadside shot which killed it on the spot. We got down when the beaters came up and I found that the tiger was a not-yet-fully grown male tiger cub.

We went to the camp and got the tiger skinned. There was great demand for tiger fat which the villagers believed to have curative power for all kinds of bodily pain like gout, arthritis, rheumatism etc. I thanked my host and hostess and returned to my work in the area.

On another occasion my security officer sought the help of SP Raipur who was also a *shikari* and the latter promised to take me to a part of the forest where horned animals, i.e. of deer family were plentiful. Accompanied by the SP we went into the jungle and could see sambars, spotted and barking deer. As the animals were easy targets, I killed two samber stags and got the horns and skins. I also got a barking deer for the pot and my cook prepared delicious kebab with the meat. The skins had always to be thoroughly cleaned of fat and blood and covered with plentiful of salt so as to prevent putrefaction.

During the course of my tours, we paid a visit to Amarkantak where from the river Narbada started from a small fountain to grow into a mighty river before reaching the sea. Amarkantak was a place of pilgrimage. We also went to Balaghat, a famous *shikar* place where hundreds of tigers had been shot in the past. I managed to get a group of men to act as beaters to flush out any tiger or other animals in the area but no animal was seen to come out.

I was interested in shooting big games only. Tiger, leopard and bison were the only big game animals available in North Bengal. Wild boars were also available. Shooting of elephants which were plentiful was totally prohibited in West Bengal, unless the elephant was declared a rogue. There were a small number of *shikar* enthusiasts like Dr Kiron Bose and one Rasiklal Dey whom the former initiated in this sport. Besides there were a few British and Indian managers of tea estates who were *shikar* enthusiasts. Amongst the latter was one Donald Mackenzie the most prominent. Dey had a DBBL rifle and was known to be a good shot. To go into and hunt for games in the government reserved forest areas I had to take out a permit from the DFO. It was anomalous that the DM/DC, SP, Divisional Commissioner and all forest officials were permitted to do shooting in the Reserve Forest but DIG of Police was excluded. I wrote to the then Secretary, Forest Department, Karuna Ketan Sen, who was my first SDO in Netrokona subdivision and a colleague in Tippera district and had remained a fast friend. He took up my case and had nearly succeeded till his proposal fell through on the L.R. raising an objection that conferring the benefit of a new category of officers will be discriminatory and against a provision of the Constitution of India which had already come into force. Consequently I confined my efforts at tiger shooting mainly in the Raja's forest for which I had a standing permission. There were also many tigers in the jungles of tall grass growing in the char areas of the Tista which was next door and could be entered into easily on an elephant. I travelled whole night in the Raja's forest and saw nothing except a cow bison which was not a game animal. In the tall grass jungle in the char areas, one hoped to see an animal like a spotted dear, a pig or a tiger in the jungle path which was clear of the tall grass. In short I had no luck and did not succeed in shooting anything in the char area or Raja's forest.

I was invited to be the Chief Guest and to speak at the annual meeting of Jalpaiguri Tea Planters' Association which had its headquarters in Binnaguri across the Tista. At the meeting I praised the work of the Tea Planters who played an important role in the prosperity of the district and welfare of thousands of tea garden labour. I added that profit should not be the only motive but equal attention should be given to taking welfare measures for the workers and their families. I also mentioned that police occasionally received complaints of unfair and aggressive treatment by the Tea Garden Management towards labour. Any one asked to speak at such a meeting had never criticised the planters even in a mild manner but I had dared to do so. My speech was received with mixed applause. One Brett was then the President of the Indian Tea Planters Association in North India with its office in Calcutta. He was the Managing Director of a well-known British Company owning several gardens in West Bengal and Assam. He was the last speaker and mentioned that he would certainly tell the planters present to remove the impression of occasional oppression on the working community but perhaps I was wrongly informed, etc. The party broke up after tea was served to all including who were present in Binnaguri.

Later IG Sarkar told me that Brett had formally complained to him about my speech which he and other European planters objected to and so on. I explained to IG what I had said that it was true as often reported in the newspapers but he did not seem to be satisfied. I am sorry to say that IG made an adverse remark on the point in my confidential report in which he incorporated the spurious complaints of my staff too. After the leave vacancy ended, Maswood, an IP officer, who was a year senior to me joined as my successor. I was in a desperate position to avoid my reversion to work as SP and approached one Hiralal Saha, the then DIG of Police in charge of Presidency Range, who was a very senior IP officer and had not gone on leave for a long time and requested him to go on leave. I had to make a good deal of efforts before I could induce him to go on 4 months' leave. He demanded a small price for doing so, namely, to pay his telephone bills during his leave. Although it was almost a blackmail and a humiliating condition for me, I agreed to his proposal and worked as DIG Presidency Range for four months. On completion of this term there was no vacancy and the IG recommended my posting as SP, Howrah. In order to avoid this posting and reversion, I applied for 4 months' leave and government granted the leave. During this period I stayed in our family house in Bhowanipur but decided to undertake a long *shikar* trip to Orissa where we had made close friendship with one Capt. A.P. Mohanty, an enthusiastic *shikari* and angler. He held the post of the Superintendent of Wireless and Transport in the police department in which the post was of an equivalent rank as that of a District Superintendent of Police. On arrival in Cuttack I called on the IG of Police and some other high police officials who assured me of all help during my stay in Orissa and in my *shikar* trips. Capt. Mohanty chalked out a plan of visits and inspection for a long period covering several weeks and took a government Jeep car with a trailer so that we could travel comfortably with the necessary utensils and other camping necessities in the trailer while Mohanty, myself and my wife would sit in the front. Mahanty drove the car and the driver and his orderly-cum-cook sat in the rear. We travelled through all the districts in western Orissa specially those well-known for tiger depredations like Kalahandi, Bolangir and Koraput. We halted at a local Circuit House to see the SP and DM and Range DIGs and Divisional Commissioner if posted there and chalked out a plan of operations. All SP's were very hospitable and they lived a life style superior to that of SP's in West Bengal nay even in undivided Bengal. Most of the superior officers came from landed gentry and businessmen's families and had extra income besides their salary in government service. Some were even from families of Rajas of native states who had to surrender their states to the government of India and drew a handsome sum of money as a paltry compensation for loss of income from their states. We spent a good deal of time in the forests both during the day and night but to our disappointment we did not see any wild animals except one black bear in Kalahandi jungles. We did not come across any horned animals either like chital, sambhar, barking deer, etc. In Kalahandi we stayed in a forest

rest house in which the window had no bars and we had to barricade the windows with stout bamboo sticks nailed to the window frame. The door could however be closed from inside. The fear that maneating tigers had created in the minds of the villagers could be gauged from the fact that on two occasions we left the guide near his doorstep but he would not alight from the car until one gunman got down and stood guard and the man ran fast into his house on each occasion. We returned to Cuttack and rested for a few days.

From there Capt. Mohanty decided to take us (my wife had accompanied me) to the bear country in Ganjam and I might be lucky to find black buck on or near the sea beach. We went there and stayed in the forest rest house close to the bear country. We made a reconnaissance of the area in day light and managed to see a couple of bears far in the hills beyond the possibility of shooting successfully. I learnt that bears came out at night and climbed up trees to attack honeycombs and to drink honey. We went out after dinner. True to information given we saw dozens of bears all over the place and I could shoot many of them. Some were small and some large, the latter likely to be males. I shot two which fell to my bullets. The bears uttered a human like cry when dying and one felt bad. As there was no prowess nor skill required to shoot these unsuspecting animals, I did not shoot more than two. I, Capt. Mohanty and the driver helped to carry the carcasses and loaded them on the car which was a Land Rover. As we approached the car, we saw some bears shuffling away from the car. My wife who was left behind in the car told me that several bears had come nosing round the car and one had stood up to peer at my wife through the glass window. She had closetted herself by closing all the doors and windows. We tried to find the black bucks but they were very scarce. They had been wontonly shot down and killed for meat by poachers and the few left stayed in jungle areas and kept off from hunters and poachers.

I returned to Calcutta and had still a month for my leave to expire. I did not like the prospect of reversion and working as a Superintendent of Police. In the newspapers I read that after riotous situation created by the clerical staff in the headquarters office of the South Eastern Railway, that the S.E. Railway had been wanting a separate Chief Security Officer for itself and from West Bengal Cadre. Till then, there was one Chief Security Officer of the rank of a DIG of Police deputed from Bihar cadre. In this case, South Eastern Railway had sought nomination of a suitable officer of West Bengal, Eastern Railway already having an officer from Bihar. I got adverse remarks communicated to me by the government against which I sent a representation stating all the facts and S.N. Roy, the then Chief Secretary who understood the malafide reasons for making adverse remarks by the IG did not agree to delete them. I approached Mriganka Mouli Basu, the Home Secretary, whom I knew very well as well as an ICS officer Jatindra Mohan Talukdar who was my Divisional Commissioner when I worked as SP 24 parganas. The latter influenced the Chief Secretary to send my name only as the State's nominee. Now was the problem of the Railway Board accepting me as the State nominee. Fortunately one Nirmal Kumar Roy, an old senior friend of mine, was a member in the Railway Board and Biswanath Lahiri with whom I had friendly acquaintance for many years and also his family members like brothers and sisters-in-law who stayed in Calcutta. He was the Head of the Security Department in New Delhi. I wrote to N.K. Roy who saw Lahiri and persuaded him to accept me and I was accepted. Hiren Sarkar, IG, West Bengal, continued with his evil designs and wrote to N.C. Kapoor, General Manager, South Eastern Railway disparaging me and asking him to object to accepting me as the state's nominee. N.C. Kapoor wrote to the Railway Board which, however, declined to change their decision. I got orders to join the post of Chief Security Officers in the rank of a DIG of Police in South Eastern Railway. I do not even now understand why Hiren Sarkar became a Devil's disciple. I took charge from T.N. Ghosh who was then working as the CSO and reported to the General Manager who was found to be somewhat cool in receiving me. A few months later after he found out what good work I was capable of doing he told me about Hiren Sarkar's disparaging letter making false allegations against me. If I had not succeeded in joining a new post equivalent to a DIG's and was compelled to work as SP and remain in the devilish clutches of Hiren Sarkar as IG, West Bengal, I had made up my mind to go on premature retirement from service, which was permitted only to officers of pre-Independence period. A lucky combination of circumstances helped me to escape from this premature end of my service career. Since then I have always told my colleagues and juniors never to fight or criticise a boss unless the fighter knew the boss's boss and was his favourite. My petition to the Government to delete adverse remarks falsely made did not get favourable reaction from the Chief Secretary S.N. Roy, ICS, who failed to act justly in this case and proved that he was a poor administrator holding the seniormost post in the state and who did not want to take responsibilities which was his duty to take.

18

An Interlude in the Railways

I spent more than five happy and useful years in the Railways from 1955 to 1961. The CSO being a senior police officer on deputation was held in more respect than other officers of his rank. CSO was a Junior Head of a Department and was considered as the bridge between the Railway and the state governments whose assistance had to be sought on numerous occasions of incidence of serious crime on the railway, strikes, riots and problems of acquiring land for new lines, workshops, etc. South Eastern Railway spanned over five states namely West Bengal, Bihar, Orissa, Andhra and Maharashtra. The important outside terminal stations were Ranchi in Bihar, Visakhapatnam and Bailadila in Andhra Pradesh, Jabbalpur in Madhya Pradesh and Nagpur in Maharashtra. The railway passed through some of the most picturesque parts of central India through hills, forests, mining areas and had two reputed seaside resorts as Puri and Waltair (Visakhapatnam). Some of the best *shikar* countries also lay in Orissa, Madhya Pradesh and Maharashtra (Chanda). Posting to this railway was very much to my liking and it gave me an opportunity to undertake *shikar* trips in places I knew in Orissa and new forest areas in Madhya Pradesh and Maharashtra.

Since the internal riots in the Railway head office in Garden Reach, the General Manager and his senior officers had developed a low morale. I had to take steps to improve the atmosphere without rousing the wrath of the subordinate staff. It took a long time to do so. I had to be in constant touch with the Calcutta Police headed by Ghose Choudhury and the Railway Police under SRP in Howrah. While in service on this railway I had to see the police chiefs of all other states, four in number as well as DIG's of police and SP's and DM's/DC's of the districts through which the Railway passed.

Superintendents of Railway Police in the five states were very important officers to help the Railway.

The post of Chief Security Officer was created when the old railway watch and ward force was replaced by a newly organised force under an act of the Parliament to create the Railway Protection Force. This was the result of a committee set up under the Chairmanship of Bhola Nath Malik, the then Director, Intelligence Bureau of the Union government. The committee was set up because the problem of crime in respect of railway property including goods carried became acute and the old watch and ward staff could not cope nor was there any machinery to coordinate activities of the watch and ward force (controlled by the Commercial Department of the Railways) with the Railway Police and the District Police. Secondly, the force needed a departmental head and a hierarchy of officers as well as a training institute. Lahiri, the first IG posted in New Delhi under the act came to my railway and gave words of encouragement as well as good advice to me. The foremost task he asked me to perform was to arrange training of new recruits who had to be taken in large numbers to fill up existing vacancies on account of retirement of old watch and ward personnel and creation of new posts. There was only a small house and the former watch and ward department in Kharagpur which was the heart of the South Eastern Railway system on the strength of having a large workshop and being an important junction station from where the SER branched out in several directions. During my discussions with IG, RPF, I protested saying that there were no facilities of housing for institutional staff to impart training and several other grounds of my inability to carry out his order. At that time I got the best ever advice in my life. He told me that it was the qualities in a good officer which enabled him to succeed against odds and never to utter the word impracticable or too difficult to achieve. He advised me to pitch up tents for the recruits accommodation and the classes could be held even in the shade of big trees. I had to find the best available officers to act as instructors and brief the instructors in my office and also to prepare an ad hoc training manual. I followed his advice which I had to pass on to the instructors also. I had to tell the GM about our scheme of recruitment and training and got his approval. GM, however, advised me to get in touch with the Chief Engineer (CE) and his office advising him of our needs and requesting him to draw up a plan for constructing the office and staff buildings, the barracks and parade ground with the help of the Railway architect. Fortunately the CE and his senior officers were very helpful and a spacious building with an indoor auditorium was planned and built. Class rooms and barracks with adequate facilities were also built. A good level parade ground was also provided. GM opened the building and took salute in a passing out parade of a batch of trainees who were trained in open space. He was mightily pleased at the display of skill and discipline of the newly trained recruits.

In the first year after opening of the new Training School building we could accommodate many trainees. The trainees were mostly Bengalees and relatives of Andhra workers in Kharagpur. I thought it preferable to recruit as many ex-army men from outside the state, West Bengal being a poor centre for getting ex-armymen. I chalked out a plan of visiting all regimental centres in Bihar, UP, Madhya Pradesh, Maharashtra, Rajasthan and Gujarat. I had earlier written to those centres stating my requirements and date of my arrival at each centre for interview and recruitment. I could not recruit many because except Biharis, most ex-Army men of other centres expressed their unwillingness to come to South-Eastern Railway far from their home state, to work. This tour undertaken in a commodious railway saloon car gave me and my wife an opportunity to visit almost all important places of sightseeing and hill stations in those states. I managed to go and see the lions in Gir forest in Gujarat. Besides each year there used to be a conference of CSO's of all the railways which used to be held in the metropolitan cities of Delhi, Calcutta, Bombay and Madras by turn. Besides I had to go to Delhi to see IG, RPF and occasionally an Addl. Member. I had occasions to go and see the State IG of Police in the state capitals. I remember that once when I was going to Bombay, my GM asked me to bring his daughter and son-in-law in my saloon. The son-in-law was the only son of the Chief Justice of Maharashtra High Court and was an officer in the Indian Air Force. On another occasion I went to Bombay and brought along my brother-in-law who was in London at the time of my visit during the Queen's coronation, his wife and mother-in-law. Those who travelled with an officer in a railway saloon had to buy 1st class tickets but they travelled with a good deal of comfort, having clean toilets, hot meals served from the kitchen adjoining the dining room and also tea, coffee and snacks whenever these were wanted.

While serving as CSO, I frequently went to the states of Orissa and Madhya Pradesh which had the largest part of the South-Eastern Railway. Actually the whole of Orissa was served by South-Eastern Railway only and so was also a major portion of Madhya Pradesh. These two states had also large forest areas and big shooting opportunity. I met Deep Singh in course of my official tour in Madhya Pradesh. Learning that I was keen to shoot a tiger, he offered to arrange a shoot for me. With information gathered by his officers, Deep Singh located two places where tigers had been seen and might be flushed out by beating. On the first day the beaters gathered in the afternoon. Deep Singh made me take my position on the comfortable branches of a tree at the head of a dry nullah or shallow ravine. Deep Singh himself took his perch on another tree at a distance. The most likely place for the tiger if any to come out was where I took my position. The second best spot was where Singh took his. As my wife accompanied me, a small *machan* was built on a tree away from us and an improvised crude bamboo ladder was provided for her to climb up. My orderly also took stand on the highest rung of the ladder just below my wife's seat. Mrs. Singh stayed back in the camp.

The beat started and for 15–20 minutes no animal came out. A magnificent blue bull or *nil gai* came out stood before me not knowing where to go. When the beaters were at only a short distance from me and there was no sign of a tiger I thought I should not miss shooting the *nil gai* and fired shot from my rifle and killed the blue bull. As soon as the shot was fired, there was a loud growl of a tiger who was approaching my position but changed direction and ran sideways. A few minutes later I heard three shots and knew that Singh has seen the animal and took shots at it. As the last shot was quite a few seconds later, I knew Deep Singh had successfully shot and the tiger was dead. The beaters came up to me and criticised my impatience. Later Deep Singh came to me and said that he had killed the animal which was a full grown tigress. As he had a small bore not so powerful a rifle namely a .280 he had to fire first two shots to stop the tiger and the last was used as a coup-de-grace. He also deplored my sense of quick despondence and consequent impatience. I learnt from my wife that she was not afraid on hearing the tigress' growl but the orderly who was quite high up had started trembling so violently that it seemed that the *machan* would crash down with my wife on it.

During my spell of service in South Eastern Railway I was invited to give a course of lectures to the Railway officers in the Railway Staff College at Baroda, Gujarat and I accepted the invitation. Accompanied by my wife I went to Baroda and stayed in the railway inspection bungalow and gave lectures on two days about problems of theft of the railway, means that can be adopted to minimise the theft as well as preventive security measures adopted by the Railway Protection Force in each railway. The problem of sabotage and disputes with the passengers also found a place in my discourse. During this visit I went to see some important parts of Gujarat State namely, Dwarka, Somnath Temple, Bhet Dwarka as well as to the Gir forest sanctuary where lions are still found under protection. During my visit the local Superintendent of Police placed police vehicles for our conveyance to all the above mentioned places. Somnath Temple had been destroyed by some Muslim invaders in the past and has been rebuilt perhaps after Independence. It is a magnificient temple worth a visit. The Rann of Kachchh is a shallow lagoon and has been the scene of many disputes and skirmishes between Pakistan and India.

Gir forest could be approached by a road running through a desert area where no sign posts or identifying trees or buildings could be seen. We reached Gir forest in the afternoon and stayed at the local circuit house which was a magnificient building in which the Maharajas and Rajas of the states as well as the Viceroy of India used to stay during their visits to see Gir lions. Besides us there were other visitors. In the evening we went to a place where it was expected that lions were likely to come to kill a bait which was tied practically every day to enable the visitors to see them. We went by car and there were several other cars and we were asked to switch on our headlights and wait. We saw a lioness come and kill a small buffalo kept as a bait. The lioness tried to drag away the kill into the forest cover but two forest guards managed to drag the kill on to the area lit up by the car headlight so that we could see the lioness feeding on the animal. Actually there was a tug of war between the lioness at one end of the dead calf and two guards at the other end. The whole thing seemed like a stage managed show because the lioness did not object to the kill being dragged away from her by the forest guards to make her feed on the kill in glaring headlights. I returned the same evening by the same route. It was a full moon night and the roads and large surrounding areas could be clearly seen. As stated earlier, the road passed through a desert area without any sign posts or identifying marks, the driver lost his way twice but managed to reach us at the railway station. Our expected arrival time was delayed by about an hour. When we reached the station we found that the train by which I was to travel in my railway saloon car was ready to start on its journey. I and my wife ran and got into the carriage when it was in a slow motion. Frankly speaking, the station master was careless and should have ascertained if we were in the carriage so the empty carriage was not hauled away. I also made the mistake of not cautioning the Station Master before we left for the Gir sanctuary. Fortunately we could catch the train and stick to our routine.

An officer of my status held a silver pass which is of the size of an Indian rupee coin which entitled the officer and his wife to travel on duty by the airconditioned first class. Except to go to Kharagpur, I was always lucky to get a railway saloon to travel on duty. An officer also got six sets of free railway passes for himself and members of his family to travel by first class and by paying a small percentage as extra fare could travel by A/C class if he or his family member travelled on private work or for pleasure. I availed of this concession to travel to Kashmir and to Ceylon.

I also went out to cover the whole of South India upto Kanya Kumarika, the states of Kerala, Karnataka, Tamil Nadu, Maharastra, Rajputana and UP by taking leave and using

Railway passes. I went to such hill stations as Kodai Kanal, Ootacamond, Coonnoor, Wellington and such places of pilgrimage and of architectural interest as Hassan, Halebid, Sravana Belgola, Ellora, Ajanta, Ajmer, Puskar, Meenakshi temple in Madura, Sanchi, Bodh Gaya, Dwarka, Somnath temple of Vishnu and many other holy places and places of tourist interest.

The new buildings of the Training School earned the envy of many important old departments which had comparatively poor accommodation. We also bought a vehicle for the school and had to recruit drivers. A large number of candidates presented themselves for the driving test. Most of them were ex-army drivers holding current driving licenses. I had arranged to hold the test in the parade-cum-football ground and found that practically all the drivers were unfit for recruitment. One driver drove the car against a goal post and uprooted it. I questioned the candidates and learnt that they had taken out a civilian license and kept it uptodate but had not driven a car since they left the Army. However, one civilian driver who was not an ex-Army man was found the best and was appointed.

I experienced another faux pas when I advertised for recruitment in watchmen's posts in the RPF and got hundreds of candidates turning up in the ground attached to the Head Office. I and two other officers feverishly worked to interview them but could not complete interviewing more than 25 per cent. We asked the rest to wait for the next advertisement but they became angry and created a riotous situation. I had to call the local police for assistance which I got quickly and peace was restored after dispersal of the crowd. I held two more interviews for recruitment but they were held in the Calcutta Maidan grounds where we took applications and photographs of candidates from amongst whom we could select those whom we considered fit for appointment and for undergoing training.

South Eastern Railway was prone to frequent small strikes by men, especially under a union leader named Biswas who had a strong hold on the railway men in Adra Section. I had a trying time to help the Administration to manage the situation. The Administration started depending more and more on me forgetting that as the CSO I had limited powers and capacity to solve such problems. I, however, had an unprecedented breakthrough when I succeeded in recruiting Biswas as my secret agent and he continued to give prior information about impending strike and troubles. He was never asked to help the Administration or to break a strike lest he lost his position of power and simultaneously we would lose a very valuable source of information. Once the President of All India Railway Workers Federation came and held confabulations secretly with the union leaders and I got all information and incorporated in the report submitted to the GM. In the report there was a plan of future action. When these plans were about to be carried out we took preventive measures as previously planned as a result of prior information received. GM, Kapoor, was highly pleased. He insisted on knowing my method of collecting secret information and this demand was not fair to an intelligence wing. He was so insistent, if not adamant, that I had to tell him on a firm and sacred assurance to forget about my information. He soon left and gave me an excellent report on my performance. Next GM was one A.K. Basu who was a saintly man and began to appreciate my service a great deal. The Railways were celebrating Railway Week every year and he made me the Chairman of the Railway Week Committee depriving Principal Heads of important departments like Operation, Commercial, Engineering, etc. I discharged the onerous duty successfully and the finale was held in a portion of the Eden Garden Stadium. To my regret A.K. Basu soon retired and one Sindhi gentleman named Mr G.P. Sahani became the GM. He was also a good man and appreciated my service. He was succeeded by one Wadhwa, the Chief Engineer of the railway who was my erstwhile colleague and promoted to be the GM in the same railway.

During my tenure in the Railway, the combined railway men's federation went on an all India strike. Before the strike call the Railway authorities chalked out an emergency scheme to protect railway bridges, workshops and other vital installations and to run a skeleton service with the officers. I was given the charge of distributing newly revised books containing the new emergency scheme and it was a Herculean task to make the copies ready, number them, put them in sealed envelopes and to distribute them by special messengers. The RPF men were forbidden by the RPF Act to be members of the railway men's union. As Prime Minister Nehru considered the strike unnecessary and harmful to national interest, the Union Government wrote to all the state governments to give all the help to the railways in their efforts to protect railway properties and loyal men from being forced to go on strike. In South Eastern Railway we took stern measures. The leaders organising the strike were summarily dismissed as per provision in the Railway Act and Rules of Service and were asked to vacate railway quarters occupied by them. With the RPF and the local police the employees and their families were forcibly evicted. This created great distress and the strikers on SER agreed to return to duty. I do not know what measures other railways took but soon the strike was called off and the leaders of the Railway unions agreed to sit with the government and the Railway Board for discussions for a settlement.

I was the seniormost CSO and hoped to be promoted to be the IG, RPF but sometimes later after my return to the parent state the choice fell on Shyam Sunder Aga, CSO Northern Railway, who being posted in Delhi was well acquainted with the Board Members as well as the then Railway Minister. I returned to West Bengal after Hiren Sarkar had left and Ghosh Choudhuri had taken over as the IG of Police. Ghosh Choudhuri got me confirmed in the rank of DIG of Police while I was still working in the railway. The period of my deputation to the Railway ended and I returned to serve in the West Bengal Police.

19

In Civil Administration

I was posted to Northern Range with headquarters in Jalpaiguri where I served as DIG of Police for the second time from 1961 to 1964. I came to be acquainted with a few British tea estate managers who were keen on hill river fishing mainly masheer in the hilly parts of the mountain rivers flowing from the snows of the Himalayas. While some fishing was practicable in the rivers Teesta, Jaldhaka, Raidak and Sankosh in Jalpaiguri and some rivers in the waters in the district of Darjeeling but those anglers who were keen to make large catches went out to Assam. A river named Manas was famous for masheer fishing and this river flowed from Bhutan into the district of Kamrup and into the Brahmaputra. Local inhabitants were known as Bodos. Experienced anglers were of the opinion that even a novice of an angler would not fail to catch fish. Accompanied by my wife I went with an English planter friend and his newly married wife in two cars to stay for a few days in a government forest bungalow on the bank of the river Manas. By reading some books including one well-known book titled *Circumventing the Masheer*, I had equipped myself with sophisticated fishing gear. I went out full of expectations of catching some fish every day. Both I and the planter's wife were both new to the game and both of us tried hard for several days but did not succeed in catching any fish. On the other hand at the same place, the planter who was an expert angler had been catching a number of fish every day weighing as much as 2 to 10 kg. It was customary to release small fish again into the river. The planter and his wife left but I decided to stay on for two more days. On the last day I was desperate to succeed in catching some fish or otherwise to abandon the idea altogether. Fortunately on the last day I caught a fish weighing 8 kg and another smaller fish and thus avoided great disappointment. Again I went to catch fish in the Manas with the Chief Engineer of North Eastern Frontier Railway and we succeeded in catching some fish but not as many as some other experienced anglers managed to do. This Manas was also a good game sanctuary where one could see elephants, tigers, leopards and wild buffaloes. I did not see any tiger but saw an elephant, a lone bull buffalo and as well as a herd of buffaloes. Actually the fishing season is in September and October as well as in February and March. A few months later my planter friend had been posted out to Tejpur, Assam and invited me to join in a fishing trip. Accompanied by my wife we became his guests and stayed for a couple of days. It was rainy season and the river was muddy and known to be unsuitable for fishing. This is so because in muddy water a masheer which feeds on smaller fish cannot see the bait, artificial or real and consequently does not take the bait to be hooked. My friend took his rubber *dinghi* and we drove to fish in the upper reaches of the river Bhoroli. Being an expert he taught me what method of angling one should adopt and what type of bait one should use in muddy water in rainy season. We adopted the method of slow trawling, or keeping the bait at rest at the bottom. With this help and guidance I did manage to catch a number of fish and both of us had quite a good day. Actually this masheer fishing is merely a sport. Fish is taken and killed and thrown away without eating because many of the non-Indian anglers did not eat fish nor did many Indians because masheer, although very tasty, was full of floating bones like in the Hilsa fish.

In Jalpaiguri on most occasions when I went out for inspection or supervision, I used to take out a gun or a rifle in the hope that I might come across some games to shoot. Once while I was inspecting a police station named Falakata by which flowed the river Jaldhaka, the O/C told me there were crocodiles in the river and if I wished I might try to shoot them. I readily agreed and hastened to go to the river. I saw some crocodiles which were not too far away. When I tried to manouvre and approach nearer, they disappeared in the water and I had no luck. On learning that crocodiles appeared and were seen very often I asked the O/C to inform me as soon as they appeared but the O/C later sent a message that the crocodiles had all gone away to East Pakistan. This he did to avoid another inspection by me. My inspections were somewhat thorough and brought out defects in running the *thana* or maintaining its registers and documents and the O/C tried to avoid such inspections conveniently.

During my second term of posting as DIG in Jalpaiguri I decided to attend the festival at the monastery at Gangtok held in winter and wrote to the *Dewan* who was one Baleswar Prasad, a senior IAS officer. He agreed to take me and my wife in as his guests and take us to the festival. His residence was on the ridge of a hill and was large enough to accommodate several guests. We attended the festival which was presided over by the old Maharaja of Sikkim. Maharaja also served luncheon to his guests. I remembered that on that occasion I spent the Christmas or New Year's day with the *Dewan* and we had a small celebration. The cold in mid-winter was not so furious so long as there was sunshine. On another occasion after the old Maharaja died, I went to Sikkim and I and my wife stayed as guests of the new Maharaja whose acquaintance we made in Darjeeling while he was a Prince.

During the Indo-China border war we were told that Chinese spies might infiltrate through hills, forests and mountains and we should arrange vigilance by the police in the border areas. After the border war was over I decided to go to Darjeeling-Sikkim border and took the Sandakpu–Phalut road. I halted in Phalut forest rest house which was at a height of 11,000 feet above the sea level. As it was the month of December water had frozen in the well which was the only source of water and we had to break the ice to get water from below the ice for drinking and cooking. I remember that we had fire during the whole night in all the rooms in which we stayed. Because of the cold we could hardly sleep. I did not allow my wife to accompany me. As Darjeeling district had borders with Nepal, Sikkim and Bhutan and infiltration had to be undertaken through hostile mountainous country and deep forest areas, the Chinese could take easier routes for the purpose of infiltration.

On another occasion during the summer months I paid a visit to Sandakpu and Phalut when Rhododendron trees were in full bloom. At the altitude of Darjeeling these trees grow up to be tall and large but in higher altitudes they become smaller and smaller till they become two feet tall shrubs full of beautiful flowers of variegated colours.

The most striking thing was a sense of nearness to the high mountains namely Kunchenjungha because there were no hills between Sandakphu range and the Kunchenjungha range and one felt as if one could stretch a hand out and touch the high mountains.

However the more interesting place to visit in this region was the adjoining state of Sikkim which provided a number of very interesting trekking tour paths dotted with bungalows for the tourists to halt and spend the night. The two rivers Rachen and Lachung have trekking foot paths running by their sides and the two paths meet at the Tibetan border where the trekker could take a different path to return to Gangtok, the capital of the state. Moreover one could see from there the third spur of Kunchenjungha which one could not see from any place in the district of Darjeeling. One could also see almost all the peaks of other high mountains like Siniolchu, Kinchinjhau, Chormiomo. Simod, Guicha Peak, Twin Peaks, Nepal Peak, Sugal Loaf. Tent Peak, Kabru, Taling Peak, Pandim which were all high peaks ranging from 21,000 to 27,000 ft. in height, Kunchenjungha was the world's biggest and most picturesque massif.

In the first early summer after the border war the new Maharaja decided to visit Nathu La along with the local general. I was invited to join and ours was a group consisting of the Maharaja, General Satarawala, GOC-in-C, myself and other army officers posted in Sikkim. We proceeded towards Nathu La. During my onward journey I saw several army vehicles which had fallen off the road which was still covered with snow and had become very slippery because snow solidified into ice due to pressure of wheels of running vehicles. While covering snow covered stretches on road, army drivers put chains on the front and rear wheels opposite the hillside so that the vehicles while driven will try to push away from the ravine. Many vehicles had become casualties and all had to be pulled out by crane. Most of the army drivers were not experienced enough to avoid accidents. I did not try to visit the other pass named Jelep La which served as another trade route from Sikkim into Tibet. At Nathu La I was asked not to take photographs but we saw Chinese soldiers just below us across the border. Unfortunately in Sikkim, the Tibetan plateau penetrated the Himalayas like a dagger in its heart at one place only, i.e. near Nathu La. During our return journey we halted at Chhangu Lake for lunch. There we tried to do some fishing. There were trout and other fish in the lake which was half frozen at that time and the Maharaja, Satarawala and I were only the three anglers. We tried trolling in separate motor boats. Satarawala alone caught one small trout but I did not catch any, nor did the Maharaja.

20

Border Skirmishes between India and China

As stated earlier on return to the state I got posted as the DIG of Police in Northern Range for the second time. Although I expected a posting in or near Calcutta, I did not object on account of my pleasant experience during my first posting in 1953–54. Actually I thoroughly enjoyed my 3 years' stay in North Bengal during this posting. As a matter of fact during my second tenure I refused twice my transfer out of North Bengal. I settled to my duties more peacefully as I knew I was not an officiating DIG of police. My tenure lasted from 1961 to 1964. I undertook regular inspections of the districts and subdivisions as per rules in the Police Regulations. These inspections had not been undertaken seriously for some years. I visited all the police stations in the districts of my Range and made part inspections. My regular inspections took quite a few days to complete. One SP enquired why I took so much pains. I told him that there were three reasons. First that I wanted the District Police to benefit from my inspection. Secondly I wanted to know fully how the District Administration with all its branches was functioning. Lastly I did not want to fail to detect any serious lacunae in the Administration so that the local officers did not feel that the DIG was a fool who got easily hoodwinked.

This time I found the roads much improved and all subdivisions except one or two were approachable by roads. I went to almost all important tea estates. Many managers were known to me since my previous tenure. As it always happens an old acquaintance graduates into a friend and frequent contacts make such friendship deep and lasting. The same held true with the prominent members of the public in the district. There were a few very successful *shikaris* amongst the European and Indian managers of tea gardens owned by European firms. Amongst the British planters there were also keen anglers who knew all about hill stream angling which was completely different from still-water fishing in tanks and small lakes. An Englishman manager got me a fibre glass rod and casting reels from the UK and another promised to take me to do angling in one of the best rivers in Assam.

Actually shooting tigers successfully is as much a matter of luck as good prior planning and organising a beat at a place known to have tigers. I cannot say I had much luck but then again I was inept too in one or two instances. As I had to take out a shooting license every time, I confined my efforts mostly outside the Government Reserve forest areas. As a matter of fact reports frequently came about a tiger killing domestic cattle and being found in a locality outside the Reserves to feast on the kill. First time on receiving report of a kill I and Rasiklal Dey went out on an elephant. I found the remnants of a cow left in the middle of a small stream and the tiger leaving the carcass and taking his stand on the other bank. On seeing us the tiger gave a low growl which made my cow elephant nervous and upset her and she started going back pushing me and my companion into a thorny bush. She was not steady at all and was most unsuitable for *shikar*. Still I took a quick shot which missed the tiger and it jumped off with a loud growl and disappeared into the bush. The elephant was so terrified that it nearly crushed us to death by pushing us on its back into a thorny bush. The *mahout* could hardly control her but when he succeeded in getting the elephant out of the tight position, the elephant nearly bolted to a place it considered safe. I am sorry to say it was a cow elephant belonging to the police department. The elephant bore the name 'Chanchal Piyari'. On another occasion I got information that a tiger was seen in a locality which had small jungle patches and bushes. We went to the place and the villagers pointed out a small bush in the midst of a plain ground dotted with scrubs. As the tiger had not been seen leaving the area, it was almost certain that it hid itself in the bush which was thick and also impenetrable even by an elephant. We beat about the edges of the bush but could not flush the tiger out. I ordered the *mahout* to make the elephant uproot a small branchless tree which was like a log and make the elephant thrust the log of wood into the bush. This was done for some time but we did not notice the tiger which went out but my companion Rasik pointed out that the tiger had managed to slip away when we were busy probing the bush with the log. The tiger was moving at a distance of 50 or 60 yards and it was risky to try to shoot it lest I wounded the beast. Moreover, its hind quarters lengthwise presented a poor target. On another occasion I learnt that three tigers had been seen and we went to the spot. As shooting from an elephant was much less convenient than from a stationary position, I decided to climb a tree. As I was stepping onto the fork of two stout branches from the elephant's back one tiger timed its flight and ran away. I was helpless but I was full of praise for the animal's intelligent observation. As all the animals had not left I took my position on the tree and asked the *Mahout* to take the elephant away. After some time I could see an animal creeping away through the wild grass. From the colour I was sure that it was a tiger and shot it. As soon as the shot was fired another tiger was seen to run away through the grass. I climbed onto the elephant and went to the dead animal which was found to be a half grown tiger cub. I should not have killed it. I felt sorry and knew that the bigger beast which ran away must have been the mother tigress. The second cub appeared and ran away but I did not shoot at it. We often roamed about in the jungle paths in the villages surrounding the town and found evidence of tigers roaming about at night and cleaning worms off their claws by scratching them on the barks of scores of trees. Actually these tigers remained in the tall grass jungle on the char and came out at night to roam in the villages or outskirts, partly to make a kill and partly to get out of a cloistered hiding place. It was well-nigh impossible to make them visible by means of beating the thick elephant grass jungles. We had undertaken beating parts of the grass jungle and could feel that some animals were occasionally moving away invisible to us. In short I did not succeed whereas one Donald Mackenzie, a planter Manager of a tea garden, was well-known for shooting many tigers successfully. Once he managed to shoot two tigers during a journey at night when he saw one tiger on one side of the road and another at some distance and managed to shoot and kill both of them.

Donald Mackenzie and others organised a shoot in a char area and tents were pitched for *shikars* for three days. I and my wife stayed in a tent and enjoyed food and camaraderie which grows rapidly in such occasions. Some pigs and does were shot. Although the area was outside the Reserve Forest, shooting a wild doe anywhere is an offence and the organisers were penalised by imposition of a fine by the Conservator of forests. Unfortunately I was mainly to blame as I had taken cine pictures every day and the Conservator of forest was present on one occasion when the cine picture was being projected on a screen saw the dead does on an elephant and decided to penalise the *shikar* party. We had taken cooks and plenty of food and meal time was pleasure even on the char. There was drinking and dinner parties round a big fire which scene was also photographed by me. On one occasion I took part in a hunt in a mountainous region in Darjeeling district. I could not shoot anything but a Nepali constable managed to shoot a thar, i.e. a mountain goat. On that occasion I and my wife paid a visit to Dr Sen and his famous writer wife Maitreyee Devi who was a favourite of Rabindra Nath Tagore who often stayed with them in the Cinchona plantation in Mungpu. We spent a night with the Sens and the night was very cold and we had to have log fire both in the sitting room and bed rooms.

The most important event during my stay was Indo-China border war which broke out in the month of October 1962. North Bengal was somewhat in the forward area although fighting was taking place in the Indo-China border between Tibet and North East Frontier districts of Kameng, Siang and Subansiri in Arunachal (formerly known as North Eastern Frontier States which were administered directly by the Governor of Assam with a Political Officer-in-Charge.) There had in the past been border intrusions by China into the Indian territory and Chinese soldiers killed our patrol men in the border within our territory and had once wiped out a post in the Western Himalayas killing all the policemen manning the post. Moreover, it was found that China had encroached upon and incorporated a large part of Indian territory of Aksai Chin claiming it to be China's own territory. As a matter of fact, the north-western border with China was not well demarcated, if demarcated at all nor was border vigilance exercised in these wild uninhabited harsh mountain areas with the result that India came to know of China's illegal occupation after China had occupied the territory and built a road to get easy access to Chinese Turkestan. When India and China had very friendly relations for more than a decade, India made the mistake of not sitting at a negotiating table to mark the Indo-China border on the basis of ground and aerial survey and the border could be demarcated by showing important land marks and hill and mountain peaks on an aerial map. When China became militarily strong and had an all powerful central government under the Communist Party, China claimed more territory for itself in some areas already held by India for many decades knowing that there was no treaty nor any map to show the boundary between the two countries. On the eastern border between Tibet and India of east of Bhutan, the British entered into a treaty declaring an imaginary line known as McMohan Line as the boundary but this line was not shown on any map, aerial or land, which would clearly show the line of boundary drawn along recognisable land marks as the actual McMohan Line. Actually it is an international convention to show the watershed in a mountainous territory to be the boundary between two independent countries but this was not acceptable to China. Moreover, China claimed that being a weak country in previous regimes, Great Britain, the strong ruler of neighbouring India, Nepal and Bhutan had forced China to sign the treaty, both sides accepting the McMohan Line as the boundary. China did not now recognise the Mc Mohan Line as the boundary between the two countries.

India was taken by surprise when China intruded into the eastern sector and occupied a large chunk of territory. India decided to fight China and drive her out by force without knowing the strength of the Chinese military machine and under-estimating the ground advantage in favour of China. China had large contingents of troops in Tibet which was a plateau at an average height of 14,000 to 16,000 feet above the sea level. The troops were well acclimatised to high altitude and more over firing artillery and mortar pieces from a higher terrain was easier and had a much longer range. India had mainly Assam Frontier Rifles, a well trained para-military regiment which was sent to meet the Chinese Army and was wiped out in the fight. Assam Rifles was not a match for a well-trained regular army unit and it was a folly to send them to fight the Chinese army. India hastily got troops from other regions in India but they were ill-equipped both physically as well as unit-wise. They had not been provided with good warm clothes nor were they supported by tanks and artillery which could not be taken up to the front due to absence of roads. The ground troops could travel by bridle paths and through jungles in which no large vehicles could move. The result was that Indian troops were overwhelmed by the Chinese and the former ran away from the front as there was no other way to escape slaughter. The Chinese came down to the neighbourhood of Assam plains but retreated on their own by declaring a self proclaimed armistice. The Chinese retreated towards the boundary but still remained a few miles along a very wide front inside India.

India then set out to organise proper army units with brigades, divisions and corps and posted suitable officers to act as the commanders of these units. The only route to Assam from the rest of India lay through a narrow strip of land between East Pakistan and Nepal and a railway and a road through the narrow strip ran and served as the only means of transport. This narrow strip could easily be occupied by Pakistan and prevent all surface transport between Indian mainland and Assam. The main rail station was Siliguri in the district of Darjeeling. I witnessed troop movements on their onward journey. Many men from regiments from South India were sent and they had no warm clothes at all. Most of the movements were undertaken by rail and there was one line in North Bengal and later bifurcated into two in Assam, one on the north side of the Brahmaputra river and the other on the south side. I also saw trains carrying troops returning from the front. During the onward journey the troops were found gay and jubilant. Soon we saw trainloads of wounded and incapacitated troops returning thoroughly dejected and demoralised. Many were injured and sick but the largest casualties were due to frost bite on account of lack of warm clothes. A special movement was started to knit woollen garments for the *jawans* but many suitable garments were not produced in the short time and by unskilled men and women.

In my range I had the headquarters of the 33 corps with Lt. General Harbaksh Singh as the corps Commander. All the corps were in the Eastern Command which had Lt. General L.P. Sen as the Eastern Army Commander. The 33 corps officers had to be in close touch with the Civil Administration to meet many of their requirements like acquiring land to stay in and set up tents and buildings, supply of water and electricity etc. Divisional Commissioner and myself were the two officers to act as the principal liaison officers between the army and the state government. India sent out an appeal for help to the international community and got very good response from the USA, the United Kingdom, Australia and New Zealand. Australia sent many good woollen blankets and jerseys for the troops and the USA agreed to give military support in case such support was needed. USSR which was not too friendly with its communist neighbour, i.e. China, also gave moral support. All this happened because China was still a closed communist country and was the 'betenoire' of the West. However the Indo-China border war was shortlived and ended with China remaining in occupation of a large territory which was long from east to west but not so much in depth. China also referred to old Chinese empire which extended southwards into India and made large territorial claims in Assam. The border dispute has not been settled as yet after 37 years and it is unlikely that it will ever be settled to India's satisfaction. India, however, failed to capitalise this international good will by aligning herself steadfastly with the Soviet Union (USSR) which did not do anything more than offering lip sympathy.

During the border war, there was an outburst of patriotic fervour all over the country. The government needed money and wanted the citizens to make voluntary contributions to the National Defence Fund. In the state of West Bengal camps were held by the Chief Minister and the Governor of West Bengal to collect donations of cash money, gold and silver jewellery and other gifts. Women made their personal contributions by handing over gold ornaments and jewellery. The whole thing was ill organised and public money should not have been collected in such irregular fashion. Thousands of crores of rupees were donated but I do not know what proportion reached the public exchequer. What government should have done was to print money receipts in duplicate in different denominations with numbers printed by the Reserve Bank of India and handed these over to the donors as receipts. RBI should have been empowered to keep account. There was no time to write or issue proper receipts because the donors were plentiful and were in undue haste to donate whatever they could. In some cases, hand written receipts were given to the donors but there were no office copies kept. Reserve Bank received the ornaments to evaluate and convert them into cash. Later government floated the National Defence Fund contributions to which were fully exempt from Income Tax.

This short war had an important fallout. China which was very friendly to India became a powerful enemy and also aligned itself with Pakistan which was always inimical to India. China has also encouraged Nepal to shake off India's partial control in any form or even any say in any matter in the form of advice by India to Nepal. China is also known to be encouraging Bhutan to take a similar stand. These countries know that with China's support they may act in any way convenient to them. We forgot that in Asia, China regarded India as its only competitor both for political hegemony as well as in the field of trade and industry. China has become a nuclear power having developed both the atom and hydrogen bombs and making them in sufficient numbers to dominate Asia. It has perhaps yet to develop the appropriate delivery mechanism to match those of the USA and USSR. Recent years have shown that China is fast becoming an economic giant and has a foreign trade surplus of several billion US dollars as against India having an adverse balance in foreign trade.

India took up road construction on the border under the specially constituted Border Road Organisation and also began to build bridges across the large and small rivers. Railway lines were extended and metre gauge lines were converted into broad gauge so as to increase their load carrying capacity to meet the needs of the Armed Forces as well as civilian needs of the several states in the north-east. In several strategic places new cantonments were built to station troops permanently. I, however, doubt if these measures will enable India to win a war against China except that she may not have to face an ignominious quick defeat as in 1962. But India's preparedness will perhaps act as a damper to Chinese misadventures in future. Building of border roads, including widening and improving existing roads and building new strong bridges across the many rivers in Bihar, West Bengal and Assam provided better logistics to the Armed Forces. These efforts involved a lot of expenditure and a large sum of money. The Divisional Commissioner, the Range DIG, District Magistrates and Superintendent of Police developed close friendly relationship with officers of the armed forces and there were social contact between the civilians and the Defence personnel.

The responsibility of this defeat and debacle and ignonimous defeat lay squarely on the shoulders of Prime Minister Nehru and his Defence Minister Krishna Menon. Nehru who was in charge of the Ministry of External Affairs considered himself as the leader of Asian countries and could not imagine any attack on the sacred soil of the country he ruled over. In Krishna Menon he found a good follower and sympathiser of his ideas. As the Defence Minister he ordered some of the Ordnance Factories in the country to stop manufacturing materials and equipments needed to fight a war or for use of the Defence Forces and personnel and instead of ordered that these factories should produce consumer goods and earn money. Secondly Nehru while on a visit to Ceylon was told about intrusion into India and replied that he would ask his Army to throw the Chinese out and thus the ill-equipped Indian Army launched their defensive action with disastrous results. In these circumstances, Nehru should have taken full blame on himself and offered to resign on the same principle as Nasser, the Egyptian President insisted on resigning later in 1967 after defeat in the six day war with Israel. Nehru did not do anything except sacking his Defence Minister and the Chief of the Army Staff General P.N. Kaul.

During my stay in Jalpaiguri I went twice to the Manas river in Kamrup district in Assam to do hill river fishing. I also did a lot of still water fishing in big and small tanks and jheels and had much success. Frequently I caught and brought large fish of the carp family namely Rohu, Katla and Mirgel and had to distribute much of the catch to neighbours. I also paid a flying visit to the Garo Hills over a weekend and managed to shoot a stag in the forest area which we feasted on. We made our base in the house of the brothers-in-law of Dr Sudhangsu Kiron Bose who accompanied me.

I got intimation from Upananda Mukherjee who had succeeded Ghose Choudhuri as IG of West Bengal that I had to move out as a new officer had been selected and appointed as the DIG of Police, Northern Range. Moreover, I had served 3 years at a stretch in one range and had to move out. I thought that before I moved out I would undertake a tour of Assam visiting all the districts I had not been to and especially the North East Frontier areas. I got a jeep station wagon of a friend and fitted it with a roof carrier and started with my wife, a cook and a police driver to act as a second driver. I induced the driver to take leave without pay and I paid his leave salary as I did not want him to waste his leave in my service.

We went to Guwahati and Dispur and then travelled further east. I visited the Assam Police Training College as well as the Kaziranga game sanctuary where I saw tigers, rhinos, elephants and herds of spotted dear. I did a lot of cine and still photography. I had taken some letters of introduction from the Head Office of two commercial houses in Calcutta which controlled a large number of tea gardens in Assam. The managers of the tea estates nearest to my likely places of halt were asked to have me and my wife as their guests and to look after our needs. In this way we had very comfortable journey and stay. We had occasions to stay as guests in two such tea estates and received excellent hospitality. One such tea estate was near Kaziranga game sanctuary and we stayed in the Manager's bungalow for three days and made several trips into the sanctuary. In the sanctuary we saw rhinos, a tiger, spotted deer and herds of elephants. I photographed all the animals except the tiger which ran away. One herd of elephants was extensively photographed. So were two rhinos who were mating while in water.

I also went to see the managers of oil exploration operation by the Oil and Natural Gas Commission in Duliajan area where the staff explained to me the modus operandi of such operations. I was also told why oil exploration was expensive. They explained that in spite of many apparently favourable conditions for locating oil bearing rocks, the engineers were successful in striking oil one in ten efforts after actual drilling in all the ten sites. The officers were mostly non-Assamese and this became a cause of grievance to a group of Assamese separatists who wanted to drive all non-Assamese officers out of the state. A few years later, several ONGC and IOC officers were kidnapped and released on ransom. A few were killed. Flow of oil by pipelines was also hindered and such acts continued. My destination was Imphal in Manipur state where the Chief Commissioner was one Baleswar Prasad, a senior IAS officer, who was to be my host during my few days stay. The CC arranged a trip for shooting game birds in a big stretch of water named Log Tak but I did not succeed in shooting any birds which always moved away beyond shot gun range.

I had chosen a time of the year when Manipur would be celebrating its famous Holi festival which was the most popular festival held all over the state. Main functions were held in the former king's palace spread over at least 3 days. There were special displays of dance, playing of the Mridanga and blowing of the conchshells. Unless one is present at these functions, one would not appreciate how much practice, tutoring and inherited experience lay behind those excellent performances. We were doused with colour on the Holi day. There were also special dance performance on the stage in the evenings. I have forgotten to mention that on our way to Manipur from the nearest rail head at Dimapur, we had to travel by road through Nagaland. We had to travel in a convoy of buses, trucks and cars which were escorted by several army vehicles under command of two officers and posses of army *jawan*s with firearms. The convoy was a long line of vehicles and a supervising party in a jeep car was occasionally patrolling the whole length of the convoy. This precaution was taken because Nagaland militants were attacking civil and military vehicles whenever they got a chance. Progress of the convoy was slow because the leading vehicle and the last vehicle had no radio communication and as a result the patrol vehicle in the rear had to travel the entire length of the convoy to find out if any vehicle had become disabled and could not move with the convoy and then go up to the front vehicle to inform that everything was allright and the convoy should move forward. We also had to stop when the down convoy moved from Imphal to Dimapur and crossed our convoy. We reached Manipur without any incident. I may also mention that some intrepid travellers went by solitary car in the firm belief that the militants knew their targets and would not attack an ordinary civilian passenger vehicle. We returned in a convoy in the same manner. On our way back evening fell and the convoy had to halt at Kohima, the district headquarters of Nagaland. On telephoning to SP he arranged for our stay in local Circuit House and also invited us to have dinner with him and this we did. During dinner the house lights were off due to a fuse blowing out. He was helpless and did not know what to do. I got a thin copper wire and fixed the fuse to great relief of the SP and his wife. During our night stay we heard intermittent rifle fire across the valley gorge and learnt that this was a daily occurrence when the army and the militants fired at targets which they believed to be militant hideouts and army locations. Most such firings were ineffective and involved the wastage of ammunition.

Our convoy ended at Dimapur, the nearest rail head for both Nagaland and Manipur. In Dimapur I called at the local army headquarters and found that a mountain division was in charge of the area. The highest ranking officer present during my visit was a Brigadier who turned out to be a cousin of a close friend of mine working in Burmah Shell regional office in Siliguri. He was very enthusiastic about me and my wife staying at Dimapur and enjoying the Army's hospitality. When I told him that we would be leaving next day, the Brigadier insisted on our joining the officers in dinner the same night. He came in a jeep car and took us to the officers' mess where we had dinner and drinks. As both I and my wife were teetotallers, there was not much drinking on our part.

From Dimapur we wanted to go into the northern territory of Assam which served as the gateway to all the divisions of Arunachal state. We crossed the Brahmaputra by ferry and landed at a place from where one could enter Kameng division. Kameng had become well-known as its capital was Bomdilla which was occupied by the Chinese during the Indo-China border war. A road had already been constructed upto Tawang which boasted of an important monastery. I had already taken out a permit to cross the inner line beyond which even an Indian citizen of the plains could not go without a special permit. I halted at a place before the hill road started. Next morning we set out along the hill road and were stopped at a place where a landslide had occurred and the road was being cleared by bulldozers. There was one huge boulder weighing nearly 50 tons or so which could not be moved by any bulldozer available there. A new strip of road had to be carved out before we could advance. In the late afternoon we reached Bomdilla and halted. I telephoned to the local Army Divisional Commander who was one Maj. Gen. Monty Palit whose father Col. Palit I had met twice in Ranchi when I had gone to the Senior Palit's house to see a domestically reared-up tiger cub which had become six months old and could easily kill a human being. General Palit invited me into his bunker which was a small room dug into the rocky hillside and buttressed with strong logs of wood driven into the ground. He offered tea and we had some discussions of mutual and official interest. We came down and halted at Itanagar which was the headquarters of Subansiri Division. From Itanagar we went upto 'Zero' quite far inside. En route I saw primitive jungles with its primitive inhabitants who lived by *jhum* (primitive form of cultivation, fishing and weaving). Government arranged to supply yarn which the tribal people wove into cloth both for wearing as lower and upper garments. In some instances I found that the yarns had not been dyed in fast colours and started losing colour when wet in rain or washing. This was a most unfortunate thing for the concerned government department to allow to happen. On our way to Zero, we had immense difficulties as the road was under construction. When nearing Zero where only bricks had been laid to serve as soling of the road, my jeep station wagon had a punctured tyre and we had to replace it in blinding rain. However, we reached Zero and rested in the Circuit House or by whatever name a good government rest house was available. Zero was in a flat plain with rice fields but one could see distant hills of almost all shapes and heights. There were not much evidence of Indo-China war as this town had no communicating road with Tibet. We returned to the plain and started for Along in Siang Division. Along was easily approachable and was situated in picturesque surroundings. The place was inhabited by Apa Tani people whose men and women looked fair and handsome. But the Apa Tani women disfigured their face by inserting cork in two holes on the soft lobes of the nose which gradually enlarged as new tight fitting corks were inserted which expanded on getting wet. It was a grotesque and crude way of beautifying one's face. In most instances the nostrils of the women got blocked and they became victims of nasal troubles and infection. After staying for two days during which I walked into the countryside and saw the Apa Tani villagers. The cattle were there but there was the ever present hybrid Goyal which was a progeny of a yak and a domestic cattle. This animal was considered a valuable property and played an important role in paying back debts or realising fines imposed or in a barter system. I tried to do some fishing in the clear water of the Siang river which was known to have plentiful of masheer but for want of live edible baits, i.e. small fish, I did not succeed. I had yet two more NEFA divisions to visit namely Lohit and Tirap/Teju, the capital of the Lohit division was approachable from Pasighat but Pasighat had to be reached from the south bank of the Brahmaputra by crossing the river.

I went back to Dibrugarh which was on the bank of the Brahmaputra and was a couple of feet above the water level of the mighty river. There were earthen embankments at many places to keep the water away but still this town was flooded first whenever water level rose in the Brahmaputra. There were a number of well-known tea estates beyond Dibrugarh some of which were owned by Brook Bond Tea Co. I went to some and saw the managers and discussed about production and law and order problems.

I tried to reach Pasighat, the gateway to Teju, but due to rise in the water level of the river Brahmaputra no ferry boat was plying. I abandoned the idea of going to Teju and turned my attention to visit Khongsha, the capital of Tirap Division. We reached Khongsha and halted. I saw the Dy. Commissioner and the Development Officer. The latter was a Bengalee gentleman who pleaded with me to exert my influence to get him out of NEFA. I told him that in the past young Britishers born and brought up in the UK and Ireland came and administered the territory at a distance of 6000 miles from their home country and in environments completely different from those which they enjoyed till they came to NEFA. Moreover, the climate was hot and humid and malaria, kala-azar, jaundice and cholera were the prevailing ailments they had to protect themselves against and sometimes unsuccessfully. As a matter of fact one Williams who was a friend and was with me in Sardah Training College got posted as a Political Officer in NEFA. He died of one of these ailments, most probably of Kala-azar. However, I told the Development officer that I would put in a word for his transfer if I got an opportunity to do so.

Tirap was inhabited by the most backward of the tribal people inhabiting NEFA but development activities were in progress. Inhabitants of Kameng division were Buddhists and had the best standard of living in the NEFA region. Unfortunately most men and women suffered from dormant non infective syphilis which they must have contracted from people of the plains. Inhabitants of other divisions were mostly animists and were gradually less progressive as one moved from the western divisions towards the east. Some of them had embraced Christianity and attended the local church service. They had remained outside the mainstream of Hinduism and the Indian civilisation as a whole. It was the short-sighted policy of Nehru government which forbade entry by Hindu missionaries and proselytisation into Hinduism. In later years India had to pay heavily for this folly and shortsightedness of the foolish liberalism of Nehru era. I may add that Mizoram, Nagaland and Manipur although more in the east were not parts of NEFA and their people were progressive and politically conscious.

From Dibrugarh I went to Digboi which was the head-quarters of Assam Oil Company whose products came from this area. Digboi was a nice small well set out and picturesque town where most people earned their livelihood from activities connected with the petroleum industry. One young man named Chanda, an Asstt. Manager in Digboi, took us around and gave us lunch. He also presented us with a small wax slab of pure Assam petroleum. He was the son of Anil Chanda who became a minister in West Bengal and Smt Rani Chanda who was in Shantiniketan and was a favourite of Gurudev Rabindranath. We met another Mrs Chanda who was the local MP and always won the election from her constituency. From Digboi we went on to Lido from where a new road had been built when the British troops under General Stilwell were planning to enter and recapture Burma from the Japanese. I went up to the border which was undemarcated and unguarded. I learnt that there was some border trade on a fixed day in the week when products of India and Burma changed hands on a barter system. Actually such trade was smuggled imports and exports but nobody cared nor did such small trading affect economy of either country. We returned to Sibsagar in Assam and eventually to Jalpaiguri from where I despatched my household goods to Calcutta.

Of the five districts in Northern Range Jalpaiguri and Darjeeling were the most interesting. Jalpaiguri had some forest areas, picturesque tea gardens and two wellknown 'Game sanctuaries' in Gorumara and Jaldapara with good forest bungalows for a comfortable stay. Gorumara had a high observation post near the bungalow from where one could see elephants, deer, pigs, leopards and occasionally tigers, who all came to a salt lick artificially provided by the Forest Department to bring wild animals within observers' view. I and my wife often went there as the place was enroute to other places of my official visit. We once saw a leopard chasing a pig. First the pig appeared and ran fast without stopping at the salt lick and we wondered why this unusual movement occurred and soon we discovered the reason when we saw a leopard stalking the pig.

Jaldapara was mostly famous for seeing rhinoceroses. For this purpose, elephants were provided by the Forest Department. One had to rise before dawn and set out when the mahouts who had acquired special skill and could trace the presence of the animal from footprints and dungs namely whether they were fresh or old and take the visitors to where the rhinoceros was likely to be found. We never failed in our attempt through the courtesy of the mahouts. Darjeeling was the most interesting of the five districts. It presents scenic views of river streams and rivers, small water falls and above all a grand view of the Kunchenjungha massif in which the world's highest mountain peaks are found in a cluster. One can also see the rising Sun on Kunchenjungha from the Tiger Hill. The rising Sun's rays first make the mountain top visible in grey which gradually changes to silver and later to golden colours. Moreover Darjeeling provided many picnic spots and trekking paths and trails.

I was not a trekker and never took long journeys by foot except in course of hunting big game. However I undertook journey to Sandakphu and Phalut in the summer of 1962 by a jeep car. My first halt was at Sandakphu which was the highest point in Darjeeling with an altitude of more than 14,000 ft. and was always cold and had snowfall every winter. The road to Phalut gradually sloped down with wild abundance everywhere of flowering plants like rhododendrons, primulax and meconopsis of many varieties growing flowers in wonderful shades of colours. There were rhododendrons everywhere bunded with thick bunches of flowers. What struck me was the gradual dwarfing of rhododendron and all other flowering and other plants. There were big trees in Darjeeling town with bunches of flowers and these trees gradually got smaller and smaller till they became dwarf plants of one foot and a half or at most two feet in height. But the sizes did not stand in the way of bearing flowers. Also the rhododendron flowers were seen in varied colours whereas in Darjeeling town the flowers were mostly red or pink.

The District Intelligence Branch officers were instructed to be on the alert. West Bengal had only a border with China through Sikkim and through Western Bhutan. Officers were scared to visit the mountain regions in Darjeeling due to extreme cold in December 1962 or January 1963.

21

In CID and Enforcement Branches—Meeting an Eminent Sculptor—Hunting and Fishing

I had in the meantime got my posting as DIG of Police, Central Range with my office in Bhabani Bhavan (formerly known as Anderson House) in Alipore. During my tour in Assam I received special attention and courtesy from all local senior police officers and wondered why it was so because I did not receive such attention on my earlier visits to the state in the past. When I joined my post in Calcutta I came to know the reason. My name had been recommended by IG Mukherjee of West Bengal to the central government for selection and appointment as IG of Police, Assam and this became known to the Assam officers. The proposal, however, fell through and an officer of Assam cadres was appointed. My service in the Central Range was uneventful and ended in a routine way.

At this time the post of DIG, IB and CID got bifurcated and I took over as DIG, Criminal Investigation Department as well as DIG, Central Enforcement Branch. This was a much coveted posting for me and I set to work to revise the CID manual and to write an Enforcement Branch Manual which did not exist till then. DIG, CID, had his offices in Bhavani Bhavan on the second floor, i.e. a floor above the office of DIG, Central Range. The Central Enforcement office was located in the top floor of a new ten storeyed building which I managed to rent and became the first occupant. Soon anti government activities in the state developed and tirades were carried on against the Congress government in the state headed by Prafulla Chandra Sen, who was known as Arambagh Gandhi for his successful Congress activities in 1942 and subsequent years till Independence was achieved. During the Chief Ministership of Bidhan Chandra Roy, Prafulla Sen was the Food and Relief Minister and he took over as the Chief Minister after Dr. Roy's death in 1962.

In 1964 Jawarlal Nehru died and Lal Bahadur Shastri took over as the Prime Minister of India. Actually Prafulla Sen's Chief Ministership lasted one full election term from 1962 to 1967 when the leftists combined with Bangla Congress, under Ajoy Kumar Mukherjee won majority in the State Assembly and formed the United Front government. The United Front government took over the reins of the state government after 1967 general elections when the Congress lost its majority. This change over did not take place smoothly. During the latter part of Prafulla Sen regime, there were widespread agitations in many parts of West Bengal and there were violent riots over food scarcity, its price and irregularities in public distribution system. There were riots in Basirhat in 24 Parganas and in Nadia. Although it was not my duty as the DIG, CID and EB to deal with riots, strikes and civil commotion, IG Mukherjee ordered me to go and deal with the more serious situations. The most serious development occurred in Krishnanagar, Nadia. The rioters could not be controlled by the local police who became demoralised under weak local leadership of the principal government officers of the district. The rioters went on a rampage and took control of the town and its surrounding and drove all local officials and most of the public to take shelter in their homes. Some government officers and Congress MLA's houses were attacked and burnt down. In short, civil administration ceased to function. IG sent me to deal with an unprecedented situation.

I left Calcutta with two platoons of the special armed police from the Armed Police Brigade in Barrackpore and reached Krishnanagar in the evening. I made my headquarters in the Local Circuit House where I posted adequate number of guards to protect my headquarters from being stormed. We got tents from the police lines and pitched them in the Circuit House compound to accommodate men who could not be accommodated in the police lines. That night my duty lay in visiting the houses of the senior officers like the DM, SP, their additional officers and the police lines. The police force was jittery and frightened in absence of a strong leadership. I got a curfew order proclaimed and curfew was clampd on the town. I sent out small contingents of policemen, some armed with rifles and some with *lathis* and gave order to enforce curfew strictly and to chase the curfew violator ruthlessly out of the streets and to force them to go indoors and to arrest the recalcitrants and send them to the local police station. A number of arrests were made but I was not keen on making arrests and later prosecution on a minor charge of violating an order u/s 144 Cr.P.C. I put more stress on using the *lathi* as a weapon and giving the arrested men, mostly youngsters a reasonably good beating and letting them go home. The whole night curfew continued and was strictly enforced. Curfew was extended the whole of the next day except for a couple of hours' ralaxation to enable people to go to bazar to make purchases, to call the doctor for treating patients, etc. I advised DM, SP and all district officers to open their offices on the 3rd day. I had to send two hourly messages to Calcutta in the first 24 hours and then four hourly messages truthfully describing the situation, the state of affairs and steps I had taken to restore civil administration. From the third day rioting stopped completely and curfew was lifted except from 7 p.m. to 7 a.m. so that policing could be easier and effective and searches could be carried on to arrest culprits whose identity became known to the police. Government seemed to be worried over the situation in spite of my assurance and a contingent of the army of the Calcutta Sub-Area arrived in Krishnanagar to help the police and civil administration. I was furious and sent wireless messages to the IG of Police and the Chief Secretary objecting to requisitioning of troops who were not necessary and had no work to do. I asked the Brigadier in charge to go back and he followed my advice. Next evening the Brigadier was back with his officers and *jawans* to aid the civil administration. On questioning I learnt that he was rebuked by his boss, the Divisioinal Commander of Bengal Area, who practically called him a fool and told him that he should not have come back, especially when there was nothing to do and the Army might have earned credit for helping to bring back normalcy in the Civil Administration. I had no arguments against this but advised the DM not to utilise the Army and he followed my advice. The Chief Secretary telephoned to me and asked me to allow the Army unit to be in Krishnanagar even if I did not need them and that in any event, presence of the Army would boost morale of the Police and Civil officers. The Army unit came and stayed for two days and left. Later I saw the Chief Secretary and explained to him that seeking help of the Armed forces in aid of the civil administration did not bring credit either to the state government or the Police Administration in the state.

A few days later the Chief Minister paid a visit and held a meeting with the senior officers and some leaders of the public. As I was not present I do not know details of discussions in the meeting but one subject was smuggling of rice out of the district of Nadia which caused scarcity and allowed price of rice soaring. In the meeting the Chief Minister rebuked several officers, especially the DM. This I learnt later when the DM came to see me in Calcutta and with tearful eyes told me the episode when he was rebuked and almost insulted by the CM in presence of his junior officers and several members of the public. DM requested me to intervene in the matter and to see that such an episode did not occur. I was flattered that the DM had come to me and not gone to the Divisional Commissioner or the Home Secretary for redress. I made an appointment with the CM and went in to see him. He asked me to sit down and enquired why I wanted to see him. I said that it was a confidential matter and wanted to speak to him alone. He asked the other officers to leave. I told him about DM's grief and grievance and added that as the CM he had every right to pull up his officers but he should have called the DM aside into a room and admonished him. CM's rebuke in public humiliated the DM who was the head of the district administration and was likely to make him less effective. CM did not at first agree with me and angrily said that an incompetent officer deserved the rebuke. I countered by saying that I agreed with him but it was not proper to humiliate him in public and lessen his effectiveness in running the district administration. Finally he agreed with my point of view and told me to convey his regrets to the DM which I did. Later some officers told me that the CM had told them that DG Bhattacharyya had mildly rebuked him. He said this in an indulgent tone but one senior police officer misunderstood and told me that I would pay heavily for my tenacity. I knew the CM and was least worried.

Episode about Acquaintance with Debiprasad Roy Chowdhury, Sculptor and Artist.

While working as DIG of Police, Central Range, an old friend of mine offered to take me to meet Debiprasad Roy Chowdhury, a famous sculptor and artist. I readily agreed and was actually delighted at the prospect of making his acquaintance. In my boyhood I was hearing about Debiprasad and his exploits in physical prowess. He was a resident of Sambhunath Pandit Street in Bhowanipur in which neighbourhood lived many Sikhs, especially of the driver class. I learnt that he was an expert flute player, body builder and wrestler and had an unusually strong physique in a big frame. In a small fight he had once lifted a Sikh over his head and hurled him on to the ground. Since then no Sikhs dared to pick up a quarrel or fight with him. I heard other stories of his drinking and smoking as well as unusual disposition to help Bengalee young men.

Accompanied by my friend I went to his house and found him doing some sketches. He was delighted to meet me and asked me to see him frequently and also take my wife along. I was introduced to his wife who was a slim elderly women who must have been handsome in her youth. I was offered some tea and sweets by the lady of the house who also urged me to take my wife along when I called again. I stayed for about half-an-hour and found Debiprasad to be a chain smoker of cigarettes of a somewhat cheap brand. He was lighting a cigarette taking two or three puffs and then extinguishing it in a bowl of sand. That day I did not enquire of him about his unusual behaviour. But a few weeks later when I saw him I enquired about his wasteful habit. He smiled and replied that he had heart problems and was forbidden to smoke. He could not do without a cigarette during his waking hours. He had adopted two means to reduce his smoking, namely make his own cigarette with tobacco in a cigarette paper, roll and seal it, then he would light this cigarette, take two or three puffs and throw it away. He repeated this process. Making a cigarette took time and reduced his actual smoking time. The other was to light a cheap brand of cigarettes, take a puff or two and extinguish it in the sand bowl. This process also reduced his actual smoking time. As I was a non-smoker, I was not in a position to advise him about how to stop smoking habit completely.

Next time I went I took my wife and Debiprasad and his wife were delighted to receive us. Mrs Roychoudhury took my wife to another room for conversation and I was left with the sculptor who was interested in hearing about some of my experiences in the police and I talked about some important events. But I was far more interested in the sculptor, his work and his varied experience in the field of painting and sculpture and as the Principal of Madras Art College.

As a first step he took both of us into his domestic art gallery where some of his paintings and sculptures were kept. There were paintings of two magnificent peacocks and beautifully sculptured bust and heads. One of the sculptures of a bust of his father was exceedingly well executed. The bust exuded strength and determination of the man it depicted. He told me an amusing story as recounted hereinafter. One rich Marwari businessman who visited his gallery wanted to buy the painting of the peacocks and enquired about the price. When told that price was Rs 10,000, the gentleman said that ten pairs live peacocks could be bought with that amount and there was no reason why he would pay such a large amount for still painting. On another day he took us into the studio attached to his residence and I found some half done sculptures. I enquired why I did not see he work on the group of statues of men and women of different states which was proposed to be set up in Delhi and learnt that the work was on a much larger scale and needed a larger studio. He had set up a new studio in a premise in Keyatala, South Calcutta and invited me to visit the studio and see how the big metal statues are made. He also requested my wife to give a few sittings to enable him to sculpt a bust of hers. She politely declined but never told me the reasons of her refusal in losing an opportunity to be a model for such a well-known sculptor. He was obviously disappointed and said that he would try to make the Bengalee woman's statue in the national group known as modern column keeping her in mind as a model. It is true that West Bengal was represented by a tall woman figure but I could not discern from a distance if her face at all resembled my wife's.

One day I went to Debiprasad's Keyatala studio and found that parts of several statues were there. He explained to me how the models are first made with good quality clay. A plaster cast is made on a part of the body. This plaster cast is segmented to the mould for molten bronze to be cast into. But before doing this another mould has to be made which will be a quarter inch smaller so that the two pieces when held together allow molted metal to be poured into to form a cast a quarter inch or so thick. The outer part is a replica of the original model. Different parts are all made in this fashion which are welded to form a rough statue and then chiesellled into proper shape and later smoothed out by applying an electric sander.

The process is elaborate, painstaking and expensive. Debiprasad told me that in advanced countries, metal is sprayed into the outer mould of plaster of paris and can be lifted out after the metal cools and hardens. Debiprasad was taking a lot of time in completing this group because Government of India failed to advance money as per schedule and he remained idle. The work was so expensive that he could not meet the expenses from his personal funds. As the sculptor had heart problems, he was afraid that he might not be able to complete the work during his lifetime. Fortunately he could do so but he died before he could set up the statues on the pedestal and display in the Capital. His four other masterpieces known to me are a smaller group depicting the march of patriots to hoist the tricolour flag on the Patna Secretariat building in 1942 in which several of the marchers got killed. This was known as Martyr column. The other is the Triumph of Labour in Madras which he executed while he worked as the Principal of Madras Art College. I do not remember if I saw this sculpture at any time during my several visits to Madras. Three other significant sculptures are the three statues that were of the Father of the Nation, Sir Ashutosh Mukherjee and Surendra Nath Banerjee, all set up in Calcutta.

When recounting tales of *shikar,* I had to refer to the Sunderbans in Khulna (now in Bangladesh) and 24 Parganas

(South). He confessed that he had visited many different forests far and wide but not the Sunderbans which he keenly wanted to visit. I promised to take him along in the government launch which I had at my disposal but unfortunately he died before I could carry out my promise.

Roy Choudhury's had one child only, a son, who was in New York and had taken training in oriental and western dancing. He was earning money by performing as an artiste with one or more dance groups who perform on the stage. When I was in the USA in 1973, I contacted him and wanted to meet him but he could not give any date or time for actual meeting and the contact ended in conversation over the telephone.

Debiprasad presented me with three valuable pencil sketches after framing them and these sketches adorn my sitting room and often remind me of the famous sculptor.

Lastly I think Debiprasad was not given recognition which was due to this master painter and sculptor, one of the Greats in modern India. In 1999 which was the year of his birth centenary, an exhibition of his paintings and sculptures was organised and seminars held in his honour.

I and my wife decided to visit Andamans and Nicobar group of islands and was joined by my brother-in-law, a Captain in the Indian Navy, who was also a keen angler. We took our equipments which had to be modified to some extent. At the end of the line, we had to attach a length of bare or plastic coated steel wire to which hooks were fitted. This was necessary as most sea fish had two rows of teeth with which they could snap a silk or nylon line and escape even after being hooked. Moreover, heavy load sinker had to be used to enable the line to go deeper in salty heavier sea water. We stayed in a comfortable bungalow of the owner of a plywood factory and industry whom I knew for many years. He was kind enough to let us use his bungalow as well as his motor boat. Actually the idea of going to the Andamans arose in a conference in Delhi where I met the then Superintendent of Police, Andamans and Nicobars one Mr Ohri who invited me to visit his territory. The Police had a beautiful sea going vessel but unfortunately this vessel was out of order during our visit and could not be used. We did some successful fishing in the dock area in Port Blair. In the dock area we did not catch any big fish. Then we took to trawling in the open sea while riding the motor boat. I did not succeed in catching any fish but my brother-in-law managed to catch a sea fish weighing about 6 kg. While on the trip into the open sea on our motor boat we had travelled many miles and saw huge sharks swimming in the clear blue water of the sea. Suddenly we realised that our boat had no wireless communication and as such it was unwise to remain in the open sea facing the risk of being stranded in case of a breakdown of the engine of the motor boat and decided to return to the camp much before dusk.

Andamans has many islands most of which are uninhabited but the main land is inhabited by Jarwas who lived in the jungles, could not be tamed to become civilised men and women and hated Indians of the main land whom they treated as foreigners. They also hated the British when they ruled the islands. The Superintendent of Police once arranged a party in a camp very much inside the forests where Jarwas lived. My brother-in-law and I set out in a small motor boat with an armed escort of several policemen with rifles. I had assured my wife that I would be able to come back by midnight. Unfortunately journey took a long time and after reaching the camp having feast with the policemen of the camp, I returned at about three o'clock in the morning. My anxious wife was still awake and awaiting my return from an area where one could get killed by Jarwas who used bows and deadly arrows.

There were many islands in Andamans Group which were connected by commercial steamer or motor boat service but frequency of the traffic was weekly or bi-weekly and I could not take advantage of visiting some of the islands where perhaps much better fishing was available.

In the Andaman main island we took the help of some fishermen who caught netful of sardines which we used as baits on the fishing line. It is a pity that there was no industry to can plentiful of sardines available in the Andamans. We get the supply of canned sardine fish mainly from Kerala. There was one peculiar thing about Andamans that it grew small coconut trees which bore many large bunches of coconut fruits which could maintain a coir industry. There was a government saw mill which was perhaps the largest in Asia. But the saw mill was running at a huge loss due to mismanagement. There was abundance of good timber wood available in the islands and these were being sawn and made into posts, planks and ply-boards but still the mill was running at a loss of about Rs 5 lakhs a year. I and my brother-in-law visited the saw mill and saw how elephants were being used to carry logs of wood from the forests which were inaccessible to any form of vehicular transport. We also watched how wood was being treated with heat and chemicals in boilers to kill the pests and to make good timber free from rot and other diseases when in actual use.

In 1967, I decided to try to do some fishing in the river Ramganga flowing through the famous game sanctuary known as Corbett Park. Accompanied by my wife, a cook and a driver I set out in my car and was joined by the French Vice Consul of Calcutta and his wife in the fishing expedition in the Corbett Park. In the river Ramganga which was shallow and clear we saw huge masheer fish swimming lazily but we could not make any of them to take our artificial baits, even when we held the baits very near to their mouth they would not take them. It seemed that the fish could see us and were also accustomed to eat live bait which we could not catch for want of a net nor procure them from any fishermen who were not allowed inside the Park. My friend, however, caught a large turtle and at first thought that he had caught a big fish but the fish at the end of the line would not fight. This absence of fight raised our suspicion that the fish caught was not masheer. My friend took half an hour to lift the turtle on the land. It was taken to our camp but it would always turn and walk towards the river. The local people who considered the turtle as sacred insisted on releasing the animal for which we had no use. We took it to the river and released it. It was a great pity that in clear water in shallow river we failed to catch fish although fish were plentiful. We went out into the forest on the back of two elephants and saw large herds of elephants and I photographed them. We did not see any tigers in two days' efforts. My friend and his wife had gone by rail and returned to Calcutta by rail.

I started on a journey to Bhopal where we stayed in the police mess. I knew the DIG of police, one P.C. Rai and he introduced me to the Superintendent of Police one Mr Qureshi who was a fine Muslim gentleman. He arranged for my stay in a forest bungalow and shooting in the forest area in the Chambal which was the scene of activities of Chambal dacoits. This area was full of large deep ravines which helped the dacoits to conceal themselves and elude the Police. During our stay in Bhopal, I received two messages, the first saying that my father-in-law was ill and the second saying that my wife should return to Calcutta. I arranged to drive my wife to Agra where she would get aboard a train to reach Calcutta. I decided to return by a car few days later. I allowed the driver to accompany her and kept the cook knowing that I could drive the car back to Calcutta but could not do the cooking for myself. Fortunately I agreed with my wife's decision to leave me and go back to see her ailing father whom she could see before he died soon after. I did not come to know of my father-in-law's death till I returned to Calcutta.

SP placed a jeep car for my use and a second jeep with six armed policemen as my personal guards both in the bungalow as well as whenever I went out for shooting. As I did not dare to walk on foot, I did not see many animals which ran away at the noise of the vehicles. I may mention here that the dacoits had declared a reward of a lakh of rupees on the SP's head who had been successfully tackling the dacoity menace. I advised him to take out an accident insurance policy which covers all unnatural deaths including death by murder or homicide from a General Insurance Company for a large amount by paying a small premium chargeable for such insurance. I did not shoot anything although deer and antelopes were available. On my return journey, I took the road south of the Grand Trunk Road marked as No. 7 route on the road map of India and drove at an average speed of 60 miles an hour without any hindrance. The road ran through some former native states in Madhya Pradesh and this journey gave me an opportunity to visit some interesting temples and forts many of which had beautiful architecture. I stayed in the circuit house of each district and the SP's were extremely helpful everywhere.

On my return to Calcutta, I learnt that my father-in-law had died a few days back. I went to Berhampore to attend the *Sradh* ceremony and for the first time in my life I suffered from a mild attack of heat stroke which caused cramps, headache and other discomforts. This occurred because I drove through very hot and dry climate during my motor journey from Shivpuri to Calcutta and I did not take any precautions against dehydration and possible attack of heat stroke.

While serving as DIG, CID, and Central Enforcement Branch I was asked by the Secretary to the Chief Minister Prafulla Ch. Sen, to accompany him to Kakdwip and Bakkhali. I alone joined him for the day and travelled in my car. Unfortunately on the outward journey, a cyclist and his companion riding on the road in front suddenly came in the way of my car and the person on the road got hit on the head by the handle of my car door in spite of the driver trying to avoid collision. I stopped and took the injured to the nearest hospital for treatment but later learnt that he died. This incident occurred because the cyclist and his co-rider tried to look back on the motorcade of the Chief Minister and in the process the cyclist lost his direction and the cycle veered and collided with my car. Beyond Kakdwip there was the area adjoining the sea and there was also a small sandy sea beach in the area known as Bakkhali which I understand the state government has been trying to build as a tourist centre.

In 1969 and 1970 Naxalites became very active in Calcutta and some districts in West Bengal, especially in Howrah, Nadia and 24 Parganas. This movement involved killing of innocent civilians, some police and civil officers, small landholders and businessmen. The movement was led by a political terrorist group called Communist Party of India (Marxist–Leninist) or CPI (ML) and owed allegiance to Communist leaders in China. The leaders in West Bengal were Charu Majumdar, Azizul Huque, Asim Chatterjee, Kanu Sanyal and Mahadev Mukherjee assisted by a few other fire brand youngsters. They wrote Marxist slogans on the walls and believed in destroying so-called bourgeois ideals by destroying and desecrating statues of national heroes like Ramkrishna Deb, Iswar Chandra Vidyasagar, Rabindra Nath Tagore, Swami Vivekananda. They wrote such slogans as 'China's Chairman is our Chairman', 'Power lies in the barrels of a gun' etc. It was not understood why they killed an eminent revered Forward Bloc leader like

Hemanta Basu, an innocent Addl. District Judge and dozens of policemen of lower ranks. Strangely enough, this despicable movement attracted young men and women of good affluent families who became misguided, neglected their studies and indulged or assisted in killing innocent people. The menace was so sporadic and manifested itself in such unexpected quarters that the police were at a loss to devise ways and means to tackle successfully. Armed police guards had to be provided to officials, legislators and policemen, policemen of all ranks were repeatedly warned not to take any risks or to give a chance of being attacked and injured or killed. The shortcoming in the police measures was lack of intelligence as to the identity of those who operated and those who were being freshly recruited. CPI (ML) became sworn enemies of the party workers of the established communist parties, especially CPI (Marxist) and workers of the party missed no opportunity to attack or kill members of the other party. In West Bengal, Congress Party failed to win majority in the election of 1967 and failed to form the government. The state government was formed by a hastily formed coalition of Bangla Congress headed by Ajay Kumar Mukherjee and Communist Party (Marxist) led by Jyoti Basu and several small groups of political parties who joined the front known as the United Front. Ajay Mukherjee became the Chief Minister and Jyoti Basu an important member of the Government and other well-known leaders of CPI (M) and CPI became ministers. They were Biswanath Mukherjee of CPI, Hare Krishna Konger of CPI (M) and Subodh Banerjee of SUCI (Socialist Unity Centre of India). This conglomerate could not work together and the government failed to rule. It was dismissed and President's Rule was imposed but the legislature was kept in a state of suspended animation. After some time another government of the United Front was formed again with Ajay Mukherjee as the Chief Minister and Jyoti Basu as the Dy. Chief Minister in charge of Home portfolio. This combination was impractical because Ajay Mukherjee had been a staunch Congressite and Jyoti Basu, Harekrishna Konger and Biswanath Mukherjee were staunch communists who held every thing that the Congress stood for in contempt. The second government came to a standstill and was again dismissed and the legislature was dissolved this time. The President's rule was imposed again for the second time in a short span of time. This rule continued till the next election in 1972 when the Congress Party came into power with Siddhartha Sankar Roy as the Chief Minister. It is widely claimed that the 1972 election was largely rigged under official patronage. This allegation is likely to be true because Congress did not win any of the five elections held in later years.

To tackle the menace of Naxalite outrages, a second post of Addl. IG was created and I was appointed to hold the post. It is imperative to mention that the Naxalite movement took its name from the agitation of landless farmers and labourers who launched a movement in Naxalbari, a village in the Police Station named Naxalbari in Siliguri sub-division in the district of Darjeeling. The movement involved attack on big farmers and burning their houses and granaries so as to frighten and drive them out of the territory. The movement was, however, tackled successfully and suppressed but those who took part called themselves communists of the Naxalite group.

In the meantime Naxalite outrages continued and killing of policemen created panic and discontent amongst the police force. A number of police officers got killed in Krishnanagar town and neighbouring areas and that was due to carelessness and foolhardiness on the part of the subordinate officers who thought that they had done no harm to the Naxalites or for that matter to any political activities and believed that the terrorists would not harm them. They forgot that the terrorists were out to demoralise the police force and the administration would adopt any means to achieve their end. Moreover, by making the police partly ineffective they would weaken or break the right arm of the state government. In theory they were right but an administration cannot be brought to a standstill by sporadic violence.

In Krishnanagar, Nadia these killings had incensed the policemen who revolted and decided to avenge death of their comrades by attacking the public and looting shops and houses of the public as if members of the public at large were to blame. They had threatened the armed sentries and taken out dozens of rifles and hundreds of ammunition to arm themselves with deadly weapons. The public shut themselves up in their houses and so did the officers who appealed to their own house guards not to join the rebels. Again I was saddled with the work and responsibility to tackle the police revolt, although there were the Range DIG, DIG IB and the other Addl. IG of Police. When I was given the order to go to Krishnanagar and to restore order it was late in the afternoon. I took two platoons of special armed police of the Brigade and one platoon of the Eastern Frontier Rifles and started in a number of vehicles. It was a longish convoy. As it was drizzling, our progress was slow. The latest news from Krishnanagar said that the rebel policemen had armed themselves and were roaming about in the town looting merchandise and setting fire to some shops and huts. When I started I was apprehensive that on reaching the town I would find policemen marauding and would have to shoot many of them to quel the revolt and to put the force back in their barracks. This would involve killing of policemen by their own comrades and in the process I started thinking seriously what to do. I, however, thought of an off chance strategy which might succeed. There was no proper SP and the Addl. SP was holding charge. I took one S.K. Singh, an IPS officer, who was a former SP of Nadia, with me besides Armed Inspectors and Sub Inspectors. All the officers and men has been warned against the risk of being shot at and getting killed if we had to take the offensive and resort to shooting the rebels or even to threaten them with shooting.

On reaching Shantipur PS about 12 miles before reaching Krishnanagar I took the first step to put my plan into action. I found the O/C of the Police Station to be in his office room. I saw him and enquired if there was any trouble in his area and learnt that there was none but he and his officers were being vigilant so that trouble did not spread from Krishnanagar to Shantipur. I asked all others except the O/C to leave the room and took O/C alone in confidence. I told him about my plan that he would telephone to the Armed Inspector and O/C Krishnanagar PS and the town outposts and inform them that the Addl. IG of Police accompanied by a large contingent of the Special Armed Force of Barrackpore and EFR who were carrying Sten and Thomson guns were proceeding to Krishnanagar by road to quell police rebellion. He had been warned not to communicate anything to Krishnanagar because it was intended to teach the rebels a severe lesson. But as a brother officer and one belonging to the district force he did not want mishap to befall any of his colleagues. His advice was to inform all those who were roaming outside in the town to return all weapons into the armoury and to return to barracks and go to sleep so that the Addl. IG would have no reasons to take action on the spot or even in a subsequent departmental enquiry. I waited for an hour at Shantipur to give the rebels sufficient time to act as per advice of the O/C and then proceeded. On reaching Krishnanagar in the early morning hours I found the town quiet and there was not one police men out, i.e. even town patrols had been withdrawn. On reaching the Police Lines, my first task was to replace District Police guards at the armoury, ammunition depot and treasury and later the guards in DM and SP's residence with EFR men I had taken with me. I asked those who were replaced not to worry but asked them to go to the barracks and sleep. There was no resistance. I then went round the barracks in the Police lines, thana, TOP's and found all constables and head constables lying on their cots but most of them were pretending to be in deep sleep as my visit accompanied by the Armed Inspector and a number of men with stenguns and rifles failed to wake them up. I was highly satisfied at the success of my strategy. I told the Addl. SP and Armed Inspector and the Circle Inspector to inform all policemen not on guard duty to be present at a meeting to be held the next day in the police line.

Accompanied by S.K. Singh, the former SP, Addl. SP and others I went to the Police Lines and presided over the meeting. I told the audience that I would speak first and then would give a chance to all who wanted to speak. I started by asking them to stand up and observe two minutes silence in memory of our comrades who had been killed by the terrorists. After this I opened my speech by expressing my genuine sorrow and sympathy for all those who had been killed or wounded and advised them not to be careless for even a minute when they are out of the police precincts. I dwelt on the hazards of police duties and helplessness of the authorities to give them full protection against sporadic stray terrorist attacks. I tried to convince them of the inherent risks men in police service faced almost on the same lines as personnel in the armed forces.

The remedy lay in helping the Administration in all manner to face the challenge of the terrorists and this challenge could not be met successfully if we antagonised the public. After all it is the public who paid for and maintained us and they had every right to demand discipline and dutifulness on part of the police force. I also cited results of police revolt in other states where the BSF and units of the Defence forces had been called in with disastrous consequences namely scores of policemen getting killed in the armed encounters. I spoke for about an hour and it was an inspired speech. After I ended I called for speakers from amongst the force who did not agree with any idea of mine or any part of my speech. None came forward and most people left with down cast eyes and the meeting was a unique triumph in the cause of police training, police morale and discipline. I stayed for 3 days to bring normalcy in the police administration and left Krishnanagar with great satisfaction that I did not have to take any brutal measures to quell a serious disturbance.

In headquarters I had to issue several orders about how policemen should conduct themselves, how the *thana* and district police and Intelligence Branch must organise and take preventive steps as well as to take measures to detect and to identify the terrorist culprits. Gradually intelligence work succeeded and we managed to find out identity of the leaders and activists and their hideouts and made successful raids and arrests. In Calcutta there were several killing of Naxalite terrorists by the police in encounters. The public claimed that the encounters were fake and were staged to kill the terrorists but the Police claimed that they were genuine encounters. However, in killing a terrorist instead of trying hard to arrest him, the risk lay in the fact that new recruits and novices got trapped and killed. There were allegations of torture of relatives of known terrorists who could not be trapped and arrested or killed. A famous case was a complaint lodged by one Smt Archana Guha whose complaint was taken up by a court of law after she fought a long drawn out battle with the police and the government for nearly two decades. One evening one probationer ASP telephoned to me saying that a hardcore Naxalite had been captured and sought my permission to kill him as if in an encounter. I did not permit his killing as the terrorist had already been arrested. There was another man named Saha, a so-called member of CPI (M) who was a *goonda,* a rapist and a terror to the public at large in Belghoria area. He always moved about with a fully loaded stengun and a loaded spare magazine and behaved like a despot in the region of Belghoria and Sodepur. He had been arrested several times but could not be convicted after trial as the victims did not dare give evidence in court. One day I learnt of an incident of extreme outrage. He had gone to the house of a widow who was living with her nearly adult son and a grown up daughter. Saha asked the brother and the mother to send the girl to him for enjoyment. The son gave information to the PS which recorded the incident in the general diary but the PS officers usually did not take any action as no criminal offence was committed. They could certainly take preventive steps to protect the family. However, Saha came to know of the report at the PS and two days later he and his gang picked up the girl and her brother. The next morning the girl was found raped and abandoned while her brother was found killed and left on the railway track. People in the area became stunned and would not make any protest. The girl and her mother told the police that Saha and his gang had kidnapped her son and daughter the previous evening. I went to the widow's house and assured her of avenging her son's death and daughter's dishonour. While a case of kidnapping, murder and rape was registered, I ordered the local police not to rest till Saha was arrested and I also told them not to arrest Saha but to kill him when found because police would not get any independent witness to prove Saha's guilt. It was easier said than done. I asked one Durga Ghosh, the local SDPO, to head the team to search for and find Saha. The first month passed but Saha could not be arrested nor trapped. When the second month passed, I was furious and getting somewhat despondent. Durga Ghosh was the only officer in West Bengal who got promoted to be an Inspector of Police without passing the departmental promotional examination because of my vigorous efforts and my strong recommendations. He was a first class executive officer but was not intelligent or studious enough to pass the departmental examination as narrated earlier. He later got promoted to be a Dy. SP and was holding the post of SDPO Belghoria. I reminded Durga Ghosh of the debt he owed me for not spending his service life in the Sub-inspector's rank and I demanded repayment of the debt by arresting or trapping Saha. He renewed his efforts with greater vigour and one evening he telephoned to me that Saha was located in a house which was surrounded by the police but he escaped from the house by jumping into an adjacent tank with a stengun in his hand. The police had surrounded the tank and there was no escape for Saha. He could be arrested although trying to arrest him was somewhat risky as he had a stengun in his hand. I ordered Durga Ghosh to shoot him dead instead of risking life or limbs of any of his men. Saha was killed and his bleeding corpse was pulled out of the tank. Hundreds of his neighbours came to see the dead body and they could not believe that the most dreaded criminal has been disposed of to their great relief. This was the only dubious case where I did not want to arrest a criminal who would not be convicted and sent to jail but would terrorise the society for all the years he would live.

Upananda retired and Sachindra Mohan Ghosh took over as IG and I continued to be his Addl. IG in a permanent post after Maswood, the permanent incumbent, had retired. There was a gap of two months between my giving up the temporary Addl. IG's post and taking up the permanent post.

During my stay in Calcutta once my friend Capt. Mohanty brought Hare Krishna Mahatab a former Chief Minister of Orissa to my residence. I felt greatly honoured and flattered by his visit. Also Biju Patnaik who later became Chief Minister of Orissa became a close friend of mine. He owned three or four Dakota aeroplanes and ran a small airline between Calcutta and Bagdogra mainly to serve as cargo carrier. I and my wife travelled by Patnaik's plane to go to Jalpaiguri. While serving as DIG in Jalpaiguri I had a distinguished visitor in the person of one Thai Royal Prince named Prince Chalerempol who stayed with us for a couple of days and enjoyed our hospitality. In return he invited me to go to Bangkok and stay with him. During this period once General Cariappa came to Jalpaiguri after his retirement. I paid a courtesy call and reminded him of the episode of his visit to the India-Pak border in 1949. I also invited him for dinner which he graciously accepted. He was staying in the local Circuit house and I sent the car to fetch him. He came in time and was received by me and my wife whom I introduced. He was immaculately dressed in dinner suit. We had some drinks and later dinner. After dinner he smoked cigarettes and so did I. General Cariappa was a perfect gentleman in private. He offered a cigarette to my wife but she politely refused saying that she did not smoke. He enquired if she never smoked not even in the privacy of a bed room or bathroom. I told him about visit to Coorg which was his native place. I related to him to the story of a devout Hindu lady marrying off her polio crippled daughter to a Muslim IPS officer and her staying in the son-in-law's house in her Hindu way with idols of Hindu Gods and Goddesses. He was immensely pleased and said that this example should be imitated by all right thinking citizens of India.

22

Intelligence Branches, Border Security and Indo-Tibetan Border Forces

When I entered service District Intelligence Branches which were started and mainly maintained in the state by the British under the Intelligence Branch, West Bengal, could not be said to have been well organised. The main source of Intelligence was to get information from people who were in the confidence of well known political parties and also intercepting and opening letters addressed to important political persons. There was hardly any direct activity by the officers of the Intelligence Branch who penetrated into political parties and got direct information. The state Intelligence Branch also worked more or less on the same line and was not, in my opinion, adequately equipped to intercept radio messages. Telephone messages were, however, tapped and recorded as I have already stated when dealing with the work of the Security Control Office in Calcutta. There was, however, a good network of Intelligence gathering persons who were in the pay roll of the District Intelligence Branches and were also rewarded for successful gathering of important information. During the Second World War intelligence work consisted of and included a lot of electronic gadgets to gather information. Intelligence gathering was done by interprid people who penetrated enemy lines or were dropped into enemy territories and managed to gather intelligence by observation and contact with local people hostile to the regime. Both warring sides managed to penetrate into the others territories and organisations. Many of these people were caught, tortured and put to death. This, however, did not happen in India till India and Pakistan became sworn enemies and fought a few wars. It was a risky job but people did come forward for the sake of their country and risk their lives. Some countries had great foresight and recruited would-be intelligence officers in peace time who later rose to important positions in government and industries of their country. Soviet Russia was more successful than others because an appreciable percentage of students and bright young people in the Western countries especially colleges and universities were communist minded and were ready to help the country which first ushered in communism in the world. Sometime intelligence gathering was done by persons, i.e. so called 'spies' who were won over by the Intelligence agencies of the country against whom they were supposed to operate and supplied false information to their original employer but the most damaging work they did was to expose identities of other comrades working in the territory. There was also Intelligence Bureau working under Government of India, Home Department and later the Home Ministry of the Union government and their job was mainly political and to keep tab over the activities of political leaders including ministers of the state and union governments and even high officials who were suspected because of their anti-state or anti-central government attitudes.

After the Second World War and after India became independent, work of the Intelligence Bureau of the central government improved vastly because of the pressing needs of the country to organise intelligence against Pakistan and China. Although a satellite had not come into existence and was not available to India till she built her own, some friendly countries like Soviet Russia might have supplied useful intelligence through observation by their own satellite. In the central government a new wing of the Intelligence Branch had been formed mainly for the protection of some very important persons like the President, the Prime Minister and also for collecting foreign intelligence on the same lines as MI5 of the United Kingdom. Having never worked in the Intelligence Wing of Government of India I am not in a position to comment on different aspects of police intelligence work. There was no doubt that we were much behind the developed countries. One thing I can say that even a simple gadget like a lie detector or psychological stress analysis machine was not available either in the state intelligence office or the branch of the central intelligence bureau located in Calcutta even in recent past.

Border Security Force was a newly formed force organised quite a few years after partition of India and was organised to entrust the force with the duties of protecting the border between India and Pakistan both in the east and the west. The force was deployed to stop cross border intrusion by people, stop smuggling of goods and cattle as well as incursion by criminals coming to or going out to commit dacoity and robbery from one territory into the other. The work of organising the force was entrusted to one K.F. Rustamji who did an exceptionally excellent job of organising a new force from scratch drafting the BSF Act and Rules thereon and developed a very efficient force and organisation which no other officer I had known could succeed in doing. In the first few years when Rustamji was incharge, the force worked admirably and succeeded in achieving objects for which they had been organised. It was Rustamji's imagination and wisdom which helped the force to acquire planes, helicopters, speed boats, wireless and radio sets so that the men working in the border did not lack any material help to perform their duties well and successfully. In later years the force was deployed to do many jobs other than protecting the border, namely, controlling internal riots and disturbances, dealing with mutiny in police forces in some states, controlling insurgency in some border states in the north-eastern region of India, which jobs must have been repulsive to the officers of the force and also lowered their morale to some extent. Besides they also lost part of the good will and respect of the other police forces in which mutiny was dealt by the BSF with a strong hand. In many instances fire arms were used by both the mutinous police and the BSF, both parties suffering casualties but such casualities were much higher amongst the mutinous police forces. In later years corruption crept in many BSF camps and they started taking illegal gratification, i.e. bribes to allow egress and ingress of people without passports and visas and turned a blind eye on large scale smuggling across the border.

On the same lines another force namely, Indo-Tibetan Border Force was organised to guard the border between India and Tibet which was taken over by China to make it a part of the Chinese territory and to establish Chinese suzerainty firmly. Life in this organisation was hard because of the terrain and environment and also full of risks but those who volunteered seldom failed in their duty and often sacrificed their lives and limbs in performing their duties. There were many incursions by China who were better equipped and often killed personnel of the Indo-Tibetan Border Force or even wiped out some camps manned by the force. Not having served in the force I am not competent to make more comments on their performance.

23

Big Game Hunting

During the leave period I decided to go on a hunting trip to Garo Hills to shoot elephants. On the eve of departure by road, I was getting ready to leave early next morning in my Fiat car when the French Consul one Marcel Bouyat who had been a friend of mine since 1947 telephoned to me to say that some burglars had entered the residence of the French Consul General on New Road, Alipore, and wounded the Consul General, his wife and his son and managed to escape. As I was residing in the neighbourhood he asked for my help to arrange medical treatment of the injured and also for police help. I telephoned to Dr Gokhale, a retired Chief Medical Officer of the Eastern Railway whom I knew and who was residing on New Road and asked for his help. I also telephoned to the Alipore Police Station and informed O/C to go to the house of occurrence and also call an ambulance to take the injured to the hospital or a nursing home. I picked up Dr Gokhale and went into the CG's house. The private durwans were there. I and Dr Gokhale went upto the first floor and found the Consul General badly injured and his son slightly injured but both were conscious. Unfortunately the Consul's wife had died of the wounds inflicted. The son told us the story of the incident. After he and his parents had retired for the night, his father sensed the presence of an intruder below his wife's bedstead. He switched on the light and peering below saw a stranger and asked him to come out. When the man came out, the CG tried to catch and detain him when the man attacked the CG with a big dagger. On seeing the intruder attacking her husband, the wife tried to grapple with the man and got fatally injured. Both shouted for help when their son who was sleeping in an adjoining room came out with a sword with which he attacked the man but the sword which was more decorative than useful caused superficial wounds on the man who escaped after attacking and wounding the son slightly. The police came with the ambulance and removed the CG to a nursing home but the son refused to go as his wounds were superficial and volunteered to stay to help in police investigation. Dr Gokhale administered first aid to the injured and bandaged the wounds. I waited till day break when the police and I looked for clues and found a faint trail of blood along the route by which the culprit escaped. It was seen that he crossed the compound, scaled over the boundary wall away from the main gate and escaped. After giving instructions to the police and assurance to the son and my friend Marcel Bouyat of doing everything we could do to detect the lady's killer, I left.

Accompanied by my wife I left for Assam about 5 hours late. After reaching Cooch Behar next day, I swapped my Fiat car with a Jeep car and a trailer belonging to a Christian missionary institution whose officers I knew. After reaching Tura, capital city of Garo Hills, I called on the DC, SP and the DFO and told them about details of my excursion and plans to shoot elephants and sought their help. I also called on the Chief Minister of Meghalaya, Capt. William Sangma who was camping in Tura. He was a native of Garo Hills. He received me cordially and enquired of police work in West Bengal and what had brought me to the Garo Hills. I replied that I was almost in love with the Garo Hills where I had come five times in the past beginning from 1937. I told him that I had come to do shooting of pigs and tusker elephants. He wished me luck and asked me not to kill too many animals, etc. After I got a license from the DFO I set out for a known place named Baghmara in the south east corner of the district near which was some well-known elephant country. In Tura I picked up a *shikari*-cum-guide to accompany me and went to Baghmara where the O/C told us about the area where elephants had been seen and explained to the guide. Leaving my wife in the Forest Rest house I and the *shikari* travelled into deep jungles all of which were, however, dotted with villages inhabited by the Garos. We spent a night in the house of a Garo village chief. There was awful smell but we managed to sleep on bare mats. Next morning, the villagers gave me exact location where elephants had been seen and we drove to those places. We walked a few miles in each area and could get evidence of elephants' presence just a shortwhile ago from warm dungs and clear foot prints. The elephants were however, moving away on getting scent of human approach. We failed to see any elephant during the day. The Garo guides promised to take us to some tuber potato fields at night which had been harvested but elephants still came to search for any tubers left behind. After having dinner we went on foot to these areas and sure enough there were a herd of elephants whose dim shapes could be seen in the powerful search light I operated on a 6 volt motor cycle battery. On our flashing the lights, some male elephants gave out loud trumpetings of warning. The sound was so deep and rumbling that it frightened me and my companions. The driver who had no knowledge about big game hunting urged me to advance and kill an elephant or two. As there were many elephants, it was too risky to approach and go into the herd and to shoot any. By the strong light of my focussing lamp we could see one elephant at a time but could not see where the other elephants were or what they were doing. If I approached I could be surrounded by several elephants and get killed. It was certainly not prudent to go into the herd to shoot at an elephant at night unless one was riding a strong elephant on the perch of which one would be almost safe especially when one could not see the position of other elephants near him. After hearing the blood curdling trumpeting of the tusker elephants we returned to the forest rest house after dropping the villagers near their home. I abandoned the idea of shooting an elephant at night. We continued our search for elephants during daylight hours but failed. Although I had been walking 4 miles everyday for a month in Calcutta before embarking on the *shikar* expedition but walking up and down hill sides brought new body muscles into play and I developed severe body pain nearing cramps. I had to rest for two days and take healing medicines before I could walk again. The driver was very greedy and wanted to eat meat of any animal I would shoot. There were hoolcks all over and we heard their cries from far and wide. One could also see them on distant trees. I saw one in a nearby tree, shot and killed it. The Garos would not eat its meat but my driver took a portion and cooked the meat. He told me that it was bitter and awful. Later we went to a plateau where we could see a number of chital deer and I shot two stags with my rifle fitted with telescopic sight. The men in the camp relished venison and the driver gorged himself in delight. My cook had become an expert in preparing *kababs* which he did over charcoal fire. My cook was one who could find food materials in all odd and unlikely places and he procured large quantities of milk to cook delicious rice pudding.

During this trip I learnt that elephant trapping was taking place in a nearby jungle. There are three methods of elephant trapping. The most common is by kheda operation in which a strong wooden enclosure is made and a gradually widening path is built from the gate of kheda into the jungle. There is a platform built round the kheda where from elephants trying to break through the wooden fencing are driven back away from the fencing. A herd of elephants is located and several dozens of beaters drive the herd into the path leading to the gate of the enclosure. When a few elephants enter the enclosure, the gate is closed by dropping a ladder like barrier built with logs falling in between strong posts. Some elephants get away from near the kheda gate and the beaters cannot stop them. This is the most successful method of catching wild elephants who are starved for a few days and weakend and then each is brought out with the help of two strong trained male or female elephants. The method is somewhat expensive and needs a few days and a few dozens of men. The second method is to put strong noose round an elephant's neck by a 'Phandi' i.e., one who puts a 'Phand' or a noose. By this means strong males or females cannot be caught but only young or immature elephants especially cow elephants can be caught and managed. The third method is to dig a big deep pit in the ground and to cover it with bamboos, saplings and grass and drive unsuspecting elephants into it. Not more than one or two can be allowed to fall into the pit. It is a cruel method because sometimes an elephant breaks its leg and all of them get a big jolt from falling into the pit. The elephants are then starved to make them weak and a sloping path is made for tame elephants to go in and bring out one elephant at a time along the sloping path after tying its neck with a strong rope ends of which are also tied tc the other two elephants' necks.

In Assam capturing elephants was mostly done by the method of noosing. I saw the party where two groups of elephant catchers were working, each group having two elephants on each of which was a 'Mahout' (Driver) and a 'Phandi' (nooser) who sat in the back. They could easily ride the elephant bare back and pass through and under forest trees, the mahout sitting in the depression in the neck between the elephants large head and its high backhump. The mahout could easily protect himself against brushing of tree branches and thorny plants and creepers by couching in the depression at the neck. The 'Phandi' sat in the rear and lowered himself by hanging on to the tail of the elephant when the elephant passed through thorny plants and creepers or went under low tree branches. When I asked them to take me they told me that one could not sit on the back of the elephant where one would get hurt or badly scratched and the team would have to go along a jungle path more or less clear. I would not be able to sit on the elephant without hurting myself badly or falling off on the ground by being brushed away by a low tree branch. Still I insisted on joining one team and sat on the back of an elephant. Soon I realised my folly. In spite of the *mahout* trying to avoid going through the deep jungles, I got my bush shirt torn and my body scratched by thorns. After an ordeal of 3 hours I asked them to take me back and they did so. They moaned that my company had robbed them of half a day's successful work as they did not go to those spots where they thought elephants would be available because I would not be able to stand the ordeal nor would I be able to keep my seat on the elephant. I paid handsome *bakshis* and returned to the camp to nurse my wounds and regret my fool-hardiness. I used to go out into the jungle every day and could only see wild pigs walking in herds at a place too distant to do accurate shooting even with a rifle. I decided to return although I had not done any hunting worth the name but I loved to be in the jungle as an enjoyable break from my urban life.

24

Victim of Machinations and Backdoor Exit

On return I joined as Addl. IG of police. A friend who had friendly relationship with one of the group of young turks in Indira Gandhi's Congress told me that there was a move to deprive me of promotion as IG of Police, West Bengal and the central government had introduced a practice of asking all state governments to seek prior approval of the union government in appointing IG, Chief Secretary and other officers to important posts. I did not believe that my friend could get such information so many months ahead before my chance came on the retirement of the then incumbent Sachin Ghosh and that with my excellent record of performance in the police in recent years when I had managed successfully to go to the rescue of the State government in dire distress, government would deprive me of my chance to be promoted as IG of Police in the state. Moreover, IG of Police had sent a proposal to the state government recommending award of the President's Police and Fire Services Medal to me fully describing my performance since award of the Police Medal in 1953. Government of West Bengal did not forward the recommendation and M.M. Basu the then Chief Secretary told me that the government wanted the award to be given to P.K. Sen, the then Police Commissioner and did not want me to compete lest the central government decided to give the President's medal to one person in one state and P.K. Sen was left out. I considered the Chief Secretary's arguments as funny. In order to ensure the award to Sen he eliminated competition and thus deprived me of the last chance to get this award. At this time P.K. Sen was about to retire and the Home Secretary B.R. Gupta telephoned to me and enquired if I would like to join as the Commissioner of Police, Calcutta. I enquired why Ranjit Gupta, who was being tipped as the next CP was not being selected and he said that government did not have much confidence in him but did not elaborate the theme. As the CP's post was still then a Senior DIG's post and below an Addl. IG's, I decided not to accept. However, I should have gauged the purpose of this proposal namely to save me from being deprived of promotion as IG, the then IG Sachindra Mohan Ghosh did not want to part with me. I always wanted to be the CP and I was unwise in refusing the offer. However, I was confirmed in my post of Addl. IG of Police. As IG Sachin Ghosh wanted to go on four months' leave preparatory to his retirement, a press note appeared stating that Prasad Bose who was serving as IG BSF in West Bengal would take over as IG by passing over or superseding me. I sent a representation to the Governor of West Bengal who was to appoint the IG and sought an interview. Before that I saw one C.C. Ghosh who was an officer of the Calcutta Port Trust and had been appointed as the Principal Adviser during a time the State was under the President's rule. I showed him a copy of my representation to the Governor and enquired why I was being deprived of my due promotion. He was silent and did not offer any reasons why he had sent Prasad Bose's name instead of mine. Later I learnt that he was told by the then Union Home Secretary L.P. Singh to do so and he complied. After all West Bengal was under the President's rule and all officers of the state were being ordered about by officers of the central government I confronted M.M. Basu, the other adviser and he too kept quiet. Both these officers were really spineless and would not or dared not protest against a wrong diktat of the Home Secretary of the central government. When I saw Governor Dhawan he said that he did not see why I should be deprived, although I had only 7 months' before retirement and assured me of going to Delhi and taking up the issue. A few days later he telephoned to me from Delhi and told me that government might agree but I must not seek an extension. I assured him that I had no desire to serve even a day after my retirement date. I paid a visit to Delhi to attend a conference on the utility of mass media to which the IG of Police was invited but he deputed me instead. In Delhi I saw L.P. Singh the then Home Secretary and confronted him with the contents of my representation but he had no answer except that he had acted on the representation of the state government suppressing the vital fact that he had asked the Principal Adviser C.C. Ghosh to recommend P.K. Bose's name. I also saw the Secretary to the Prime Minister Indira Gandhi one P.N. Haksar and explained to him how injustice was being done to me by depriving me of my due promotion. Moreover, I had a much better record in field performance than P.K. Bose. He pleaded his helplessness because the file had already been sent to the P.M. and he did not dare to recall the file and give a note for consideration of my suitability along with P.K. Bose's. I also saw Hooja who was the Director, Intelligence Bureau and he behaved stupidly by assuming superior airs. Both L.P. Singh and Hooja had feet of clay which they could manage to hide till they were found out and both the officers were booted out of their posts by Prime Minister, Indira Gandhi. In the state it is a coincidence of fate that both C.C. Ghosh and M.M. Basu soon died. However, my efforts as well as Governor Dhawan's efforts failed. Before actual appointment of Prasad Bose I consulted one of the eminent lawyers in Calcutta High Court, named Sankardas Banerjee, who loved me as if I was his younger brother and he advised filing a constitutional writ petition. His junior colleague D.N. Dass wrote the petition which was finalised with my approval. The petition was filed in the Court of Justice Sabyasachi Mukherjee who later became the Chief Justice of India. Governments of West Bengal and of India were the opposite parties in the suit. The Advocate General of West Bengal Banamali Das represented the state government and the Solicitor General of India represented the central government. They were assisted by a few lawyers of the Calcutta High Court. Altogether there were six lawyers on the side of the two governments. Sankardas Banerjee assisted by D.N. Das was the only Counsel for me. The hearing lasted 12 days. During all those days the court room was packed with both senior and junior lawyers who were interested to hear pleadings of both sides. The Judge gave a decision in my favour stating that I should be fully considered by the government before deciding who should be appointed. Sankardas Banerjee received congratulations from his colleagues in the bar and the press reporters wanted to give a big write up eulogising his advocacy. He sternly forbade them to do anything of the kind saying it was justice which had won and any write-up of eulogy would annoy the judges and jeopardise my chance of winning the appeal, if any. As a matter of course government went up in appeal which was heared by a Division Bench consisting of one Justice Ghosh and a junor Judge. As soon as the Appellate Division bench was constituted, one of the Opposite Party lawyers gave out that they had already won the appeal. This utterance astounded my Senior Counsel and he became very suspicious of the confidence exuded by the O.P. As predicted by the O.P. lawyer, the appellants won but the judgement was not delivered in writing till I retired when a second appeal in the Apex Court became infructuous. During hearing of the appeal I had a chance of reading the annual confidential reports written by some of the Inspectors General of Police. Hiren Sircar gave bad reports and incorporated false insinuations and conclusions. As we did not like each other, I could understand his doing so as his own reputation was far from enviable. I have, however, wondered why Upananda Mukherjee whose regime benefited most from my acts of extra police work gave grossly false and malicious reports. I suppose his family background and up bringing in conditions of poverty and deprivation did not allow him to be a high minded person and he cared to lend his ears to those who became his sycophants and surrounded him. He used to call a particular IP officer "A snake in the grass" but I know that this snake was non-poisonous but the man who said this became a venomous snake in the latter part of his career. He was even hated by the ministerial staff of his own office with the result that they refused to organise or take part in a farewell party for him at the time of his retirement. Mukherjee often referred to me as "Super IP" because of my proud and non-subservient attitude and comparatively better standard of living all of which perhaps displeased Mukherjee.

Thus I quit service not in an expected manner although I never doubted that justice was denied to me. I may, however, add that I had got post-retirement justice when the post I retired from was upgraded to the rank of the Inspector General of Police and I began to get pension of the same rank as in the case of other officers who actually retired from the post of IG of Police. I also learnt that Ranjit Gupta, who became C.P., Calcutta after P.K. Sen ingratiated himself with L.P. Singh by giving false and exaggerated tales about his own good achievement. That L.P. Singh believed him was proved by Singh's note about Gupta in the Government of India file for selection of the IG West Bengal after Sachin Ghosh's retirement. On the other hand the state government officials could size up Gupta correctly and had little confidence in his abilities or character. That was the reason I was offered the post of the next Commissioner of Police which post I foolishly declined. Their estimation was justified when Gupta was unceremoniously dismissed from the post of CP and Rabindra Nath Chatterjee was appointed. After a while Gupta was appointed as IG of the state from which post he was also kicked out by the then CM, Siddhartha Sankar Roy, who was a classmate of Ranjit in their college days.

The West Bengal Police had alternately good and bad periods of administration under good and bad Heads of the Force. Sukumar Gupta who was the first Indian IG was a good man without having strong likes or dislikes or indulging in nepotism. He was succeeded by Hiren Sarkar who was IG for ten long years. He was technically the ablest policeman but had pride and prejudices at wrong places. He was vindictive and did not shrink from lying and writing false reports both good and bad about the officers serving under him. He was succeeded by Hari Sadhan Ghose Choudhury who was upright and straightforward but did not apply himself seriously to any problem so long as his own reputation was safe. He was succeeded by Upananda Mukherjee who unfortunately was the first policeman in the state to get the benefit of extension of service by 3 years when the age of retirement was increased from 55 to 58. He was an able general administrator but poor in technical matters i.e., did not have knowledge, initiative or energy to improve working of the police force. He knew which side of the bread was buttered and won over Mriganka Basu, the Home Secretary and later the Chief Secretary of the State. He managed to get extra vehicles, extra telephones and wireless equipments and large extra force sanctioned by the government but could hardly put them to good use. Later he formed a small coterie of senior officers and kept himself surrounded by them and was often guided by their reports and advice. He had a nitwit lady Smt Biva as his wife who had a tremendous and unbelievable stronghold over her husband who often conducted himself foolishly at her bidding. They had no children nor did I and my wife. Once in a party in the government house Mrs Mukherjee approached my wife and enquired why she had no children and my wife's prompt reply was that the same question could be put to her. This reply did not please the lady. In the same party Mrs Mukherjee, wife of the then Governor of West Bengal Harendranath Mukherjee came to Mrs Biva, poked her forefinger into her belly and enquired why she had no children. As a matter of fact the Governor had no children either. My wife who witnessed the whole episode had a hearty laugh when recounting the story to others. Upananda's wife was unscrupulous in small matters and often took valuable gifts from the officers who gave *saris* to her during the Durga Puja festival and other things during the course of a year. Upananda was a witness but did not protest. Rumours had it that the Mohanto of Tarakeswar often sent gifts to Mukherjees which they accepted without hesitation. Mukherjee was succeeded by Sachin Ghosh who was succeeded by Prasad Bose. Both were good and extremely scrupulous officers. I should cite here an instance of Sachin's scrupulous honesty. One day I entered his chamber and he was arguing with someone on the telephone and repeatedly insisting on getting a bill sent to him and also threatening to send back the goods. After he finished talking I enquired about the subject matter of the hot discussions and learnt that he had acceded the request of his daughter to buy a gramophone disc player for her and such purchase was then laced with a free gift of three ordinary discs, each side playing 3½ minutes. He placed the order with the office of the Gramophone Co. Ltd. in Dum Dum. On opening the parcel his daughter was delighted because instead of three ordinary discs she had been given three long playing discs each side having 5 to 6 songs recorded. These discs were worth 3 or 4 times more than those ordinary short playing records. Sachin Ghosh was immediately on the alert and wanted to pay an extra sum of money for these costly discs but the Sales Manager would not accept the payment and hence the long conversation and argument over the phone. The Company was actually made to send an extra bill for the balance amount and Sachin paid. Very few officers would behave in the same manner in the same circumstances. Prasad Bose was succeeded by Ranjit Gupta who was a big talker and did not hesitate to bluff and was in the habit of hunting with the hound and running with the hare. Of all the three officers who reined over bad patches it was Ranjit who got caught and made to leave the post unceremoniously. My deprivation of the post of IG made me furious but I could do little to avenge myself.

I, however, promised to myself that in my retired life I would prove that I was worth much more than what government thought to be my worth. I set up an organisation to offer security consultancy, security guard service and detective investigation work. I have been greatly rewarded in my efforts to render useful service to the public in these fields and also earned considerable sums of money compared with what I earned in government service. I have spent and intend to spend almost the entire sums of money I earned towards charity. I established three charitable institutions, two big ones for public charity and one for private charity to help some not so affluent relatives of mine. I have now spent 30 years in this private profession. My work and membership of the World Association of Detectives, Inc. USA and my desire to see other countries have taken me nine times out of the country covering the USA, Canada, Hong Kong, Singapore, Thailand, Indonesia, Philippines, Australia, New Zealand, Russia, Israel, Egypt, Greece, Turkey, Yugoslavia, Hungary, Austria, Germany, France, Spain, the UK and Ireland, visiting some countries more than once. I shall end my reminiscences here and now instead of extending them to cover my post retirement years. My great sorrow is that the greatest tragedy in my post retirement life occurred when I lost my wife in her 51st year in 1979 which deprived me of sharing with my wife a life of comparative affluence and my wanderings over many foreign lands. Fortunately I was able to take her to Ceylon, the whole of Europe, the USA and Canada which visits were fruitful and very satisfying to her.

25

Thoughts on the Country

When I heard of India attaining Independence, like many others I became jubilant and thought that Indians would become citizens of a Utopia or a near Eldorado.

The first surprise to me came when the framework of the British Administration with all the enacted laws were adopted and moreover rights and privileges of the government employees increased under the new constitution and so did the rights of the people to sue the government and semi-government institutions even on filmsy grounds.

Adoption of the British framework certainly pleased most employees of the government and semi-government institutions because they had still then not been aware that the honest and efficient employees could not discharge their duties effectively. Soon the upright and honest employees found out that they could not discharge their duties efficiently or effectively.

Moreover, the masses, i.e. the public at large thought that by attaining independence they had acquired the liberty to do even wrong things. In Calcutta this became apparent when on August 15, 1947 the visitors to the Raj Bhavan (Government House) in Calcutta took away and misappropriated many valuable items and objects d'art. Similarly, travelling by public transport and on railways without ticket increased manifold. Crime and problems of law and order vastly increased with the result that in the first ten years of independence the Police had to resort to shooting at unruly mobs on more occasions than they did during the previous 100 years of the British Rule. Leaving Jalianwalabagh out, more rounds of lethal ammunition were fired in that short time than in the previous hundred year.

The first severe shock came to me and all non-Muslim Indians and nationalist Muslims in the form of knowledge and realisation that India might be partitioned on the basis of Hindu and Muslim majority areas to be named India or Bharat and Pakistan and that the native states which were numerous might choose to remain independent or opt to become a part of India or Pakistan. Most native states took time to take a decision but Vallabbhai Patel who became the Home Minister exerted pressure on most states inside the territory which formed India to join India. I do not know what kind of pressure was put on them but it must have been made clear that things would be unpleasant and life of the Rulers and their subjects in the states would become unpleasant, if not unbearable. All states inside the Indian Territory joined except the large state of Hyderabad ruled by the Nizam, a Muslim ruler in the heart of Deccan plateau and a small state Junagadh ruled over by another Muslim Nawab. India had no hesitation to send her armed forces and force Junagadh to become a part of India. Another large native state of Jammu and Kashmir which comprised of the regions of Jammu, Kashmir, Ladakh and Gilgit formed the northern most territory of India; had a predominantly Muslim population with a Hindu ruler named Maharaja Hari Singh. The state was on the border between India and Pakistan and had the easy option of joining either India or Pakistan. The ruler sat on the fence and took no decision and efforts of the Indian government failed to induce the ruler to take a quick decision. Noticing the Ruler's hesitancy, Pakistan invaded Kashmir to take the state by force. This move frightened the Maharaja who thought it prudent to leave his seat on the fence opted for India and signed the instrument of accession on 26.10.47 and sought help of India to save his state from Pakistani invasion by regular personnel of the Pakistan Defence Forces and irregular fighting personnel provided with arms and ammunition by Pakistan. India responded quickly and rushed troops and armaments by air-lifting them from India and landing them on a small aerodrome in Srinagar, the capital city of Jammu and Kashmir. The Maharaja's troops could only give a feeble resistance which however, proved to be useful in delaying advance by the forces from Pakistan so as to give the Indian armed forces to be in Srinagar which would otherwise have been overrun by the

Pakistanis if there was delay by a couple of days in intervention by the Indian Armed Forces.

The Indian armed forces took very prompt action to halt the advance of the enemy and waited for more reinforcements to arrive before taking the offensive to push back the intruders. It is important to mention that the usual route to Srinagar was from the town of Rawalpindi, then in Pakistan and the road ran along a gradual slope and was kept in good condition for thousands of Indian and Foreign tourists visiting Srinagar and other parts of Kashmir. While it was much easier for the Pakistanis to approach the State Capital from Pakistan side, the Indian armed forces had to be airlifted in small batches; still they managed to gain ground and gradually pushed back the intruders. But Prime Minister Jawaharlal Nehru suddenly declared unilateral ceasefire perhaps on the advice of the then Governor General Lord Louis Mountbatten. No doubt India's Armed Forces were facing difficulties in logistics to make headway to drive the intruders out but India need not have declared a ceasefire and halt Indian Army efforts. At that time India was militarily much stronger than Pakistan and should have taken only a breathing time to make further advance. Pakistan had a very great advantage in the fact that the region of Kashmir including the areas round Gilgit, Hunza, Ishkuman and Baltistan had a large majority of Muslim population while the valley of Kashmir had both Hindus and Muslims as its inhabitants. Jammu was inhabited mostly by the Hindus and Ladakh had mainly Buddhist population. The areas in occupation of the Pakistanis were considered to be the Pak occupied Kashmir (POK) and the dividing line between POK and the areas under control of India was treated as the line of ceasefire and later as the Line of Control. This line ran through areas which were too near Srinagar and the town of Leh the capital of Ladakh region. Pakistan could easily cross the LOC. and disrupt and destroy lives and properties of the people in the regions under Indian Control and cut off an important road connecting Leh, the capital of Ladakh. By declaring ceasefire, India invited perpetual troubles for herself. Government of India made another serious blunder by referring the dispute to the United Nations and declaring that it would seek a referendum amongst the people of the former state of Jammu and Kashmir provided Pakistan vacated the areas illegally occupied within six months. The dispute started in 1947 and has still been raging in 2002. In between there have been four wars between India and Pakistan in all of which Pakistan got worsted. But Pakistan has constantly claimed that the State of Jammu and Kashmir specially Kashmir having a Muslim majority should rightfully belong to Pakistan and insists on the promised referendum being held without mentioning the important proviso that Pakistani intruders must have left and vacated the occupied areas within six months. Actually foreign countries have nearly forgotten the proviso and think that the promised referendum should have been held in the last fifty years to know the wishes of the Kashmiri population. The then Indian Prime Minister must have been day dreaming if he thought that Muslims living in a state contiguous to Pakistan would opt for India and discard Pakistan if a referendum was held. Nehru depended on the then Kashmir leader Shaikh Abdullah swaying the entire Muslim population to opt for India. Later it proved doubtful if Shaikh Abdullah himself would have opted for India. As a matter of fact for his anti-India activities in later year Abdullah was deposed from the post of the Chief Minister and put in confinement for as long as eleven years. This dispute will not be solved in forseeable future and cannot now be solved by use of force in a war between the two countries. Five decades ago Pakistan was militarily much weaker than India. In the last three decades Pakistan has won the friendship of the USA as well as of a very strong China who was friendly with India in the past. Pakistan has developed nuclear weapons as has India. The rich and developed countries are more favourably inclined towards Pakistan than India because of the latter's too friendly relationship with the USSR. USSR has broken up in twelve constituent states and is now known as Commonwealth of Independent States. Russia is still the most powerful member of the Commonwealth. Of the original fifteen states the three Baltic states namely Latvia, Estonia and Lithuania broke away from the Russian Federation and became three independent states. Russia has, on the other hand, become an impoverished country and seeks loan and donations from the rich countries of the west. There is little prospect of India getting any help from Russia which has only been able to keep her nuclear arsenal as a counterbalance to western aggressive hegemony especially by the USA.

Shaikh Abdullah was released from confinement and he assumed leadership of Kashmiris but became more careful in his dealings with India. There was a hostile truce between Kashmir ruled by Abdullah and India as long as the Shaikh lived. Kashmir was awarded a special status under Article 370 of the Constitution of India which confers special status on Kashmir which tantamounts to being autonomous in many respects. Several Acts passed by the Indian Parliament are not applicable to Kashmir until the Maharaja or the Head of the State approved of adoption of the provisions of the Acts.

When British India was partitioned practically all the Hindus of Sindh, Northwest Frontier Province and of the partitioned Punjab which later formed the West Pakistan were compelled to leave and go over to India. Similarly the Muslims of that portion of the Punjab which formed part of India and many Muslims of West UP, Gujarat and native states which later formed Haryana and the Punjab left India. Thousands of Hindus left the Muslim Part of undivided Bengal and Assam, the latter comprising district of Sylhet and part of Silchar which went to East Pakistan. Few Muslims left Bengal in India. It may be added that Mahatma Gandhi and Abul Kalam Azad the then President of the Indian National Congress were vehemently against partition of the country but the Mahatma yielded to the persuasions of Nehru who was more than a son to him.

Nehru and his senior colleagues made the great mistake of continuing with some pernicious custom of the British Rule and did not allow the Hindu refugees to settle down in Jammu and Kashmir including parts of Gilgit. Similarly the old practice of people of the plains of Assam and Bengal were prevented from settling in the sparsely populated regions of the five North East Frontier districts namely, Meghalaya, Manipur, Nagaland and Mizoram and the large frontier territory known as NEFA, with the result that these districts had to be given statehood and further that there were militancy and insurgency in Nagaland, Manipur and Mizoram and the terrorist activities are still raging. The militants and insurgents do not observe international law on human rights but India has to do so. The result has been that Indian policemen and para military and defence force personnel are getting killed in large numbers without being in a position to retaliate. Even a small area which had Bodos in Darrang district in north Assam is claiming independence from India. It was in the interest of China, East Pakistan and even some countries of the Western World to instigate the militants and separatists so that India could be dismembered and these countries could get a foot hold.

After 1949 war with Pakistan the next war broke out in 1965 during the Prime Ministership of Lal Bahadur Shastri who proved to be a better statesman than Nehru. Indian Armed Forces sought his permission to go into West Pakistan and complete a pincer movement to defeat and drive out the Pakistanis. Shastriji agreed and this manouvre helped India to defeat the Pakistan armed forces without too much trouble. The next war was fought in 1971-72 when the Bengalees of East Pakistan were fighting for Independence and India received crores of Bengalee refugees. Pakistan also invaded India in the West and India which was giving direct help to the Bengalees in East Pakistan had to fight a war in the West too. Indira Gandhi was the then Prime Minister and she allowed the Indian Armed Forces to enter some areas of West Pakistan after driving the Pakistani out of India. She declared a unilateral ceasefire and withdrew the Indian troops into India. She perhaps followed in the footsteps of China which declared unilateral ceasefire and withdrew from a major part of Assam invaded by them but China retained a huge chunk of the Indian territory which she claimed to be hers which the British had taken away from China by force. Indira Gandhi lost the last opportunity of bargaining with Pakistan. Indira might have continued to occupy parts of Pakistan and asked Pakistan to withdraw from the Pak occupied Kashmir or at least to agree to shift the Line of Control from the dangerously close areas of Indian Kashmir. Indira Gandhi did not do so and India lost the last opportunity to force Pakistan to come to reasonable terms over Kashmir dispute which will remain a cause of dispute and border wars between the two countries in forseeable future years. India entered into an agreement with Pakistan which is known as Shimla agreement to define the Line of Control precisely but in doing so the Line of Control was delineated to be too near the important road link from Srinagar to Leh in Ladakh. The folly of allowing this LOC overlooking the Leh Road was proved by the severe border skirmishes in 1999 when Pakistan managed to occupy the Indian bunkers inside the Indian territory and could be dislodged by fighting many battles in which India spent crores of rupees in using Bofors Howitzer guns and thousands of rounds of ammunition and mortar shells. It was further proved by behaviour of Zulfikar Ali Bhutto, the then Prime Minister of Pakistan, who came to Shimla where a meeting with the Indian Leaders took place on the subject of release of prisoners of war taken in East Pakistan. After the formal meeting Bhutto had a tete-e-tete meeting with Mrs. Indira Gandhi alone in which nobody else was present and nobody knew the final terms and conditions agreed upon to establish peace between India and Pakistan. After getting down from the aeroplane in Pakistan Airport Bhutto gave a broad smile and said that he had got 93 thousand Pakistani P.O.W.s and the territory occupied by the Indian Army back and in exchange gave a scrap of paper which was later known as the "Shimla Agreement" which only contained a clause that India and Pakistan would respect the Line of Control and shall not enter into each other's territory. This clause has been violated time and again and there have been acts of cross border terrorism creating an insoluble problem for Kashmiris, both Hindus and Muslims. As a matter of fact practically all Hindus numbering as much as three lacs of Kashmiri Pandits have left hearth and home in Kashmir valley. India also lost several officers and many soldiers. The only good thing that resulted was for Pakistan to realise that it was not yet a match for India in war games and that India was swept by a strong wave of patriotism which was not evidenced since Sino-Indian war in 1962. The Government formed by the Bharatiya Janata Party and its allies headed by Atal Behari Bajpai earned esteem and loyalty of a large section of Indians.

Instead of elaborating on the mistakes I might as well as briefly list the 'Himalayan Blunders' that can be traced to Jawaharlal Nehru's folly, vanity, indiscretion and even greed for power.

(a) The *first* was the agreed partition of India, the whole of which formed the country under the British Rule for 200 years. In order to avoid partition India might have allowed Jinnah to be the first Governor General and a Muslim to be the Prime Minister till a constitution for a Republic was formed. After all the Hindus were in a majority and would have ruled the Parliament as well as most of the state assemblies. Indian politicians and Intelligence units did not even know that Jinnah was suffering from terminal illness of tuberculosis or cancer.

(b) The *second* mistake was to hasten the Independence day by almost a year to make Liaquat Ali the Finance Minister, the Indian politicians being fully ignorant of the power of the man who controlled the purse strings and could close and open the purse according to his principles.

(c) The *third* blunder was to keep and allow Lord Mountbatten who was the former Viceroy and Governor General of British India to be the first Governor General of Independent Dominion of India. Nehru allowed himself to be advised by Mountbatten with whose wife he had much too close a relationship than was good for India or Nehru's own reputation.

Nehru always had weakness for smart and beautiful women and allowed them the privilege of being photographed together.

(d) The *fourth* was to call a ceasefire in the Indo-Pak war over Pak invasion of Kashmir in 1948. After all the Indian troops had gradually been advancing and driving the Pakistani invaders. India should not have declared a unilateral ceasefire when Pakistan had grabbed a large area of northern Jammu & Kashmir in spite of our claim to the whole of the former native state of Kashmir under the Maharaja Sir Hari Singh. In this connection the biggest folly was for Nehru to refer the case to the United Nations Organisation and to promise to hold a plebiscite, although holding the plebiscite was subject to the important clause that Pakistan would vacate the occupied areas within six months after which the plebiscite would be held. Nehru depended on the influence of the then Kashmiri Leader, Shaikh Abdulla but most Indians think that even Shaikh Abdulla and India lovers like him could not have swayed the Muslim majority public in Kashmir to vote to become a part of

India. In course of decades people and the International Community have forgotten about the important provision of vacating Pak occupied region and have remembered only the clause of holding a plebiscite. I do not know whether Mountbatten influenced Nehru to declare a unilateral ceasefire but Mountbatten certainly played a part in bringing the two sides to sit together at a table and discuss the terms of truce. The Congress which represented the Hindus and nationalist Muslims had no important leader from Bengal with the result that Bengal was partitioned much to the detriment of the Hindus. Although the Hindus formed 47 per cent of the population India got 1/3 of the old Bengal. Chittagong Hill Tract which was contiguous to parts of Assam and Manipur was also given away to East Pakistan in spite of the population being Chakma Buddhists. It was during partition of India that Bengal missed the strong presence of Subhas Chandra Bose. He dreamt of winning Independence for India with Japanese help but he would have been thrown away like a piece of waste paper if the Japanese won the war in the East. Perhaps he would have been put in prison and later killed in an unobstrusive manner. Some people think that India might not have been partitioned if Subhas Chandra was in India or at least India would have got much better terms. Unlike Nehru and Vallabbhai Patel he would not have been in an undue hurry to achieve Independence over partition in which India did not get her fair share of the territory. The two nation theory of Jinnah fell apart because crores of Muslims stayed back in India which believed in secularism. After formation of Bangladesh in 1972 India has the second largest Muslim population next to Indonesia.

(e) The *fifth* Himalayan blunder committed by Jawaharlal Nehru was when India ceded the islands of Great Coco and Little Coco in the Bay of Bengal to Burma, now Mynamar which has renamed them Cow and Calf. It is strange that Nehru decided and Parliament agreed to cede these islands to another country when these two islands were in the territory of India. Now Burma has allowed the use of these two islands either on lease or rent to China which is using these two islands as radar base and may later convert them into naval base too. These two islands are situated in north of the Andaman group of islands between Andaman and India. The result has been that the Naval and Submarine bases of India in the Andaman islands have become greatly vulnerable by the presence of China which is not too friendly to India. When people all over the world are fighting for small patches of land it was the height of folly to hand over these two strategically situated islands to Burma and one fails to understand the reasons or purpose of doing so. This misdeed will be a permanent source of trouble to India and greatly weaken defence capabilities in the eastern seas.

(f) The *sixth* blunder was to adopt a hundred per cent democratic constitution on the lines of that in the UK. Indian politicians forgot that seventy-five per cent of the population are illiterate excluding some semi-literates and they are more moved by personal charisma of political leaders, rather than their policy. Moreover, the majority think in terms of caste, creed sect and religion and have little regard for principles or larger good of the country. The result has been formation of several national parties and later formation of many regional i.e., provincial state parties who think of their own good and evil, want to make money by dishonest means, mostly by cheating illiterate people and misappropriating state funds meant for improving the lot of the poor and downtrodden. There has been horse trading to buy members of the Parliament and the State Assemblies and the Governments at the centre and in some states have had to resort to unfair means to remain in power. If India had adopted a constitution like that of the USA then the government would have remained in power for at least four or five years and the ministers would have been appointed from amongst those most suited for their jobs on account of their expertise or suitability. The horrible consequences of the Indian Constitution were witnessed during two periods. One between 1977 and 1980 during which a state of emergency was in force in the country and again between 1997 and 1999 during which periods several prime ministers and cabinets took charge of the country. Similar were the cases in almost all the states except Maharashtra, Kerala and Assam. The President's rule had to be imposed several times in most of the states because no party had a clear majority and minority or coalition governments had to be formed which did not last long.

(g) The *seventh* blunder of Nehru was to try to play the role of a Big Brother to the Third World countries. This attitude annoyed China which was known to be a sleeping giant but Nehru was forgetful that the giant had been waking up under the Communist Rule and the Chinese politicians had more practical sense of adopting right means to improve their country and its people than being dogmatic. India and China had very friendly relations and each called the other a brother and the word Hindi-Chini Bhai-Bhai was coined and was in vogue. At that time India should have known the strength, of the monolithic communist regime and the strength, loyalty and devotion of the Peoples army. If Nehru had done so then he would have known that India and China had considerable undemarcated border and that China had been rejecting the border known as Macmohan Line which she said had been imposed on her by British force of arms on a weak China. India should have conceeded parts of Aksai Chin or allowed China the right to build a road to approach Chinese Turkestan through the Indian territory and settled the border line in the eastern parts between the UP, Nepal, Sikkim, Bhutan and North East frontier districts amicably by drawing a border line on an aerial survey map. Instead of doing so Nehru claimed that he had a verbal discussion with Chou En Lai, the Chinese Prime Minister, that both parties accepted the McMohan Line as Sino-Indian border. China wholly denied this claim of verbal agreement. Secondly Nehru should have known that these things are settled by drawing up documents of formal agreement. The result was that the Chinese claimed that India had set up border posts inside China (Tibet) attacked and slaughtered policemen of Indo-Tibetan Force manning some of the border posts. The dispute escalated and ended in Sino-Indian border war in 1962 when ill-equipped and mentally unprepared Indian troops were killed and routed to India's great shame and humiliation.

(h) The *eighth* blunder was that the USA extended help and offered a helping hand during 1962 Sino-Indian border war which would perhaps have lasted long but India let go the hand grip and reverted to her old stand to side with the USSR when the cold war was at its height.

(i) The *ninth* blunder was not to have diplomatic relationship with Israel with which India had no enemity nor any conflict of interests. While the USA, Great Britain and most western countries had diplomatic relationship India did not recognise Israel nor agreed to have diplomatic relationship with her. Israel was keen to have this recognition and friendly relationship with India but India was obstinate in her refusal just to please the Islamic countries which she did not want to antagonise. India thought that if she had diplomatic friendly relationship with Israel the Muslim countries especially Iran and the Arab World would support Pakistan against India. In spite of India's futile efforts, the Arab countries and Iran offered help and sympathy to Pakistan during the Indo-Pak war in 1965. Nehru had died by that time but his successors were disillusioned at Nehru's obstinacy and shortsightedness. For reasons not fully known to this author, Israel was very keen to have diplomatic friendly relationship with India all the time. She sought the help of Pritish Nandy, a well known journalist and later editor of the *Illustrated Weekly of India* and Pritish had promised help during his visit to Israel but on return to India he did not do anything. As a matter of fact when this author visited Israel to attend a conference in Jerusalem in 1987, he was requested to go to the Foreign Ministry Office for an important discussion. The author obliged and met a high official who expressed his country's desire to develop friendly diplomatic relationship with India and sought the author's help in whatever way he could. The author was frank enough to admit that he had retired from government service long time back and so had his colleagues in the Ministry of External Affairs. He could not be of much help but would make enquiries. The Israeli officer said that his country could assist India in improving her agriculture, making use of desert lands, adopting drip irrigation, manufacturing some high grade small arms, etc. It was at this time that this author learnt about the episode of Pritish Nandy. Moreover, siding with Israel would have pleased the USA a great deal and India would have benefited but she foolishly denied herself a justifiable opportunity.

(j) The *tenth* mistake, if not a blunder, was in India's planning of the five year plans. In the first few plans too much stress was laid on industrialisation and little on improving the agricultural sectors. The stress on industrialisation made Government of India spend thousands of crores of rupees to set up not only core units to produce steel, copper, zinc, etc., and heavy and light machinery, armaments, etc. Except production and trading in petroleum and petroleum products all the Public Sector units lost heavily and became industrially sick. Some monopolistic units such as those producing or dealing in petroleum and its products and telephone industry for providing telephone facilities could not possibly lose being in a position to force the consumer to pay whatever price the government fixed. Still the government had to subsidise petroleum industry by several thousand crores of rupees each year. Then the government planned to set up large dams and barrages to conserve water and to aid agriculture by a system of open canal irrigation in lean months of the year but the grandiose schemes destroyed large tracts of forest cover and made refugees of local residents, especially the tribal people to move out of their ancestral homes and villages and try to settle in new places where they were strangers and the environments did not suit them. From healthy cheerful although poor residents in their ancestral villages, these people became jobless beggars and were exploited by those who had land, industry and wealth. Moreover, the sites for building dams were often not wisely chosen as in several instances capacity of the dams has decreased fast due to heavy silting making the dams half useless in two decades or less instead of lasting half a century as originally planned. The irrigation canals were in open dug channels exposed to the sun and this caused loss of water by evaporation and seepage into the earth and loss of good farm lands. In contrast China adopted the policy of water distribution by channelling the water through large pipelines well embedded into the soil so that there was no loss of water by evaporation or seepage. Above all the farm lands were restored by a thick cover of earth on top on the pipe lines. Although more expensive, this alternative wiser method has given all round benefit to the people of China. On the other hand smaller dams and barrages would have destroyed much less forest areas, would have made less number of people homeless and could be well managed by the people themselves.

It is a bad reflection on the character of the Indian people that public sector units have almost all become industrially sick and unviable and many have remained closed or been working as loss making units. Although we blame the industrial workers but the main fault lies in the management. The incontrovertible evidence lies in the fact that a privately managed industry with the same type of labour is profitably run whereas the public sector units mostly run at a loss or become sick and have to be closed down. There are other factors too, namely, absence of accountability for inefficiency and mismanagement, nepotism and too much protection being given on account of caste, creed, religion, sectarianism and political patronage.

Nehru's two successors namely Lal Bahadur Shastri and Indira Gandhi did much better, being untrammelled with too much socialist idealism and having less hauteur about their own wisdom and position. Shastri showed great statemanship in permitting the Indian troops to cross the Indo-Pak border to carry on the war successfully and ended the war quickly in 1966. Indira Gandhi made the mistake of nationalising the Banking and Insurance sectors resulting in deterioration in service and proliferation of branches of these institutions on a dogmatic rule of having a branch according to the population of the area. Her greatest triumph lay in helping the Bengalees of East Pakistan to throw out the suzerainty of West Pakistan and to create a new independent state named Bangladesh. There is controversy over her action in declaring a state of emergency in 1975 which did not bear any good fruits and resulted in ignonimous defeat of her Congress Party in 1977. The opposition which came to power in 1977 only lasted three years and Indira came to power again in 1980. She committed the blunder of using force against the Sikhs in the Punjab, especially sending in troops in battle tanks into the Golden Temple. As a result she became an object of hatred by the Sikhs and was assassinated by her own Sikh guards in October 1984. She had great pride and confidence in herself and would not yield to persuasion not to have Sikh armed guards round her or in her precincts of office and residence. Her eldest son Rajiv Gandhi who was not keen to enter serious politics was persuaded to succeed his mother as the Prime Minister in 1984. He was known as Mr Clean and won the 1984 election for the Congress Party by an unprecedented large majority. He was inexperienced and committed many mistakes including using force against the government of Sri Lanka, a friendly neighbour and later by sending Indian troops to fight the Tamils who became his sworn enemy. By his ill-advised measures and inducting wrong persons into his cabinet, he lost the confidence of the people and the Congress Party lost the election in 1989. He was later assassinated by a group of the Tamil Tigers known as LTTE in 1991 when electioneering for his party in Tamil Nadu. LTTE which had fanatics in its ranks killed Rajiv with a human bomb who was a female member of the party.

Although the Congress formed the largest party with 197 member in the lower house of Parliament, there were as many as 24 other parties who had sent members to the ninth Lok Sabha. A hastily formed conglomerate of parties which opposed each other formed a government with V.P. Singh as the Prime Minister. V.P. Singh tried to be popular by bringing in legislation to reserve government and semi-government jobs for other backward classes as per the recommendation of the Mandal Commission. There was countrywide agitation of a violent nature by members of the upper castes especially students who faced bleak future in government service. V.P. Singh resigned and was followed by Chandrasekhar who also resigned after the Congress withdrew support. The Lok Sabha was dissolved and preparations were afoot for election.

As already mentioned a very tragic incident occurred during electioneering by the Congress president, Rajiv Gandhi in Tamil Nadu when a female member of LTTE acting as a human bomb killed him in May 1991. However, Congress got a large number of seats though not having a simple majority and managed to form a government under Narsimha Rao which lasted its full term from 1991 to 1996. Narsimha Rao was a shrewd politician who managed to win over several MPs to get a simple majority in Parliament. Between 1996 and 1998 there were two general elections and three governments under premiership of Atal Behari Vajpai, Devagowda and Gujral and again Atal Behari Vajpai, all of which fell because the Congress pulled the rug from under their feet. In 1999 another general election was held to form the thirteenth Lok Sabha. The main contending parties were the Bharatiya Janata Party and its allies and the Congress (I) under Mrs Sonia Gandhi, widow of Rajiv Gandhi and its allies. The Bharatiya Janata Party and its allies won a simple majority and formed a Government which, may, hopefully stay a full five year term. There has been controversy over the legitimacy of Mrs Sonia Gandhi's Indian citizenship because under the Italian law she has remained a citizen of Italy too.

From an elite Parliament in the 1950s and 1960's, the Lok Sabha has degenerated into an institution in which criminalised politicians and politicised criminals have become members and muscle and money power including bribery play an important role.

India is facing numerous serious problems, economically, politically and ethnically. Its industries have become sick, from a few, more than two score political parties are in the national arena and ethnic groups are fighting to have their own independent states, although some have smaller areas than an average district in India. Terrorist activities have increased manifold and the police and para-military forces whose strength had to be increased several times have been having a very hard time. Personnel of these civilian forces as well as those of the Defence Forces are getting killed in ambushes and explosions and by land mines. There is hardly much sense of nationalism not to speak of patriotism amongst those who do not form the core of the majority population. Observation of Human Rights stands in the way of punishing the terrorists except through a lengthy judicial procedure.

Nehru's love for the elitist community was amply proved by his giving tickets to and inducing high flying professionals from all walks of life to join the first Lok Sabha. Many of them were not nationalists and some were vigorously pro-British and wanted British rule to continue. These MP's did not bother about politics and did not even attend sittings of the Parliament in either house. Nehru realised his mistake and did not give tickets to such persons for the second Lok Sabha which was formed with useful members. Non-Congress parties sent some stalwarts as their representatives and some of them were great debators and Parliamentarians in the Opposition.

One great omission on the part of Nehru and his famous colleagues was that they forgot their erstwhile brothers and sisters in arms in the freedom fight and never thought of them and the miserable conditions of poverty and deprivation they lived in. Most of them had left their schools, colleges and vocations and many sacrificed their lives leaving widows, dependent mothers and sisters who had no decent or dependable means of livelihood. It goes to the credit of Nehru's daughter Indira Gandhi who was a mere child during the years of freedom struggle who thought of the Freedom Fighters, recognised their struggle and sacrifice by awarding Tamra Patra as a sort of Freedom decoration medal and arranged to pay pensions to the fighters if they were alive and presumed dependents of those who sacrificed their lives or died in the meantime. Whatever be the shortcomings of Indira Gandhi the country should remember her with gratitude for this one act of hers alone which was never thought of by Nehru, Vallabbhai Patel, Morarji Desai, who were all satisfied with winning Independence and holding positions of importance. I wonder how the Mahatma who had so much wisdom and foresight, both wordly and spiritual forgot about the freedom fighters. In his defence it may be said that he died within five months of attaining Independence.

On the other hand, Indira Gandhi destroyed the Congress by Kamraj Plan by which she drove out important Congressite stalwarts in her cabinet like Morarji Desai.

Not having the courage to admit their own deficiencies like inefficiency, lack of scruples, principles, corruption and criminalisation of politics and politicians many of national leaders have taken refuge under the expediency of resorting to the exercise of tracing most of the country's ills and shortcomings to the British colonial rule. This author served a few months short of 36 years in the superior cadre of the police in India which had to do so-called dirty work for all civil governments unless the government deployed the defence personnel on such occasions when the police failed or the job was too difficult for the police to carry out successfully. The author had served 12 years under the British and nearly 24 years in Independent India. During the British rule he had seen the waning years of terrorism in Bengal, the Bengal famine of 1943 and above all the country spread movement of Quit India in 1942 which took violent turns in many places. He had served in several districts during the six years of the Second World War when the United Kingdom had very difficult times to preserve its own existence while nearly the whole of Europe was under the heels of Hitler and his junior partner Mussolini. Indian territory was imperilled after Japan occupied the whole of littoral China and all the countries of Eastern Asia including Indo China, Cambodia, Hong Kong, the Philippines, Dutch East Indies, Burma, Malayasia, Singapore. Thailand was the only country which was not occupied by the Japanese. Japan set foot on Indian territory in the northeast region in easternmost parts of the district of Nagaland and Assam.

Although Quit India movement ceased but the British government carried on negotiations to confer much greater autonomy if not outright Independence in a dignified manner. Except some die-hards, the rulers in Britain or those British rulers including high officials in India did not lose their heads nor asked the Police and other officers of government to behave except in a lawful manner. During the Quit India movement there were excesses on both sides indulging in unnecessary violence and some police and civilian officers did indulge in violent and unnecessary excesses. Some police officers panicked and behaved irrationally. Midnapore district in Bengal had almost declared independence and civil government including the police became so much afraid of their physical existence that they panicked or became revengeful and committed illegal acts. Shooting down of a patriot like Matangini Hazra who was merely carrying a Congress flag and advancing towards the police camp was outrageous. Matangini could be immobilised and arrested when she walked into the group of police personnel. Police who panicked because they were not sufficient in number and feared being overwhelmed shot and killed her. Such incidents had happened in other places too. But so far as the author and many of his colleagues were concerned, they were briefed from time to time and were advised to follow the extant laws of the land and provisions of the special acts during the war and were always advised to use force in the manner they were trained in. They were asked to exercise the law of right of self defence of person and properties, bearing in mind the special duties of the police to protect the citizens' life and properties especially public properties. That meant one was obliged to use minimum force required to meet the ends of law and order. In his autobiography Jawaharlal Nehru claims to have seen the middle category of police officers, especially British and Anglo-Indian policemen, to behave like brutes and their face and eyes looked like ferocious animals. Although Calcutta Police had the largest concentration of British and Anglo-Indian policemen, the author does not share Nehru's opinion. In those days brutality was punished and not rewarded as in post-independence India. After independence this author has seen Bengalee police inspectors, sub-inspectors, sergeants and a few police constables to be brutal in using force wantonly beating small groups of workers, dispersing rallies and processions organised by followers of their political opponents. This the author had witnessed many times during the Left Front's rule in West Bengal against unarmed unorganised protestors belonging to the Congress. They do so perhaps with the idea that their masters in government will reward them for showing this wanton cruelty and brutality.

Death of a prisoner in police custody was a serious incident whether he died of police torture or by suicide. O/C of the PS and a couple of others would face suspension and departmental proceedings. Even the Superintendent of Police was placed in an awkward position. It was strongly presumed and rightly so that once a person was taken into police custody, it was the police who were fully responsible for his safety and welfare.

Another good practice was in vogue. If a man or woman died of starvation because of poverty, the District Magistrate and the Subdivisional officer were asked to explain why they did not arrange some subsisting diet for him or her because death by starvation was a slur over the whole government. The area had to be declared a famine area and relief work to help the poor people to earn a livelihood had to be started with government funds. Such work usually consisted of building new or repairing old roads and *bundhs* (embankments) to stop floods.

In the fields of the Police and District Administration we have abandoned many necessary and wholesome practices of the Colonial *Raj*. I shall give a few examples. Whenever a Hindu or Muslim religious procession had to go along the street and lanes in a town or even in a village, they would have to follow the customary route and not deviate therefrom. These routes could be found written in official records of the district. Similarly there would be no music or shouting by Hindu processionists when passing by a Mosque or other Muslim or Christian religious places and similarly the Muslim processionists would not be allowed to shout any slogans or words in praise of Allah when passing by a Hindu temple or religious site. If a new Hindu temple or a mosque or even a Christian Church had to be built, the fact had to be notified in the official gazette and also circulated in the locality and objections had to be invited from local residents and members of other communities. These healthy practices have all been abandoned and Hindu temples are sprouting up in dozens and large mosques are being built in scores in mixed localities without ascertaining the wishes of and inviting views of the residents of the locality. Even municipal plans are not prepared and submitted. Every sober and wise citizen should question if these were bad colonial practices.

Even in the field of education the British made Sanskrit, mother of all North Indian languages, compulsory. So was the study of elementary Roman, Greek, English and Indian histories. These have been discarded in the education systems of the state and central governments in independent India. Even the study of English grammar idioms and proverbs has been abandoned. Unless an Indian in North India studies some Sanskrit he will find it difficult to be proficient in his mother tongue. Unless a person reads the Greek and Roman history which form the basis of the Western civilisation he cannot be an educated person in the western style. Were these bad and unwholesome colonial practices and have we done a good thing by discarding them? Even patriotism and nationlism in the modern sense were unknown in ancient India and middle ages and these we learnt during the British Rule. It is the British both members of the ruling community and British civilians who taught us to preserve our Indian heritage. In Calcutta alone, the Asiatic Society, the Indian Museum, the Zoological Garden, the Botanical, Geological, Archaeological and map making survey departments and the Imperial Library later named the National Library were all set up by Englishmen and still we talk of evils of the colonial heritage.

It is the British who introduced the railway segment, steamer services, the telegraph and telephone systems. Certainly the British made huge commercial gains by manufacturing and selling the vehicles, equipments, vessels and on the other hand they did not, however, encourage steel and textile industries in order to protect the British steel and textile industries in their selfish interest. Nationalistic Indians, however, started these industies. Jamshedji Tata founded Tata Iron and Steel Co. and enterpreneurs like Birlas, Mafatlals started cotton textile mills. Britishers, however, founded many jute mills in Bengal on both banks of the Ganges, the best jute being produced in Bengal especially East Bengal. After Independence control of these industries and their trading fell into Indian hands namely houses of Jatias, Goenkas, Poddars, Jalans.

The main harm that the British did was in fixing the gauge of the Railways in India while England, America and the whole of Europe except Russia had standard gauge railway lines having a width of 56½ inches or 1.435 metres. Four odd different gauges namely broad gauge with 5'6", metre gauge with one meter or 39.37 inches and two narrow gauges with diffferent widths of 0.762 and 0.610 metres were introduced. Broad gauge line was laid in the plains of India, meter gauge in somewhat hilly areas or in those areas providing comparatively smaller quantities goods and passengers for transportation by rail and narrow gauges for steep hill regions like Darjeeling, Shimla, Wootacamond and other hill stations. The great commercial self interest that the British *Raj* served was that locomotives, wagons, passenger bogies, rails and other accessories needed to run trains in all the guages had perforce to be bought from the UK. Although India had started manufacturing locomotives, wagons, passenger rakes and rails in India but there were 20,000 miles of broad gauge and another 20,000 miles of metre gauge in the subcontinent i.e. including the regions of Pakistan and Bangladesh, formerly East Pakistan. There was need for transhipment of goods, i.e.

unloading from broad gauge wagons and loading in metre gauge wagons and vice versa at many places in the country. This caused delay, expenses and loss by breakage and theft. Passengers had also to move from trains of one gauge to the other by disembarking and embarking to their great inconvenience and annoyance. India has therefore embarked on the expensive but necessary task of converting metre gauge lines into broad gauge. This involves replacement of railway lines, modification of station layout, building new bridges besides discarding all metre gauge locomotives, wagons, passenger rakes and rails and selling them as scraps. So far as water transportation is concerned it did not present any such problems.

If the Britishers had decided to introduce and establish railway lines of width of 4 ft. 8½ inches known as the standard gauge as in their own country, then such line could serve the whole of the subcontinent except the small areas served by narrow gauge lines. As a matter of fact, road transport should have been organised for reaching the hill stations. Even with the trains on the narrow gauge, road transport both for goods and passenger traffic is cheaper, faster and more popular.

Although the British system of justice was introduced the rulers allowed unconscionable delay in dispensing justice. I do not know how the then rulers or the enlightened public from amongst whom hundreds of elitist lawyers and judges were born tolerated this delay. The fault lay and still lies in the lawyers seeking adjournments and the judges and magistrates being over indulgent without a thought for the well being of the parties seeking justice or waste of their money and time and fattening the pockets of the lawyers.

The worst feature of present Indian polity is the all pervading corruption which has tainted men and women in almost all walks of life from some prime ministers and chief ministers to the lowly policemen and office peons of the lowest rank and in the different strata of employees of all departments of the government, among businessmen, industrialists, doctors, politicians and their followers including social workers. Certainly the British colonial rule did not impart us lesson in this terrible vice.

A greater curse has been an unmanageable explosion of population. From nearly 300 million population before partition it has increased to1000 million in 1999 in partitioned India alone. This population growth has thrown all planning and improvements ineffective while India has managed to grow enough food to feed its population but has been unable to provide a roof over the head, health and educational facilities. Even Muslim countries in the Middle East have been surprised at India's failure to put any check on its population growth nor she has been able to adopt a stern policy like in the Peoples' Republic of China. While this author visited the Islamic countries in the Middle East some discerning people told him that India's unchecked growth of population will nullify all its efforts at improvement in the living standards of the masses.

All is not black in the panorama of the country. The governments at the centre and states have also done very good work in some fields. First comes improvement in agriculture, especially in production of food grains which are staple food of the people especially rice and wheat. India is self sufficient in food in spite of burgeoning growth in population. Serious and successful efforts have been made in oil exploration but the need of the country far exceeds the country's production.

Great improvements have been made in extending roads, railways and rural electrification as well as means of mass contact like television and telephone systems. Small scale industries have been encouraged and sprouted up in large numbers. New industries especially in chemical products and consumer goods have been set up successfully in many states. Successful efforts have been made in introducing new disciplines in education, setting up more universities, colleges and schools to bring higher education to more people and literacy to the masses. New hospitals in the public sector and nursing homes as well as hospitals in the private sector have been established to bring modern treatment for diseases to more people. Unfortunately the drug manufacturing industry has hiked prices of medicines to unprecedented heights to make unconscionable profits. While Indira Gandhi was the Prime Minister, she reined in the pharmaceutical industries as well as large remuneration to the Directors, officers and other employees in the private sectors, no other Prime Minister or his ministers have made any efforts. Some states have failed to take advantage of the improved atmosphere. As for example, West Bengal which was in the vanguard of industrial states and centres of education and medical services have fallen far behind because all important industries have become sick or have closed down and most educational and medical institutions of the Government being in shambles. It is difficult to find good reasons for this state of affairs because the state has been governed by one Party namely Communist Party of India (Marxist) and its allies for the last 23 years with Jyoti Basu as the longest serving Chief Minister in India.

In analysing many events and happenings and propensities of a large section of the population one is apt to think that the history of ancient India seems to be repeating itself but the elite and the educated hope that the dark days will be over. Otherwise the subcontinent will share the fate of Yugoslavia which was held intact as long as Josif Tito remained alive and in power. This author and millions of his thinking hope and believe that this great country will survive the turbulent years to rise to great heights again.

Index